D1483195

Women and the Rise of the Novel, 1405–1726

Other Works by Josephine Donovan

Sarah Orne Jewett

*New England Local Color Literature:
A Women's Tradition*

Feminist Theory: The Intellectual Traditions of American Feminism

*After the Fall: The Persephone-Demeter
Myth in Wharton, Cather, and Glasgow*

Gnosticism in Modern Literature

Uncle Tom's Cabin: Evil, Affliction, and Redemptive Love

Edited Works

Feminist Literary Criticism: Explorations in Theory

Animals and Women: Feminist Theoretical Explorations
(with Carol J. Adams)

*Beyond Animal Rights: A Feminist Caring
Ethic for the Treatment of Animals*
(with Carol J. Adams)

*P.O.W. in the Pacific: Memoirs of an
American Doctor in World War II*
(by William N. Donovan, M.D.)

Women and the
Rise of the Novel, 1405–1726

Josephine Donovan

St. Martin's Press
New York

WOMEN AND THE RISE OF THE NOVEL, 1405–1726
Copyright © Josephine Donovan, 1999

ISBN 0-312-21827-3

Library of Congress Cataloging-in-Publication Data

Donovan, Josephine, 1941–
    Women and the rise of the novel, 1405–1725 / Josephine Donovan.
        p.   cm.
    Includes bibliographical references and index.
    ISBN 0-312-21827-3
    1. Fiction—Women authors—History and criticism.   2. Women and
literature.   3. Frame-stories—History and criticism.   I. Title.
PN3404.D66   1998
809.3'99287—dc21   98-41947
                                                                              CIP

First published: December, 1998
10   9   8   7   6   5   4   3   2   1

To the Memory of My Mother
Josephine Devigne Donovan
(1916–1992)

Ne obliviscaris

I had rather be a meteor,
singly, alone, than a star in a crowd.

—Margaret Cavendish
The Duchess of Newcastle

Contents

Introduction

IT IS A TRUTH (NEARLY) UNIVERSALLY ACKNOWLEDGED among literary historians and theorists that women played a special role in the rise of the novel. Most critics, beginning with Madame de Staël, attributed women's particular relationship with the new genre to their allegedly privileged access to emotion, which there found unique expression. It was not just "sensibility," however, that women brought to the literary scene in the early modern period, but also, and more importantly, "sense"—an attitude of irreverent realism that manifested itself as a feminist prosaics. This book is largely the story of the emergence in the fifteenth century and growth into the eighteenth century of this women's literary tradition; of how it contributed to the genesis of novelistic discourse; and of how it stands on its own as the first women's tradition in Western prose fiction.

From their earliest secular literary writings in the twelfth century, women offered a critique of ideological formations that objectified them in stereotypical roles or commodified them as objects for patriarchal exchange, as in arranged marriages, for example. Their critical standpoint was rooted in the realization that they were treated as inferior because they were women. Their resistance to that treatment required them to identify with each other (in some cases over borders of social rank and race) and to protest their mistreatment as a class. Although the term *feminist* was not current at the time, I use it to characterize their attitude. By *feminism* I mean affirmation of female agency and subjectivity; recognition of patterns of domination and abuse of women by men; and, most importantly, the perception of women as a class that has common interests—namely, to protest the harms they experience *as women*.[1] The harms most vigorously protested in this body of women's literature are: rape, what is today called sexual harassment, and the pejorative stereotypes that were repeatedly served up in the extensive misogynist literature of the period.

In a preface entitled "To All Noble, and Worthy Ladies" to her collection *Poems, and Fancies* (1653), Margaret Cavendish makes a plea to women readers for support by comparing herself to a fictional abused woman who similarly asked women "to help her, to keep their *Right,* and *Priviledges;* making [her situation] their owne *Case.* Therefore," Cavendish implores her women readers, "pray strengthen my Side, in defending my *Book.*"[2] Cavendish's appeal betrays a feminist perspective: women are viewed as a class with common interests. By embracing one woman's injuries as a class case, she argues, women may make common cause and sustain their rights.

Relying on Russian critic Mikhail Bakhtin's theories about the novel's formation, I argue that the women writers of the realist tradition I identify in this study articulated a feminist standpoint in the *querelle des femmes,* the centuries-long "debate" about women's place. The establishment of such a standpoint contributed importantly to the constitution of the dialogic mentality that Bakhtin considered a precondition for the rise of the novel. These women's critical perspectives on patriarchal exchange systems and misogynist "theoretism" produced the kind of subversive antiauthoritarian irony that Bakhtin heralded in the novel. Their critical irony took the shape, in some cases, of anti-romance burlesques and, in others, of satirical treatment of what has been called marriage-marketing, in which women were little more than goods up for barter.

The dominant genre in this women's tradition of prose fiction was the framed-novelle, a collection of stories encased in a narrative frame. As early as Christine de Pizan, these women authors recognized the dialogic potential of the genre, and used the frame for feminist comment on and/or ironic treatment of the inset materials. In many cases they used the frame for the expression of a feminist standpoint.

Finally, many of the women in this tradition seized on the theological method of casuistry to particularize their arguments in defense of women. Emerging in the late Middle Ages, casuistry is a method whereby general rules are adapted, modified, or interrogated through the investigation of a particular case that problematizes the rule. The term *casuistry* got its bad reputation from the fact that to accommodate particular cases the rules often became so riddled with exceptions that they were no longer rules; moral relativism was the result. The women writers' interest in casuistry, however, lay in the fact that it afforded them an opportunity to present particularized cases of women whose stories controverted and interrogated misogynist generalities, rules, and norms about women. Such individualized cases not only challenged harmful cultural attitudes, they also created particularized literary characters, thereby introducing one of the novel's most unique features. Such particularized realism about ordinary people's common life contributed perhaps the most important ingredient to the novel's "prosaics," another Bakhtinian term, which he used to designate the ethical and aesthetic "poetics" of the novel.

"Circumstances Alter Cases," the title of chapter five, was a byword of casuistry. It claims that a case is not to be judged in the abstract but always relative to its particular circumstances. Circumstantial details can change the purport of any given case and thus an understanding of them is necessary for fair ethical and aesthetic judgment to take place. Paying attention to the particularities of an individual's situation necessarily challenged and enlarged ideological norms and abstractions, allowing for a more complex appreciation of individual behavior.

Presenting the details of a woman's case (or, in fiction, her story) allowed for a fuller understanding of her situation, thus preventing reifying abstractions from obscuring her truth. It allowed her story, told from her viewpoint, to be heard. The novel itself, as explained in chapter one, is the genre that best allows for the expression of particularized individual cases. That particularization is inherently subversive of "theoretistic" authoritarian dogma, as Bakhtin contended. What Bakhtin and others failed to realize, however, is the extent to which women writers, particularizing the cases of women in the *querelle des femmes*, contributed to this important dimension of the novel's prosaics. In so doing these women not only helped constitute the new genre, they furthered the cultural work of ideological transformation—the destabilization of dominant authorities— that occurred in the early modern period. The structural preferences of these women—for the framed-novelle as a genre, for example, and for a non-Latinate rhetoric—also contributed importantly to the emergence of novelistic discourse.

The principal heroines of my study are Christine de Pizan (1365-ca. 1430), whose *Le Livre de la cité des dames* (ca. 1405–1407) pioneered the tradition of women's critical realism that I treat here; the anonymous author of *Les Évangiles des quenouilles* (ca. 1466–74); Jeanne Flore (fl. ca. 1537); Marguerite de Navarre (1492–1549); María de Zayas y Sotomayor (1590?-ca. 1661/1669); Margaret Cavendish, the Duchess of Newcastle (1623–73); Delarivier Manley (1663–1724); Mary Davys (1674–1732); and Jane Barker (1652–1732). The contributions of many others—from the twelfth-century women troubadours to Madame de Lafayette to Jane Austen—are also part of my story. But my main focus is the evolving tradition of Western women's prose fiction in the framed-novelle genre from 1405 to 1726, the year Jane Barker's *The Lining of the Patch Work Screen* appeared.

While genres similar to the novella or tale may be found in many non-European cultures, the realist novel is a Western phenomenon. Therefore, in this study I focus exclusively on the Western tradition. Consideration of the rich Arabic, Indian, African, and Asian (particularly Japanese) narrative traditions is regrettably beyond its scope.

In chapter one, "The Case of the Novel," I examine the fundamental characteristics of both the novel and Bakhtin's theory of prosaics in order to establish how the above-mentioned women writers contributed to the novel's emergence. In the chapter two I elaborate on the connections between critical irony, as expressed in literature, and the establishment of a political standpoint. Here I use contemporary feminist and Marxist "standpoint theory" to buttress my claims.

Chapters three and four trace the evolution of the women's framed-novelle tradition from Christine de Pizan in France to María de Zayas in Spain to Jane Barker in England. In chapter five, "Circumstances Alter Cases," I explain how these authors used casuistry to make their fictional cases, and how it in turn shaped their fiction.

In chapter six I focus on a group of British women writers—Catherine Trotter and Aphra Behn, in addition to Davys and Manley—who constituted an important literary wave of the 1690s; they created a feminist prosaics that did much to shape the realism characteristic of the English novel. Chapter seven considers the genealogy, from the fifteenth to the eighteenth century, of a novella about a woman; its evolution illustrates changing aesthetic and ethical attitudes and serves to chart the transitions in women's literary history of the period. Those transitions are further examined in chapter eight, where I trace the history of the women's anti-romance from the troubadours to the nineteenth century. A final chapter, chapter nine, treats these women writers' relationship with the once dominant Latin rhetorical tradition, how it affected them and how their resistance to it was another factor in the emergence of the familiar conversational, non-Latinate prose style used in the novel.

This study is unique in theories about the novel's origins not only in its focus upon women writers,[3] but also in its attention to the continental tradition of women writers, which enormously influenced the British women (and men) who have been the focus of most earlier studies. The impact of Marguerite de Navarre's *Heptaméron* on the English women writers of the seventeenth century was palpable, and the influence of María de Zayas—whose name was erased in the translation process and thus unfortunately deleted from English literary history—was also considerable. Certain of Madame d'Aulnoy's works similarly had a marked impact on the British women writers. I treat this influence in chapter six.

I also depart from recent (and feminist) predecessors in the field who tend to lump Jane Barker together with Penelope Aubin and Elizabeth Rowe as didactic moralists to be distinguished from earlier, more outspoken feminists, such as Behn and Manley.[4] Instead I see Barker as part of a continuing feminist tradition; her satiric treatment of marriage-marketing is much closer to Cavendish, Behn, and Manley than to Rowe and Aubin. I do agree, however, that the assertion of a feminist voice, still strongly available in Barker, was largely eclipsed soon after by the moralistic sentimentalism that came to dominate prose fiction in succeeding decades. In chapter seven, "The Case of Violenta," and chapter eight, "Women Against Romance," I discuss these literary transitions.

This study began in the early 1980s as a chapter in my book *New England Local Color Literature: A Women's Tradition* (1983), in which I sketched through several centuries the genealogy of what I called women's literary realism. I first taught my graduate seminar "Women and the Rise of the Novel" in 1982 at the University of Tulsa's Graduate Program in Modern Letters. It was Germaine Greer, then Director of the Tulsa Center for the Study of Women's Literature, who proposed the title for the course, which is now the title of this book. Since then I have continued to read and study the astonishing numbers of works written by women of the early modern period. My doctoral training in comparative literature, under Fannie J. LeMoine at the University of Wisconsin, facilitated my access to the continental women writers.

Many people contributed to the completion of this book. In particular, I would like to acknowledge the students in my courses on early modern women writers at the University of Tulsa and the University of Maine, as well as the following scholars, who have generously contributed information and support: Ruth Perry, Deborah Rogers, Fannie J. LeMoine, Germaine Greer, Ulrich Wicks, and Esther Rauch. In addition, I would like to express my appreciation to the National Endowment for the Humanities for a fellowship that enabled me to complete portions of the manuscript; to the University of Maine for three faculty research grants and a university sabbatical that greatly facilitated my research efforts; to Maura Burnett and the editing staff at St. Martin's Press, and to Marilyn Emerick. Finally, the Reference and Interlibrary Loan staffs at the University of Maine; the Portsmouth Public Library; the Houghton Library, Harvard University; the Huntington Library, San Marino, California; and the Newberry Library, Chicago, were very helpful.

I hope that this book, along with my works in American women's literature, will contribute in a significant way to the intellectual task that has fallen to my generation of scholars: the construction of women's literary history.

Chapter One

The Case of the Novel

THE NOVEL, A GENRE THAT HAS DOMINATED Western prose fiction for more than two centuries, is a unique literary form that has its own distinguishing properties. Specifying what they are is not an easy task, however. One way is to contrast it with earlier literary forms, in particular the epic, a classical genre (which was revived in the medieval period), and the romance, a medieval form.

Georg Lukács famously defined the novel as "the epic of a world that has been abandoned by God" in his *Theory of the Novel* (1920),[1] thus identifying the novel in terms of the post-medieval dissociation of sensibility and the rise of secular empiricism that emerged as the medieval cosmic synthesis was fatally challenged by early modern astronomy. Similarly, in his still-classic study, *The Rise of the Novel* (1957), Ian Watt correlates the emergence of the novel with what he calls "philosophic realism," a new secular nominalism where Cartesian individualism and Lockean empiricism combined to establish the particular sense experience of the individual as a valid epistemological source.[2] The novel, Watt contended, is grounded in this empiricist epistemology: "The novel arose in the modern period, a period whose general intellectual orientation was most decisively separated from its classical and mediaeval heritage by its rejection—or at least its attempted rejection—of universals" (12).

In 1785, one of the earliest theorists of the novel, Clara Reeve, contrasted the novel with the romance in order to develop one of the first definitions of the new genre.

The Romance is an heroic fable, which treats of fabulous persons and things.—The Novel is a picture of real life and manners, and of the times in which it is written. The Romance in lofty and elevated language, describes what never happened nor is likely to happen.—The Novel gives a familiar relation of such things, as pass every day before our eyes, such as may happen to our friend, or to ourselves; . . . represent[ing] every scene, in so easy and natural a manner, and . . . mak[ing] them appear so probable, as to deceive us into a persuasion . . . that all is real.[3]

Like most theorists, Reeves highlighted the novel's realism: "The Novel is a picture of real life and manners," recounting everyday events in a "familiar" way.

By the latter half of the seventeenth century even authors of romances were beginning to call for more probable or more realistic characters. In various theoretical statements made in the mid-seventeenth century, Madeleine de Scudéry, the leading French romancier, proposed that writers should attend to probability, thereby invoking an Aristotelian criterion, which soon became codified as *vraisemblance*.[4] In French neoclassical criticism, however, *vraisemblance* emerged as a doctrine of propriety—authors should depict characters who are realistic according to social norms of appropriate conduct. Unfortunately, this notion precluded the kind of particularized idiosyncratic realism that twentieth-century critic Mikhail Bakhtin and others appreciate as one of the novel's most important characteristics.

Early English theorists of the novel also critiqued the romance from the point of view of everyday realism. One of the earliest and most cogent defenses of realism occurs in Delarivier Manley's preface to *The Secret History of Queen Zarah, and the Zarazians* (1705). Manley, like de Scudéry, calls for more probable characters, but, unlike the French *vraisemblance*, her notion of probability is not synonymous with propriety. Indeed, her principal example critiques what she feels is the unbelieveably virtuous female behavior seen in most romances. "*It wou'd in no wise be probable that a Young Woman fondly beloved by a Man of great Merit, and for whom she had Reciprocal Tenderness, finding her self at all Times alone with him . . . cou'd always resist his addresses.*"[5] Similarly, romantic heroes "*have nothing in them that is Natural*" (A6[r]).

Manley argues that a reader "*who has any Sense*" wants to see someone like herself "*represented*" in the work (A6[v]), for "*we care little for what was done a Thousand years ago among the* Tartars *or* Abyssines" (A3[v]). Finally, and most importantly, Manley critiques the abstract generality of romance characters. "*Most authors are contented to describe Men in general . . . without entering into the Particulars . . . ; they don't perceive Nice Distinctions*" (A7[r]). Manley here adumbrates an idea that is at the heart of Bakhtin's "prosaics" theory of the novel, which "focuses on quotidian events that in principle elude reduction to 'underlying' laws or systems."[6] We will return to this theory shortly.

Earlier, Margaret Cavendish, the Duchess of Newcastle, had anticipated Manley's critique in scattered negative comments about the romance and the epic. In the *Sociable Letters* (1664), for example, itself one of the earlist examples of familiar realism, Cavendish says of epic and romance authors, "my Reason believes they Writ Unreasonably, not only of their Feigned Gods, or of their Feigned Fights, and of their Feigned Fortunes or Successes; The truth is, they . . . contain . . . more Impossibilities than Probabilities,"[7] thereby reinvoking Aristotle's probability criterion. Characters' actions, she believes, "should be Natural," noting the improbability of many heroic deeds in the epic and romance: "for what One man can Disorder, or Rout an Army, with his Single Strength or Courage?" (257).

Cavendish also modifies Aristotle's theory of *mimesis* to articulate the idea that the artist should "imitate" contemporary reality as realistically as possible. She complains in the above-cited passage that heroic deeds "cannot be Imitated." And she offers instead her own work, the *Sociable Letters*, which "are an Imitation of a Personal Visitation and Conversation" (C2ᵛ).

In an essay in her *Natures Pictures* (1656), Cavendish contends that poets are "Natures Painters,"[8] which explains the title of the work. They should copy nature, that is, the immediate environment, directly, rather than copying ancient texts. Those who imitate or rework the classics in their writings are "like a company of Ravens, that live upon dead carckasses [*sic*], so they upon old Authors, and some have been like Maggots, that have been bred in their dead flesh, which is the living works of dead Authors . . . but very few [are] rightly begotten from Nature" (*Natures Pictures* 361). By this criterion she criticizes Virgil, for example, because he was not a "true Naturall Poet . . . he was rather an imitator of Homer, than of Nature" (361). In this essay, "Heavens Library" (where Cavendish has Jove ranking the great works of literature, throwing out some and elevating others), she proposes that "all Romances should be cast out" (360).

Like these early women critics, Bakhtin, in his essay "Epic and Novel" (1975), also stressed that the novel operates in a "zone of familar contact";[9] whereas the epic is an abstract monolithic genre that exists on a "distanced plane" (20) that is "walled off" from the present (15). "There is no place in the epic for any openendedness, indecision, indeterminacy" (16), attributes readily apparent in the novel, which manifests a "spirit of process and inconclusiveness" (7). Significantly, Bakhtin sees the epic as the product of a "patriarchal social structure"; it "canoniz[es]" the events of "the world of fathers" (15). Conversely, to extend Bakhtin's argument, the novel valorizes events from the everyday world of mothers.

As a secular genre, the realist novel focuses on the happenings of this world; its connectives are horizontal and largely paratactic. No providential transcendent force controls things from above. Causality is secular and material. Thus, the dominant trope in realist prose fiction becomes metonymy, as opposed to metaphor. And the dominant style is the plain style, a familiar, paratactic, conversational mode.

Unlike the epic, the romance, classical tragedy, or other poetic genres, the novel pays attention to economic realities; indeed, one could argue that economic forces and motivations become the primary focus of the realist novel. We will return to this aspect of the genre shortly.

The novel also evinces a critical irony that is unique and definitional. The word *irony* derives from *eiron*, a figure in Greek comedy who undercut the boastful *alazon*. This etymological connotation is readily apparent in the novel's irony as reified official doctrines and sanctimonies are routinely undercut and debunked. It is perhaps Bakhtin who has most insisted on the novel's inherent irreverence. Parody, satire, travesty—these are the fundamental responses the novel has toward institutionalized dogma, according to Bakhtin.

In novelesque treatment "the object is broken apart, laid bare (its hierarchical ornamentation is removed): the naked object is ridiculous; its 'empty' clothing . . . is also ridiculous" (23–24). By contrast, the presentation of the epic hero is nonironic (34); there is only one, adulatory, perspective in the epic: "the epic world knows only a single and unified world view" (35).

There were undoubtedly several sources for the mentality of critical irony that emerged in the early modern period. It has been argued that the economic base for the ironic ethical perspective found in the novel was use-value production. A Marxist term, use-value production refers to the production of goods that are used by the producers and/or by their immediate associates. Women have long been associated with use-value production because in pre- or noncapitalist sites, such production took place in the home and involved traditionally female labor, such as cooking, clothes-making, sustenance gardening, etc. Production for exchange is, conversely, the production of goods for sale or trade. Any large-scale monetary-based economic system is based upon production for exchange; however, the exchange ethos is particularly evident in industrialized captialism. Theorists of the novel, especially those with a Marxist bent, have connected the novel's rise with the emergence of the exchange ethos of early modern capitalism, seeing the novel as a site of resistance to that culture. Lucien Goldmann, for example, in *Pour une sociologie du roman* (1964) has effectively argued that economic production for use, which was increasingly being replaced by production for exchange during the seventeenth and eighteenth centuries, provided an ethical standpoint from which to criticize and ironize the increasingly dominant ethos of commodity exchange.

Another probable source of the novel's critical irony lay in a kind of folk-culture resistance to the growing colonization of everyday life by nation-state bureaucracies and by the increasing dominance of scientific and pseudo-scientific regulation and/or (in Michel Foucault's terminology) "discipline" of the everyday life-world. While this resistance became more acute in the nineteenth century, it may be seen as early as the fifteenth century in various folk parodies, such as *Les Évangiles des quenouilles* (ca. 1466–74), which I treat in chapter three.[10]

A third source for the novel's critical irony—one that has not been sufficiently acknowledged—lay in women's growing resistance to misogynist ideologies and sexist practices that reified them as objects for exchange and abuse. In chapter two I further explore the contribution of women writers to the emergence of critical irony as a dominant perspective in prose fiction.

To my mind the most important defining attribute of the novel, however, lies in its character as a form of ethical knowledge. Because of its unique blend of realism and critical irony, the novel can foster ethical understanding of individual characters' plights and of the forces responsible better than perhaps any other medium. The remainder of this chapter will be devoted to exploring further this crucial aspect of the novel.

Unlike other literary modes, the realist novel provides a detailed sense of the density of worldly life, its *quidditas,* its whatness. We have already noted how Delarivier Manley identified the novel as a genre that particularizes, that recognizes and embraces distinctions and differences. The realist novel exults, in fact, in the multifariousness of the particulars of the world. The novel's characters are much more complexly individualized than characters in earlier genres, and they are rooted in particularized, qualitatively differentiated, space and time (what Bakhtin calls the *chronotope*)—in *particular* circumstances.

The novel emerged in part out of the theological method of casuistry, where generalized rules are adapted or refracted by individualized cases that challenge a general principle.[11] A focus on the details of a case, on the circumstances of a life, is inherently subversive to doctrine, for no rule can be stretched to accommodate all the particularities of an individual case. Because of its emphasis on individual and particularized circumstances, the novel is therefore in this sense necessarily a subversive genre, as Bakhtin and a number of other theorists contend.

The novel provides, in effect, an ethical defense of the individual against tyrannical norms. Its antiauthoritarian "Galilean perception . . . denies . . . absolutism," according to Bakhtin (*Dialogic Imagination* 366), valorizing instead the irreducible uniqueness of the individual and her or his situation. Bakhtin's analysis of Dostoievsky's character Devushkin in the novel *Poor Folk* points up the novel's ethical dimension. Devushkin, himself poor, resents all attempts to fix him, to stereotype him, to objectify him as a poor person. "Already in his first work Dostoevsky shows how the hero himself revolts against literature in which the 'little man' is externalized and finalized without being consulted." Devushkin is "*personally* deeply insulted . . . and outraged" by the characterization of poverty in Gogol's *Overcoat;* he felt that "he had been defined totally once and for all."[12] In short, Devushkin had been erased in all his particulars, reified into an object in someone else's textual exchange. With Devushkin we see the expression of a kind of fierce critical irony—rooted in a subject's resistance to reification—that characterizes the novel and establishes its ethical perspective. Devushkin also manifests the awakening of the critical consciousness that is necessary to the emergence of a standpoint, as elaborated by Georg Lukács in *History and Class Consciousness*—to be explored further in the next chapter.

Bakhtin, in other words, conceives the novel in ethical terms as the site where the particulars of experience refuse to be dominated or objectified by what he called *theoretism.* As identified by Gary Saul Morson and Caryl Emerson, *theoretism* is systems thinking, generalizing theories that elide the singularity of events. "When 'theoretists' of ethics or action consider the world, they generalize to patterns, norms, and rules in which these singularities are lost" (53). "As Bakhtin uses the term, theoretism always understands events in terms of a set of rules to which they conform or a structure that they exhibit. . . . [T]heoretism thinks away the 'eventness' of events" (50).

As opposed to theoretism, Bakhtin proposed an ethical and aesthetic response he termed a *prosaics.* Unlike a *poetics,* which since Aristotle has been conceived as a largely formalist and purely aesthetic theory, a prosaics integrates the ethical with the aesthetic, focusing on the moral thematics of a literary work, rather than on its formal aesthetic properties.

As an ethical approach, prosaics entails a casuistical ethic: that is, it does *not* focus on abstract principles, and its methodology is *not* deduction; rather it emphasizes the particular case, and its method is induction. As Morson and Emerson explain, "prosaics focuses on the quotidian events that in principle elude reduction to 'underlying' laws or systems" (33). It is in fact "suspicious of systems," meaning any "organization in which every element has a place in a rigorous hierarchy" (27–28). Tolstoy expressed a "prosaics," a casuistical ethic, through his characters Levin and Pierre (in *Anna Karenina* and *War and Peace,* respectively); "instead of a system, they come to rely on moral wisdom derived from living rightly moment to moment and attending carefully to the irreducible particularities of each case" (25).

Bakhtin came to see the novel, "the most prosaic of prosaic forms, [as] occupy[ing] a special place in ethical education" (27). "Far superior [to abstract philosophical discussions] would be case studies extending over hundreds of pages . . . and describing all . . . events within their multivalent social milieu. Far superior, in short, would be the rich and 'thick' accounts found in great novels" (27). The novel thus comes to be seen as a form of ethical knowledge. "If ethics is (as Bakhtin contends) a matter of particular, concrete cases, and not of rules to be instantiated, then novels may be the richest form of ethical thought" (366).

Though she seems to have developed her ideas independently of Bakhtin, British author and critic Iris Murdoch in effect amplifies his *prosaics.* Like Bakhtin, she rejects "theoretism" (without using the term, of course): "What makes metaphysical ('totalising') coherence theories unacceptable is the way in which they in effect 'disappear' what is individual and contingent by equating reality with integration in system."[13]

Murdoch believes that moral sensitivity or moral awareness requires a knowledge of, an ability to see, the particulars of one's environment, whether those particulars be other people, animals, nature, or other aspects. A great novel teaches one to attend to these particulars. It trains the mind to see and to respect "the great surprising variety of the world."[14]

The kind of "morally disciplined attention" (*Metaphysics* 23) that Murdoch is talking about derives from Simone Weil's concept of "attentive love." In 1942 Weil explained:

> The love of our neighbor in all its fullness simply means being able to say to him: "What are you going through?" It is a recognition that the sufferer exists, not only as a unit in a collection, or a specimen . . . but as [an individual]. . . . For this reason it is . . . indispensable, to know how to look at him in a certain way. This way of looking is first of all attentive.[15]

As Murdoch continues, an attentive focus on realities beyond the self makes one realize that the other is a being with "needs and wishes" of her own; this awareness makes it "harder . . . to treat a person as a thing" (*Sovereignty* 66). In her view, great novelists can lead one to this kind of awareness because they are not "afraid of the contingent."[16] They are able to achieve "the extremely difficult realization that something other than oneself is real," expressing thereby a "non-violent apprehension of difference."[17]

The imagination that is exercised in both writing and reading a novel is thus "a moral discipline" that makes us aware of others' situations, their suffering, and their coping. Such awareness should induce not only ethical compassion or sympathy; it may also "help people not to become embittered or brutalised or stupefied by affliction" (*Metaphysics* 322).

In her recent book *Poetic Justice* (1995), Martha Nussbaum has enunciated a similar theory, linking the novel and the moral sensitivities it encourages to the practice of law and the formation of public policy. Nussbaum reflects that "our society is full of refusals to imagine one another with empathy and compassion" and considers that this kind of moral imagination can be fostered by novels.[18]

Like the theorists treated above, Nussbaum remarks that the novel enacts a kind of casuistical ethic (without using the term): "the novel constructs a paradigm of a style of ethical reasoning that is context-specific . . . in which we get potentially universalizable concrete prescriptions by bringing a general idea of human flourishing to bear on a concrete situation, which we are invited to enter through the imagination" (8). "We see the novel's abstract deliberations . . . as issuing in each case from a concrete human life" (28). Nussbaum also promotes a "prosaics" of fiction in which the ethical and the aesthetic are co-present: the novel's "moral operations are not independent of its aesthetic excellence. [*Hard Times*] binds us to the workers because it causes us to take pleasure in their company" (35).

In another recent work, *The True Story of the Novel* (1996), which traces novelistic discourse back to antiquity, Margaret Doody sees the novel's prosaic attention to the familiar, particularized details of the physical world—or what Doody calls "presence" (as opposed to "dry transcendence")—is what makes the novel "the 'feminine' literary form *par excellence*."[19] To read a novel "is to tune in to the wavelength of the Feminine" (461).

It is the goddess Demeter, the goddess of earth, who, Doody claims, inspires and informs the novel. "The Goddess of prose narration stands for the subscription—on the part of author, readers, and characters alike—to the physicality of the narratable world" (440). The novel offers a kind of subversive "celebration of the Goddess, and of the mundane world" and proposes a "new nonphallic religion" that affirms "the divine powers of nature" (462). Here Doody promotes what is probably the first ecofeminist theory of the novel.

Furthering her argument, Doody insists that the novel's focus on the messy, disorganized details of life make it inherently resistant to established systems of order. "The mess in the Novel is not to be cleaned up by the broom of the Law" (478). It remains "the repository of our hope in something that can be stated as 'feminine' if the State and Establishment

are thought of as 'masculine,' under the sign of the phallus" (473). "It re-
joices in a rich muddy messiness that is the ultimate despair of *Fascismus*"
(485). In an earlier article Doody had similarly concluded, "there is always
something uppety about the novel," which is a genre that "opposes the official, the public, the 'masculine' and the governing, and speaks for the
marginal, the dispossessed, the emotional."[20]

Virginia Woolf proposed a similar aesthetic of contingency. In an article entitled "Everyday Use and Moments of Being: Toward a Nondominative Aesthetic" (1993) I suggested that in various writings—particularly in
A Room of One's Own (1929)—Woolf articulated an aesthetic wherein the
contingent details of the messy everyday world are valorized over generic
abstractions that would ignore them.[21] In her famous visit to the British
Museum in *A Room of One's Own* Woolf perceives that venerable institution as a synecdoche for patriarchal knowledges and methodologies.
These teach one, she realizes, to "strain off what was personal and acci-
dental . . . and so reach the pure fluid, the essential oil of truth."[22] "The
student who has been trained . . . at Oxbridge has no doubt some method
of shepherding his question past all distractions till it runs into its answer
as a sheep runs into its pen" (28).

Conversely, Woolf herself uses a methodology that adapts to the ran-
domness and messiness of life itself. "I take," she says, "only what chance
has floated to my feet" (78). In another essay, "Modern Fiction" (1925),
Woolf urges, "Let us record the atoms as they fall upon the mind in the
order in which they fall, let us trace the pattern, however disconnected
and incoherent in appearance, which each sight or incident scores upon
the consciousness."[23]

Thus, Woolf maintains that the writer of prose fiction should be faith-
ful to the anomalous particulars of reality and not rush to cram them
into a pen of preconceived doctrine. In this she affirms a metaphysics of
presence. Woolf's reluctance to shape reality into artificial abstractions is
shared by a number of women writers from Dorothy Wordsworth to
Clarice Lispector, as I document in "Ecofeminist Literary Criticism:
Reading the Orange" (1996).[24] "*Tell the thing!*" exhorted Sarah Orne Jewett to aspiring writers; her advice could serve as the byword of a prosaics
of literature.[25]

The affirmation of the value and validity of the contingent world's singularities may be seen as an important countervalence to the Gnostic
imagination of contemporary existentialism and poststructuralism,
wherein the real physical world is dismissed as alien, threatening, and
slimy (Jean-Paul Sartre's *Nausea*), and/or nonexistent (contemporary discourse theories wherein reality is seen as being filtered through linguistic
constructs to the point that it exists only as an *absent* referent).[26]

A prosaics of the novel not only affirms a metaphysics of presence; it also proposes, as we have seen, a casuistical ethic, whereby the moral response is governed not by universal rules and abstract doctrines but rather by a particularized evaluation of the circumstances of each individual case. This kind of casuistical moral reasoning is an important aspect of Carol Gilligan's "ethic of care" (as opposed to a rights-or rule-based ethic); it is a "mode of reasoning that is contextual and narrative rather than formal and abstract."[27]

Such contextual reasoning is well illustrated in Susan Glaspell's short story "A Jury of Her Peers" (1917), a work that Gilligan herself has analyzed as exemplifying an ethic of care (but to somewhat different purposes than I do here). The story concerns a moral dilemma faced by two women who come to understand that their neighbor has murdered her husband. By attending to the evidentiary particulars, which their husbands, the police investigators on the case, overlook, the women come to realize their neighbor's guilt. In the process, however, they also piece together the circumstances that led to the murder; namely, that the woman had been severely emotionally abused, and had snapped when the husband had killed her only emotional connection, a pet canary.

Rather than convict the woman according to a universal ethical and legal principle (all murder is wrong), the women tacitly pardon her (by harboring the incriminating evidence, the dead bird), feeling that in this particular case the murder was, if not justified, at least defensible. In fact, the women consider that within the context they themselves bear some responsibility, because they neglected to maintain communication with the woman, thus contributing to the emotional isolation that fostered the crime.

It is prose fiction—sometimes short stories but particularly the novel—that allows for the nuanced exploration of circumstances that is necessary for this kind of moral reasoning. That is why Nussbaum, Murdoch, Bakhtin, and others promote the novel as an ethical form, and perhaps the only form in which casuistical reasoning can be fully enacted.

The idea that fiction can be used as a tool for the inculcation of moral sentiments is not a new one. Indeed, by the mid-eighteenth century, as Catherine Gallagher points out in *Nobody's Story* (1994), this conception of fiction had been well explored by philosophers like Hume and Adam Smith, as well as by fiction writers.[28] Most of the women writers I will be concerned with in this study conceived of prose fiction as a means of transmitting moral and political positions. As early as Christine de Pizan's writings at the turn of the fourteenth century, prose narrative was seen as a vehicle for the refutation of misogynist perspectives and for the advocacy of the moral recognition of women. Emile V. Telle suggests that for

Marguerite de Navarre the novella became "a means of teaching . . . feminism."[29] And numerous women writers conceived of their work as cautionary tales. Marie de Gournay wrote in her dedicatory preface to *Le Proumenoir* (1594) that her novella serves "to warn women to be wary" ["l'utilité d'advertir les dames de se tenir en garde"].[30] Similarly, María de Zayas, a seventeenth-century Spanish writer, said she wrote her framed-novelle to present "case histories" ["casos verdaderos"], which are designed to "enlighten, or disenchant, women about men's deceptions" ["y que tuviesen nombre de desengaños"].[31]

Early writers also recognized the potential prose fiction had to arouse readers' sympathy for characters, even to encourage their identification with them (as seen in *Don Quixote* and the numerous "female quixote" figures; see further discussion in chapter eight). Such sympathy could well work then, as theorists claimed, to enlarge readers' moral sensitivities—a position similar to that maintained by Martha Nussbaum today.

In her 1671 "Preface" to *Natures Pictures,* for example, Margaret Cavendish says that she hopes her work will "beget chast Thoughts, nourish love of Virtue, kindle Human Pity, warm Charity, encrease Civility."[32] While pity was an emotion Aristotle recognized as an appropriate response to tragedy, Cavendish's linkage of the concept with "warm Charity" suggests a significant transformation of the classical idea, one that anticipates the conception of literature as a vehicle for the inculcation of moral sentiments, which, as we have noted, came to dominate in the eighteenth century.

One direction that emerged from this view of literature was the sentimentalist tradition, which was a dominant strain of women's fiction well into the twentieth century. While I do not treat it here, sentimentalist literature was premised on the idea of using fiction to sensitize readers to the plight of disadvantaged and oppressed protagonists—usually, in the earliest examples of the genre, women, but in later works, animals, slaves, and impoverished lower classes.

Unfortunately, however, most sentimentalist works reimposed a kind of reductive theoretism, turning characters into specimens, of the type Devushkin protested against in Dostoievsky's *Poor Folk.* And while sentimentalist fiction has been enormously influential in changing social attitudes or performing "cultural work" (consider, for example, Harriet Beecher Stowe's *Uncle Tom's Cabin* [1852], which Abraham Lincoln only half-facetiously credited with having caused the Civil War), it does not have the inherently subversive character of the realist works favored in prosaics theory. The reason for this is that sentimentalist fiction failed to particularize characters and circumstances as anomalous cases, instead inscribing (and thereby reifying) them in prefabricated constructs. (*Uncle*

Tom's Cabin should not be taken as prototypical in this respect, however, because it remains in many ways a realist novel.)[33]

My thesis in this study is that while women have long been identified—both as writers and as readers—with the sentimentalist tradition, their contribution to the rise of the realist novel has not yet been recognized. That contribution included the development of a critical irony that was rooted in women's marginalized standpoint and resistant to dominant misogynist ideologies, and the articulation of a kind of feminist casuistry wherein case studies of women's circumstances, realistically conveyed, were used to refute misogynist generalities and maxims. Women contributed to the formation of this inherently subversive genre by articulating their own critical voice and particularizing their own circumstances, in order to resist misogynist reifications that cast them as objects within the dominant discourse of sexual exchange. They thereby helped to fracture the univocal discourses that dominated in pre-modern eras, establishing the kind of dialogical counterpoint that was essential to the emergence of the novel.

Chapter Two

Critical Irony, Standpoint Theory, and the Novel

IRONIC PERSPECTIVES DEVELOP WHEN PEOPLE SENSE a discontinuity between the official version of events and their own experience of them. When an unofficial, marginalized position becomes agreed on by numbers of people in a group, it gathers strength and provides some countervalence to the dominant perspective. Once members of a group identify their perspective as that *of* the group, the position approaches that of a political standpoint, a critical point of resistance to oppression.

Women writers in the early modern period, who were nearly all members of or associated with the nobility, evinced early on a resistance to discourses that cast them as inferior beings, objects for exchange in dynastic power struggles. In fact, that resistance is apparent in the earliest Western works by women: the debate genres used by the twelfth-century women troubadours (see chapter five) and, around the turn of the fourteenth century, the writings of Christine de Pizan (see chapter three).

With the rise of capitalism and the emergence of a merchant and banking class, the urban bourgeoisie, the exchange of women that had functioned to seal patriarchal kinship relations under feudalism became used to solidify needed economic alliances between the landed (but cash-poor) gentry and the cash-rich but land-and-prestige-poor bourgeoisie. The marrying-off of daughters was an important way these economic relations were mediated. As one historian noted, "the marriage settlement [became] . . . the sacrament by which land allied itself with trade."[1]

Women who were the objects of these negotiations—often without their consent or even knowledge—for the most part disliked the system.

Much of the critical animus in seventeenth- and eighteenth-century women's prose fiction is directed against the marriage market in which women were in effect commodified goods for sale. Daniel Defoe, often considered the first novelist, realized the inherent drama in this situation and used it to frame two of his earliest novels, *Moll Flanders* (1722) and *Roxana* (1724), although somewhat ambiguously.[2] As Ellen Pollak has noted, Moll Flanders manifests a clear "desire to short-circuit or withdraw from 'normal' bourgeois relations in which women are circulated as objects among men."[3]

Moll Flanders was by no means the first woman character to indicate resistance to the marriage-market exchange system (and indeed Defoe's treatment of both her and Roxana tends to undercut the seriousness of their positions); that resistance is much more clearly stated in the works of Margaret Cavendish, who wrote half a century before Defoe. Indeed, Cavendish herself was preceded by the continental women writers, such as Marguerite de Navarre and María de Zayas, of the framed-novelle tradition, which effectively began with Christine de Pizan in 1405. These women also critiqued the marriage exchange system (still principally the feudal, kin-based system in their day), as well as other abuses of women such as rape, wife-beating, and what is today called sexual harassment.

As noted, critical irony can be rooted in what has been labeled a standpoint, which is the political perspective that an oppressed group may come to have. The notion of a standpoint was originally articulated by the Hungarian, Hegelian-Marxist theorist Georg Lukács in a section of *History and Class Consciousness* (1922) entitled "Reification and the Consciousness of the Proletariat." Lukács believed that when a person is treated as a thing, an inherent contradiction emerges because the person as subject knows that s/he is not an object; from this contradiction may emerge a critical consciousness, a resentment of being reified, and a rejection of the process and forces that are responsible. When several people in an objectified class share their resentment, the process of "consciousness-raising" begins, and a political standpoint develops wherein it is recognized that the treatment is shared by members of the group *because they are members* of that group. Lukács was principally concerned with industrial workers, or the "proletariat," who are reified on the assembly line as cogs in the machine; subsequent feminist theorists have applied Lukács's ideas to women.

In the capitalist production process, Lukács claimed, the worker "is turned into a commodity and reduced to a mere quantity. But this very fact forces him to surpass the immediacy of his condition."[4] Beneath "the quantifying crust," however, lies a "qualitative, living core" (169), from which emerges the critical class consciousness that Lukács deemed both epistemologically privileged and revolutionary. "[I]n the proletariat . . . the process by which a [person's] achievement is split off from his total personality and becomes a commodity leads to a revolutionary consciousness" (171). "Corresponding to the objective concealment of the commodity form, there is the subjective element . . . that while the process by which the worker is reified and becomes a commodity dehumanizes him . . . it remains true that precisely his humanity and his soul are not changed into commodities" (172).

I will argue that early modern women writers developed a critical feminist consciousness because they too were reified in misogynist ideologies that cast them as inferior beings, objects of sexual exchange and abuse. As contemporary feminist theorist Catharine MacKinnon has effectively argued, sexual reification may provoke the emergence of a women's standpoint: "What is it about women's experience," she asked, "that produces a distinctive perspective on social reality? How is an angle of vision and an interpretive hermeneutics of social life created in the group women? . . . Sexual objectification of women . . . provides answers."[5]

It would seem further that the emergence of critical consciousness is enhanced if the subjects have a point of comparison from which to determine that their own treatment is unjust. In the case of these women writers, that comparative perspective came from their upper-class status. Why should they, who enjoyed privileged treatment by virtue of their class, be subjected to abuse and derogation because of their gender?

Contemporary feminist theorists have adapted Lukács's standpoint theory to women. In general, however, these theorists, notably Nancy Hartsock, have developed a more Marxist and less Hegelian version of standpoint theory than Lukács. Reverting to the Marxist theory of historical materialism, they assume, like Marx, that "the mode of production of material life conditions the social, political, and intellectual life process in general."[6] When standpoint theory is grounded in this premise, it holds that a group's consciousness is rooted in that group or class's relationship to the mode of production, or its economic base, and in particular to the labor experience of its members. Feminist standpoint theory, therefore, holds that women's labor, their place in the economic system, conditions or shapes their consciousness. Nancy Hartsock finds, for example, in material practices "the structural determinants of [women's] experiences"; these are "the common threads which connect the diverse experiences of women."[7] In particular, Hartsock has focused upon women's historical connection to use-value production, seeing that as a base from which emerged a critical position toward the increasingly dominant ethos of commodity exchange. As noted, use-value production generally means domestic labor, such as cooking, knitting, weaving, spinning, and subsistence agriculture—tasks that even royal women such as Marguerite de Navarre often performed. Such labor is generally less alienating than that of industrial workers or of those involved in commodity exchange, and therefore constitutes a more holistic, personalist consciousness, according to this vein of standpoint theory.

I have come to believe (revising a position I took in an earlier article)[8] that while both of these branches of standpoint theory—what we may call the Lukács (Hegelian) version and the Hartsock (Marxist) version—provide relevant explanations for the presence of a critical feminist irony in the writings of early modern women, the Lukácian theory is the more important. The primary animus for these women writers' development of a critical standpoint and for the critical irony manifest in their work was their intense resentment of their sexual objectification as women. The Hartsock use-value production theory remains nevertheless suggestive, and I wish to explore further some of its ramifications before returning to the other, which I do in the next chapter. Lucien Goldmann has proposed that the novel arose as a dialectical critical response to the emergence of capitalism, with its exchange-value ethos and the attendant marginalization of production for use and its personalist ethos.[9] He saw the novel's thematics as an ethical reaction against the alienation inherent in commodity exchange; and argued that the artist retains a connection to the world of use-value production and that this provides the critical basis from which she or he criticizes the abstractions and immoralities of the world of commodity exchange. While Goldmann does not explain why or how an artist retains a connection to use-value production, it is apparent that artistic production resembles use-value production in that the latter retains an artisanal character in which products are valued for their personal, "sacred" qualities rather than for their abstract commodity worth. What Goldmann does not specify, however, is that much of women's domestic use-value labor is on the edge of artistic production. Indeed, the line between use-value product and "art" is blurred in many of women's household tasks such as knitting, baking, needlepoint, quilting, etc.

An interesting contemporary work that explores the relation between women's use-value production and art is Alice Walker's brilliant story "Everyday Use" (1973). The mother in the story values a family quilt for its personal connections, its sacred character, reflecting a use-value ethos, where the daughter, Dee, values it in terms of its exchange value as an aesthetic commodity. The story revolves around the conflict between the two women on this issue.[10]

As we have noted, Bakhtin contrasted the novel with the epic, which he claimed was "walled off" from the "continuing and unfinished present," where the novel presents "a zone of maximally close contact between the represented object and contemporary reality in all its inconclusiveness."[11] The novel, he thought, was a genre on the boundary between the literary and the non-literary, routinely incorporating "extraliterary genres," such as letters, diaries, etc. within its fabric (33). I argue that the "zone of contact" between women's use-value production and their artistic production is uniquely close. Early women writers such as Cavendish and Jane Barker in fact appropriated use-value practices (spinning and needlework, for example) in their aesthetic theory to explain aspects of their own literary composition (see further discussion below).

A sense of irony toward patriarchal exchange systems, with their inherent commodification of women, was one of the principal contributions women writers made to the rise of the novel. Women's historical connection to use-value production appears to have been a primary source for this irony. The conception of art as a use-value praxis held by many early modern women writers was accompanied by an ethical perspective that was functional in use-value relations. Qualitative rather than quantitative, personalist, and unalienated, it provided a likely basis for women's resistance to the commodification of relationship that attended production for exchange.

Although early modern women writers came predominantly from a group of upper-class women who had a somewhat problematic relationship with use-value production, they retained an identification with it, and with the domestic sphere. Women's base in use-value production, therefore, provided a critical, ironic standpoint from which to judge the machinations of the exchange system. This viewpoint was, I contend, an important basis for the irony seen in their early literary production, and it contributed importantly to the dialogical consciousness Bakhtin posited as essential to the rise of the novel.

Theorists who consider the emergence of the novel primarily in literary historical terms, such as Maurice Z. Shroder, see the form arising as an ironic reaction against the romance, constituting itself as an "anti-romance." Shroder suggests that the archetypal character relationship in the novel is between an *alazon* figure, who expresses a romantic (or mystifying) sensibility and an *eiron* figure, who expresses a commonsensical, realistic viewpoint.[12] Don Quixote is the classic romantic *alazon* and Sancho Panza the sensible *eiron*. In early women's novels the *alazon* figure took the form of the "female quixote," a character who imbibes romances to the point that she mystifies the underlying commodity relationship of the marriage-market exchange. She is usually coupled with a sensible sister or servant who debunks her pretensions (*eiron*).

It may well be that the irony inherent in this pattern was rooted in women's historical connection to use-value production. Once again Goldmann provides the necessary link when he argues, in effect, that the novelist is herself an ethical *eiron* to the ideological *alazon* of the marketplace. Goldmann remarks, "In the economic world, which constitutes the most important segment of modern social life, every authentic relationship between objects and human beings, [which is] qualitative, tends to disappear; at the same time relationships among people [are] replaced by a mediated and degraded connection, [one based on] . . . the purely quantitative values of exchange" (38). The artist, however, for reasons, as noted, that Goldmann does not explain, retains a connection to a use-value, qualitative ethic, and this forms the critical or ironic standpoint from which she or he takes an oppositional position to the dominant exchange-value ethic of capitalism.

Like Lukács and Hegel, Goldmann sees the novel as a "fallen" form because it reflects a world where authentic values have been compromised by the secular, amoral Machiavellian ethic of commodity exchange. The romanesque hero, then, has the problematic task of seeking "authentic values in a fallen [dégradé] world" (26). But those values, reflecting the relatively unalienated experience of use-value production, are no longer accessible; they can only be achieved or even imagined through the mediation of the quantitative ethic of exchange production (39). Don Quixote is a good example of a figure whose desire for unalienated experience is mediated by false, reified images that intrude. Goldmann deplores the profane character of exchange-value thinking, arguing that it negates the sacred (or the qualitative), functioning entirely in terms of "anaesthetic" rationalism (55).

In his study *Popular Fiction before Richardson,* John Richetti follows Goldmann in seeing that there is a moral dialectic in the novel between what he calls religious and secular values. Unique among scholars of the novel in drawing attention to such early modern women writers as Delarivier Manley and Jane Barker, Richetti sees that in their works the religious-versus-secular thematic connects to a feminist critique of patriarchal society. Although he does not explain it in explicitly feminist terms, Richetti recognizes that these women criticized the "financial and sexual materialism" that "reduces love to a biological impulse and marriage to a profitable alliance."[13] In other words, they resisted the commodification of relationships that resulted both from the growing extension of exchange-value consciousness into all areas of life and from the marriage-market exchange system in which women's bodies were reified into implements for male gratification; into what are now called "sex-objects." By contrast, the women envisaged (sometimes implicitly) an oppositional ethic, one rooted in spiritual love, in a personalist relationship that does not entail the commodification of women.

The writings of Margaret Cavendish and Jane Barker reveal that women writers of this period consciously connected the idea of literary production with use-value production: they both draw analogies between the traditional use-value roles of women and the role of writer, and they both seek models in use-value production for their art. They thus locate their literary production in that blurred "zone of contact" between reality and literary representation—and between use-value and artistic production—whose emergence Bakhtin saw as critical to the rise of the novel.

While their relationship with use-value production was clearly problematic, they nevertheless both personally identified with the subjective and valued roles it had provided women (as opposed to the devalued objectification that attended women's relegation to commodity status in marriage-market ideology). Their attempt to appropriate writing to such use-value labor as spinning and needlework suggests a desire to validate their new craft and thereby to legitimate the critical, ironic perspective expressed therein.

Jane Barker's *Patch-Work Screen for the Ladies* (1723), one of the most important, if most ignored, works in women's literary history, vividly appropriates use-value production to literary production. Barker's linkage of the two realms—women's work and art—provides a critical standpoint for the author's ironic view of the received "word of the fathers" (Bakhtin, *Dialogic Imagination* 342).

In apologizing for her inadequate poetry, Barker suggests that perhaps her "Fingers ought to have been imploy'd rather at the Needle and the Distaff, than to the Pen and Standish...."[14] Barker uses, however, this self-deprecatory remark (with its suggestion that women's proper identification is with use-value production rather than with literary production) to criticize a received masculine literary tradition—the Pindaric ode, a classical verse form. The reason she ought to return to the needle and distaff is that she has had difficulty trying to compose a "Pindarick," whose aesthetic she then proceeds to debunk. Its "irregular Jumps, and Starts," she observes, its "sudden Disappointments, and long-expected Periods ... deprive ... the mind of ... Musick " (7). Thus, Barker ends by ironically undercutting the received "word of the fathers" from the viewpoint of one trained in use-value production.

Like Cavendish and most other early modern women authors Barker decries women's exclusion from formal education. "A learned Woman," she laments, "is like a Forc'd Plant, that never has its due or proper Relish" (11). Nevertheless, she implicitly sees women's training in use-value occupations as relevant to, indeed indispensable to, literary production. Indeed her very concept of what a work of literature, in particular a novel, should be is based on a use-value product, the patch-work screen. Not only is such a creation quintessentially women's work, it also exhibits the "unofficial," random, folk character that Bakhtin saw as essential to the novel's dialogic discourse (*Dialogic Imagination* 20).

In her introduction Barker expands the patch-work analogy to a dialogic discussion among women: "*whenever one sees a Set of Ladies together, their* Sentiments *are as differently mix'd as the* Patches *in their Work . . . they* divide *and* sub-divide, '*till at last they make this Dis-union meet in an harmonious* Tea-Table Entertainment." Barker carries the metaphor still farther, remarking a correlative to "the Clashing *of* Atoms, *which at last* united *to compose this glorious Fabrick of the* UNIVERSE" (v-vi).

Barker, however, apologizes for this flight of fancy (reminiscent incidentally of Cavendish's similarly undisciplined and extravagant analogies) immediately thereafter: "*Forgive me, kind Reader, for carrying the Metaphor too high; by which means I am out of my Sphere and so can say nothing of the* Male Patch-Workers; *for my high Flight in Favour of the Ladies, made a mere* Icarus *of me . . .*" (vi). Barker is not only referring to celestial spheres here but to her proper sphere as a woman. Being a writer meant she was venturing out of her sphere and risking thereby a fall from social grace.

Barker had earlier explained that she chose the patch-work form "*the better to recommend it to my female readers, as well in their Discourse, as their Needle-Work*" (iv). In other words, Barker connects women's "discourse" directly to their use-value practice, assuming that their aesthetic understanding derives from their domestic labor. Barker thus anticipates a female readership and the frame of the novel is that of one woman, Galesia, narrating the events of her life to another, presenting them to her as patches that contribute to the patch-work composition. Some of these patches are poems, some are essentially short stories, some are stretches of narrative, some are indeed recipes (czar's punch, p. 92; Welsh flummery, p. 96; French soup, p. 109).

Barker is clearly positioning literature in what Bakhtin called the "zone of contact." In Barker's view the boundary line between literature and non-literature was blurred. Not only did she include what we consider non-literature (recipes, for example) as "patches" in her work, she also wrote them in verse—thus according them equal status with "serious" literary work.

Moreover, in a poem on how her protagonist became an herbalist apothecary, Barker connects medical prescriptions with poetry—another blurring of boundaries. Calling upon her muse to inspire her in the writing of prescriptions (recipes), Barker comments,

. . . if my Muse, will needs officious be,
She must to this become a *Votary.*
In all our Songs, its Attributes rehearse,
Write *Recipes,* as OVID *Law,* in Verse.
To *Measure* we'll reduce *Fibrific-Heat,*
And make the *Pulses* in true *Numbers* beat.
Asthma and *Phthisick* chant in lays most sweet;
The *Gout* and *Rickets* too, shall run on Feet. (58)

Barker seems here to see poetry as a healing art that has a direct physical effect on illness. Thus, literature, in her view, retains a direct practical connection with the real world and does not assume the institutionalized official character of earlier patriarchal forms. Barker's praxis seems to confirm Bakhtin's insight that the novel emerged from such an anti-authoritarian consciousness, rooted, as here suggested, in a marginalized use-value ethos.

An incident in Cavendish's *Sociable Letters* (1664) serves, however, to indicate that at least some women of the nobility had a problematic relationship to use-value production. Cavendish nevertheless legitimates her writing as a use-value occupation, seeing herself finally as a spinster in words.

In this episode, which is narrated in indirect discourse (see further discussion of the significance of this convention in chapter nine), Cavendish sets herself (or her persona) up as *alazon* to her servant, who serves as *eiron.* Cavendish, herself apparently neither skilled in nor interested in "Huswifry," is chastened by neighbors' criticism that she and her servants rarely engage in domestic crafts. Acknowledging that she has spent most of her time in studies, Cavendish decides that she and her maids will embark upon a course of spinning.

Upon hearing of this scheme her chief servant smiled. "I ask'd her the Reason, she said, she Smil'd to think what Uneven Threads I would Spin, for, said she, though Nature hath made you a Spinster in Poetry, yet Education hath not made you a Spinster in Huswifry."[15] After proposing various similar plans, such as making silk flowers and preserves, which are similarly debunked by the servant, Cavendish decides "to Return to my Writing-Work" (314).

Cavendish's idea of engaging in use-value production is here presented as fantastical as Don Quixote's various dreams. As in Cervantes's work, the commonsensical view is presented by a servant. It is clear that Cavendish is herself disconnected from the domestic practices that constitute use-value production; they are alien to her, and she is economically superfluous, supported by her husband. Writing is the practice that has clearly filled the void. As she says in her preface to the *Poems, and Fancies,* "our *Sex* hath so much waste time."[16]

Yet she continually appropriates her writing to use-value production. In her dedication to *Poems, and Fancies,* for example, Cavendish analogizes poetry to "Huswifery" and to spinning, noting that her lack of skill in the latter made her turn to the former: "*True it is,* Spinning *with the* Fingers *is more proper to our* Sexe, *then* [sic] *studying or writing* Poetry, *which is the* Spinning *with the* braine: *but I having no skill in the* Art *of the first . . . made me delight in the* latter" (A2[r]; see also A7[r]). By using this analogy Cavendish is clearly ironically undercutting traditional female roles and attendant ideologies from a position that posits writing as a use-value occupation.

Cavendish did not publish primarily in order to support herself, as most subsequent women novelists did, beginning with Aphra Behn. (Cavendish said she published principally because she wanted to be famous, and probably because she wanted thereby to exert power.) It is clear nevertheless that for her writing has become a substitute for use-value production: she has become a spinster in words.

Returning to Lukács's Hegelian theory that there is an inherent human resistance to being treated as an object, another, and perhaps more important, source of women's critical irony was their resistance to sexual objectification. While sexual objectification of women was not new, it was reinforced by the exchange ethos that accompanied the rise of capitalism. As noted above, changing economic conditions fostered the emergence of "marriage markets"—places like Bath, a recurring site in novels, where women went to meet prospective spouses. Such a system involved more overt commodification of women than did the arranged marriage, in which women were objects for exchange but at least did not have to sell themselves. Under the new system women increasingly had to advertise themselves in order to attract potential mates. Ruth Perry cites a diarist who in 1654 remarked how London women had begun "to paint themselves, formerly a most ignominious thing, and used only by prostitutes." As Perry notes, "by the end of the seventeenth century the amount of oils, rouges, perfumes, and cosmetics being sold was dizzying." Late seventeenth-century feminist Mary Astell remarked how while men make their fortune, "with us Women [it is a matter of] the setting ours to sale, and the dressing forth our selves to purchase a Master." Anyone who has read a number of eighteenth-century novels knows that they are centrally concerned with the marriage-market processes; with, as Perry puts it, "the politics of [women's] sexuality."[17]

In her study of late eighteenth- and nineteenth-century women's novels, *Women, Power, and Subversion* (1981), Judith Lowder Newton argues similarly that the writers she studies—Fanny Burney, Jane Austen, Charlotte Brontë, and George Eliot—evince in their writings a consciousness that is "alternative or oppositional to dominant values." She locates the source of the authors' critically ironic attitude toward patriarchal ideology in their own experience. "Each writer . . . appears to be working through some painful personal encounter with culturally imposed patterns of male power and female powerlessness. In Burney this is specifically the shock of being reduced to merchandise in the marriage market."[18]

Probably the earliest extended critique in English prose fiction of the marriage market from a woman's standpoint occurs in Cavendish's novella "The Contract," which appears in *Natures Pictures* (1656). (Since Cavendish uses the method of casuistry in this story, I treat it more extensively in chapter five). It is also apparent in another novella in the same work, "Assaulted and Pursued Chastity," where the female protagonist embarks on a series of far-flung adventures in order to escape being prey to what Cavendish calls the "marchandiz[ing]" of women (*Natures Pictures*, 220).

But perhaps the best early example of feminist critical irony occurs in an episode in Cavendish's *Sociable Letters*. It is related in a form of indirect discourse Bakhtin (or V. N. Vološinov) calls "quasi-direct discourse," or the *style indirect libre*.[19] In his analysis of Bakhtin's theory, Gary Saul Morson notes as an example of indirect discourse the opening sentence of *Pride and Prejudice*: "It is a truth universally acknowledged that, a single man in possession of a good fortune must be in want of a wife." Morson remarks the critical irony inherent in this mode. "This sentence does not make an assertion, it reports one; and reported speech is already the beginning of a dialogue. Considerable irony is implicitly directed at the group that might make such an assertion and identify itself with the universe."[20] The patriarchal voice that so universalizes itself, of course, views women as exchange objects, as Austen pointedly infers in her opening sentence. Neither Bakhtin nor Morson recognize, though, that the critical irony inherent in such use of indirect discourse—which Bakhtin sees as a sine qua non of the novel—derives from the woman's perspective as the *subject* who is being *object*ified in the reported speech.

In the *Sociable Letters* Cavendish uses indirect discourse (or technically "quasi-direct discourse") to describe a scene where she is overhearing a ponderous and lengthy dialogue among several male pundits about the origins of the universe. As the discussion winds down, she notes,

> N. N. said, that if the World was Eternal, it was not made by Chance, for Chance proceeded from some Alteration, or Change of some Motions, and not from Eternity, for Eternity was not Subject to Chance, although Chance might be Subject to Eternity, and to prove the World and Worlds

were Eternal, he said, the Fundamental Frame, Parts, Motion, and Form, were not Subject to Change, for they Continue One and the Same without any Alteration. Thus, Madam [the addressee of Cavendish's letter], the Sages Discoursed, but they perceiving I was very attentive to their Discourse, they ask'd my Opinion, I answered, they had left no Room for another Opinion, for the World was Eternal or not Eternal, and they had given their Opinions of either Side; then they desired me to be a Judg [*sic*] between their Opinions, I said, such an Ignorant Woman as I will be a very unfit Judge, and though you be both Learned, and Witty Men, yet you cannot resolve the Question, it being impossible for a Small Part to Understand or Conceive the Whole, and since neither you, nor all Mankind, were they joyn'd into one Soul, Body, or Brain, can possibly know whether the World had a Beginning or no Beginning, or if it had, When it was Made, nor of What it was Made, nor for What it was Made, nor What Power Made it, nor What the Power is that Made it, nor whether it shall Last or Dissolve; wherefore said I, the best is to leave this Discourse, and Discourse of some other Subject that is more Sociable, as being more Conceivable: Then they Laugh'd, and said they would Discourse of Women, I said, I did believe they would find that Women were as Difficult to be Known and Understood as the Universe. (224–25)

We have in this passage all the ingredients that Bakhtin saw as essential to the rise of the novel: indirect discourse ironically reporting the "word of the fathers" from the critical point of view of the marginalized other, a woman who, interestingly enough in this passage, is speaking to another woman in tones of unmistakably Austenian irony. The pompous assertions of the men serve as *alazon* to the woman narrator, the *eiron*.

Moreover, the narrator calls attention to her inferior status. By implicitly debunking at the end of the passage the men's projected theories about women, Cavendish effectively resists the imposition of any patriarchal objectification upon her. The characterization of women as a "Subject that is more Sociable" is not only rejected by the narrator; it also inflects a certain irony upon the title of Cavendish's collection, the *Sociable Letters*, suggesting a note of bitterness and anger at being an intellectual subject relegated to the status of a sociable object—a resentment that is expressed throughout the work.

Elsewhere Cavendish pointedly rejects the patriarchal exchange system with its inherent commodification of women and their accompanying devaluation. Letter XCIII in the *Sociable Letters* provides her critique of marriage and motherhood. First, "a Woman hath no . . . Reason to desire Children for her Own Sake, for first her Name is lost . . . in her Marrying, for she quits her Own, and is Named as her Husband." Nor does the estate descend through her line, "for their Name only lives in Sons, who Continue the Line of Succession, whereas Daughters are but Branches which by Marriage are Broken off from the Root from whence they Sprang, & Ingrafted into the Stock of an other Family, so that Daughters are to be accounted but as Moveable Goods" (183–84). The perception of women (daughters here) as objects for exchange could not be more acute.

Similar feminist assertions pervade Cavendish's work. A comment in "To the Two Universities" (1655) is representative:

> . . . so as we [women] are become like worms that onely live in the dull earth of ignorance, winding our selves sometimes out, by the help of some refreshing rain of good educations which seldom is given us; for we are kept like birds in cages to hop up and down in our houses . . . we are shut out of all power, and Authority by reason we are never imployed either in civil nor [sic] marshall affaires, our counsels are despised, and laught at, the best of our actions are troden down with scorn, by the over-weaning conceit men have of themselves and through a dispisement of us.[21]

An acerbic critique of the commodification of relationships associated with exchange-value production is provided in another important work of the period, Delarivier Manley's *Adventures of Rivella* (1714). In this autobiographical novel Manley vigorously opposes the exchange-value ethos of capitalism (for example, see her discussion of the financial machinations surrounding the will of Lord Crafty's wife),[22] urging in its stead a relationship ethic wherein women would be treated as subjects, not sexual commodities. Manley's critique of Lord Crafty's mercenary mentality is representative:

> This Lord us'd to . . . [trust] no person with his real Designs: What Part he gave any one in his Confidence when they were to negotiate an Affair for him, was in his own Expression but tying 'em by the Leg to a Table, they cou'd not go farther than the Line that held them. He was incapable of Friendship but what made for his Interest, or of Love but for his own proper Pleasures: Nature form'd him a Politician, and Experience made him an Artist in the Trade of Dissimulation. (56–57)

Rivella's (or Manley's) own ethic entails refusing to play the game of commodity exchange—whether it be in the commercial realm, as seen in Lord Crafty's exploitation of his assistant, or in the marriage-market exchange of women. Rivella is unwilling to abandon her printer and publishers, for example, when they (and she) are the target of a libel suit brought against the *New Atalantis,* an earlier work by Manley. A friend (the narrator) urges her to flee to Europe in order to avoid a prison term. "I us'd several Arguments to satisfy her Conscience that she was under no farther Obligation, especially since the Profit had been theirs; she answer'd it might be so, but she could not bear to live and reproach her self with the Misery that might happen to those unfortunate People" (112). Thus, Rivella refuses to allow a financial consideration—that the profit for her book had accrued to the printer and the publisher—to override her personalist concern for their welfare.

Earlier she had declined to play the marriage-market courtship game with the narrator, who remarks that while "she did not return my Passion yet [she did so] without any affected Coyness, or personating a Heroine of the many Romances she daily read" (18). Rivella's insistence upon honesty in relationships—that they be based on affectional ties rather than economic interest, free of the ideological mystifications that sustain the marriage-market trade—proves costly, however. She becomes increasingly cynical and pessimistic and appears to feel trapped in a secularized Machiavellian exchange-value reality. Sir Charles, the narrator, reports, "She told me her Love of Solitude was improved by her Disgust of the World" (41). She develops a philosophy of self-interest and becomes a "*Misanthrope*" (109). In the end she withdraws from politics, declaring that it is not the place for women and resolving from this point on to write only of "more gentle pleasing Theams" (117). John Richetti summarizes Manley's vision as follows:

> [Her] ideology, with its distrust of the complex world of financial power and aggressive economic manipulation, reinforces the female distrust of a masculine world where a woman is either only another pawn in the struggle for power and influence or a commodity to be possessed and devoured by the same ruthless individualism of a society whose highest values are economic laws. (149)

In *A Patch-Work Screen for the Ladies* Jane Barker also treats the rituals of marriage-market courtship with intense critical irony. She includes as subplots (or "patches") the stories of several "seduced-and-abandoned" women (what Nancy K. Miller has identified as the "heroine's text," a staple of eighteenth-century fiction);[23] the main character Galesia's own abandonment by a lover Bosvil forms a leitmotif. But Galesia refuses to "act the *Coquet*" (40) or engage in similarly stereotypical behavior expected of the courted woman ("the Curtesies, the Whispers, the Grimaces, the Pocket Glasses, Ogling, Sighing, Flearing, Glancing" [46]).

In a particularly significant scene Galesia overhears (or has reported to her) a discussion between her father and a suitor's father regarding a marriage contract in which they assess her market value. Like Cavendish, Barker casts the episode in a form of indirect discourse. Interestingly, she uses quotation marks in conjunction with the "that" subordination, but the effect is clearly that of indirect discourse, overheard or reported conversation.

> So the good old Gentleman was overjoy'd at his Son's own Proposal, and took the first Opportunity with my father, over a Bottle, to deliver his Son's Errand. To which my father answer'd . . . and told him, "That he was very sensible of the Honour he did him in this Proposal; but he cou'd not make his Daughter a Fortune suitable to his Estate. . . ." To which the old Gentleman reply'd, "That Riches were not what he sought in a Wife for his Son . . . A prudent, vertuous Woman, was what he most aim'd at." (34–35)

Once again the ironic effect is achieved by the fact that a subject, Galesia, is looking in upon her own commodification in a marriage-market exchange. She thus is the *eiron* to the fathers who are *alazons*. In this way the literal "word of the fathers" is undercut or problematized in accordance with Bakhtin's insights.

Galesia rejects the suitor, despite parental encouragement, and indeed eventually retires from the beau monde of courtship rituals, choosing solitude instead. She finally becomes an herbalist healer, a use-value occupation dominated by women to the present day. Galesia's reservations about early modern capitalism are expressed in her warning to her woman companion not to invest in the "*South-Sea* . . . Bubble" (111–12), an investment scheme of the period that collapsed. In the end, Galesia secures a room of her own—a place of solitude on the margins—in which to ruminate and to write. This position reinforces her peripheral standpoint, from which she continues to criticize patriarchal society and its exchange-value ethic.

We see manifest therefore in Barker's work, as well as in Cavendish and Manley's, a feminist critical irony that is rooted in a women's standpoint of resistance to the reification forced upon them by patriarchal exchange systems. In the next chapter we will trace an important source for this resistance, the women's framed-novelle tradition. As Erich Auerbach remarks in his study of the early modern novella, only with the emergence of the framed-novelle does one have the possibility of the expression of a standpoint; in earlier folk forms, such as the fabliau, "one has no standpoint but [only] naïve, unreflective, uncritical folk poetry" ("haben gar keine Standpunkt, sondern sind naive, nicht reflektierende, unkritische Volkspoesie").[24] The standpoint that emerges in the women's framed-novelle is feminist.

Chapter Three

The Women's Framed-Novelle: The French Tradition

THE FRAMED-NOVELLE WAS THE DOMINANT genre in prose fiction in the late medieval to early modern period, until it was superceded by the novel. It is an assemblage of short tales that are linked by a frame narrative, usually that of the social interaction among the story tellers. The best known example is probably Giovanni Boccaccio's *Decameron* (1353). Chaucer's *Canterbury Tales* (ca. 1387–1400) uses the frame format but the inset tales are in verse and therefore are not novellas, which are in prose. Like the early novel, the framed-novelle was "a literary genre without status, often alleged to be written for women and thus not to be taken seriously."[1]

The major theorists and historians of the rise of the novel—Ian Watt, Michael McKeon, and J. Paul Hunter, for example—have overlooked the framed-novelle as a progenitor of the novel, probably because their focus tends to be Anglocentric, and possibly because the genre has been trivialized by its association with women. By and large these theorists ignore continental sources, which are considerable, for the rise of the English novel. Russian critic Victor Shklovsky, however, in his *Theory of Prose* (1925) recognizes the important link that exists, both historically and structurally, between the framed-novelle and the novel.[2]

The Shklovsky thesis is summarized by Morson and Emerson as follows:

> According to Shklovsky, novels arose from collections of short stories. First, authors wrote stories separately, then they found ways of combining them

in a "a common frame." . . . The next step was to find a better way to link stories. Authors discovered the "stringing together" . . . of stories: instead of framing them as separate narratives about separate people, they transformed them into episodes of a single character's life. In this way, the modern novel was born.[3]

While this is an oversimplification, Shklovsky's claim that the framed-novelle was an important source for the novel is a position reinforced by this study. The Shklovsky thesis is in fact considerably strengthened by a consideration of the women's framed-novelle tradition. As I argue in chapter five, casuistry provided the writers in this tradition with a theory that identified stories as "cases" that were used to prove, disprove, or modify received theses. Among the later writers in this tradition—that is, by the mid-seventeenth century—writers were beginning to conceive of their own life-histories as cases or series of cases, which provided the conceptual model for what are considered the first English novels.

In this chapter I will focus on the early examples of the women's framed-novelle tradition, which was in fact the first women's literary tradition in Western prose literature. I will argue that these women used the framed-novelle format to articulate a women's standpoint, which they forged in opposition to the dominant ideological voice of misogyny that characterized the men's novella tradition. Such articulation established a dialogical counterpoint between subordinated and authoritarian idioms, which contributed to the dialogic mentality that Mikhail Bakhtin identified with the rise of novelistic discourse.

While the framed-novelle format—short tales enclosed in a larger frame narrative—was well established by the early modern period,[4] the women writers modified the genre considerably, expanding the discursive frame greatly and using it for feminist purposes. This device, where frame characters comment on and analyze the inset stories, was pioneered as a feminist practice by Christine de Pizan in the *Livre de la cité des dames* (1405) and perfected as a dialogical form by Marguerite de Navarre in the *Heptaméron* (1549). As seen in the *Cité des dames,* it enabled the expression of feminist ideas and the articulation of a women's viewpoint (which was also sometimes expressed within the stories themselves).

The male writers in the tradition, the most notable of whom was Boccaccio, did not use the discursive frame to the same extent or the same effect, or for feminist purposes. Indeed, by the time of the *Heptaméron* the men's framed-novelle was characterized by a virulent misogyny, especially in the French tradition.[5] It is clear that the women writers seized the genre in order to counter this misogyny. The feminist framed-novelle tradition originated, therefore, in France—possibly facilitated, ironically, by quasi-misogynist parodies like *Les Évangiles des quenouilles,* which I discuss below. It spread to Spain and England undoubtedly through the influence of the *Heptaméron.*[6]

Although other factors may have attracted women writers to the framed-novelle—such as its roots in oral culture and a gift economy, as discussed below, and its nonLatinate, folk character (see chapter nine)—I believe the main reason was that it enabled the articulation of a feminist standpoint in the *querelle des femmes.* In expressing a critical position against abusive treatment of women, the women writers established the kind of dialogical critique that Bakhtin saw arising in the early modern period and culminating in the novel. Bakhtin, however, ignores the contribution of these women. Not only does his failure to appreciate their work limit his dialogic theory,[7] but insufficient attention to the framed-novelle and its role in the emergence of the dialogic led him to overestimate the dialogical character of the novel. In fact, the novel is structurally a much less dialogical form than the framed-novelle, even though it may evince a subversive dialogism in its thematics. But the inherent structural tension between the inset stories and the frame commentary sets up a dialogical potential in the framed-novelle that is eclipsed in the novel, where the narrative focus is more unified.

Bakhtin's concept of the dialogic is, however, more a matter of thematics than structure. As articulated in *Rabelais and His World* and in *The Dialogic Imagination* the dialogic is presented as a form of discourse in which the subversive antiestablishment standpoint of marginalized, oppressed groups is represented. Their "Galilean" perspective is perceived as being inherently critical of the "official" monologic culture of established institutions, notably the Church and the crown. As we have noted, Bakhtin is particularly interested in forms of speech, such as profanity or the ironic use of indirect discourse, that debunk or destabilize the "word of the fathers,"[8] thereby establishing the "relativity of prevailing truths and authorities" (*Rabelais* 11). The novel is, according to Bakhtin, a particularly subversive genre because of the "dialogized heteroglossia" (*Dialogic* 273) it exhibits. "Diversity of voices and heteroglossia . . . constitute . . . the distinguishing feature of the novel as a genre" (300). Unlike earlier literary genres, such as the epic, which are characterized by "unitary" discourse, the novel decenters monolithic ideological forms (367).

While Bakhtin is undoubtedly right to recognize subversive irony and parody as inherent in many early novels (*Don Quixote,* for example), he is wrong to see it as a form that retains a "diversity of voices," a "dialogized heteroglossia." On the contrary, the novel as it finally took shape in the eighteenth century is characterized by its focus on one or a group of individuals whose voice dominates—to whose story digressive narratives are subordinated. This indeed is the distinguishing difference between the novel and the framed-novelle. In the latter the inset narratives exist in dialogical counterpoint with the frame narrative, and the frame voices exist in dialogical relationship with one another. While the frame thesis—its hypotaxis—can subordinate the stories (and does in certain feminist examples of the genre), in the most genuinely dialogical of the framed-novelles, for example the *Heptaméron,* no one voice dominates, and no voices are dominated. In some of the women's use of the framed-novelle (notably Christine de Pizan and María de Zayas's) one voice—a feminist one—does come to prevail. But because that voice is itself inherently critical of the "word of the fathers"—ideologies that legitimize the exchange and abuse of women—it maintains the subversive viewpoint Bakhtin identified with the dialogic.

The women's framed-novelle tradition, therefore, represents one of the first dialogical formations in Western literature. These literary works are dialogical on two counts: the first is that the structural counterpoint that exists between the frame and the inset stories is inherently dialogical; the second is that, as noted, the women writers' handling of the form allowed the articulation of a feminist standpoint, which provided an ideological counterpoint to the prevailing misogynistic monologue.

On the first point, the frame perspective opened up the possibility for ironizing the stories, though this possibility does not seem to have been exploited by the male authors in the genre. Rather it comes into play as the women writers attempted to critique a received body of misogynist folk tales and fabliaux, which reified women in stereotypical molds; as against this monolithic discourse the women counterposed a view that values women as diverse subjects—thus establishing the dialogical heteroglossia Bakhtin identified with the novel. As noted, Bakhtin indeed conceived the dialogic in political terms as arising from the clash between authoritarian absolutist discourses (the "word of the fathers") and anti-authoritarian perspectives. What he failed to note was that in the early modern period a primary ideological source of resistance was feminism, women claiming their voice in the *querelle des femmes.*

It may be that women writers were drawn to the framed-novelle format in part because of its roots in oral culture and in a gift economy—the socio-economic habitat of nearly all women in the early modern period. The frame story almost always involves a group of people gathered together to tell each other stories (oral culture) and/or to discuss their meaning. As a genre, the framed-novelle marks the transition between an oral and a print culture. The works may be written down, but until the seventeenth century they were not "published" in the modern sense; rather they circulated by manuscript.[9]

The genre thus has its origins in a gift economy. Gift economies are precapitalistic or noncapitalistic systems, seen in small communities, such as extended families, small towns, tribes, or, in sixteenth- and seventeenth-century France, in court circles and salon society. Historically, in most societies women's economic functions have been restricted to gift economies and use-value production. Their role in gift economies has been two-pronged, however. On the one hand, women have been participants in gift economies as the exchangers of gifts, particularly as the donators of gift or unpaid service labor, which helps to keep the economy operational, and as the producers of items for noncommercial use, rather than for the market.[10] But, on the other hand, women are themselves used as gifts or exchange objects in patriarchal kinship systems. Indeed, some theorists see women's "*cultural utilization as exchange objects*" as definitional of patriarchy.[11]

Both aspects of women's role in gift economies are relevant to their literary production, as seen in the framed-novelle. First, its oral conversational style is, as Elizabeth Goldsmith (and others) have noted, a "gift-giving" mode; that is, it involves collaborative literary production and a free exchange of ideas on a given topic.[12] No one "owns" the topic as property; it remains in circulation in a kind of open-ended process. It does not become alienable as a commodity is reified in a market economy. The frames in the framed-novelle convention retain this kind of gift economy conversational mode. Margaret Cavendish's assertion that she wrote *Natures Pictures* "not . . . so much for sale, as pleasure"[13] suggests a conception of literature rooted in a gift economy, not a capitalist exchange economy.

On the other hand, one of the principal ideas that emerges in these discussions is a critique of the marriage exchange system in which women are commodified as exchange objects whose subjective opinion counts for nothing. A central component of the feminist thesis that dominates early modern women's literature is a vociferous protest against this system and its silencing of women. Along with this protest, these women writers also demanded greater educational opportunities, they protested against male violence against women and misogynist ideologies, and to a surprising degree they rejected or ironized conventional roles, in particular such domestic roles as sewing (as we have seen with Cavendish), which were seen as precluding women's participation in such traditionally male roles as writing for circulation.

In short, these writers are asserting women's voice as a subject in a world where they are more often treated as objects. As Patricia Francis

Cholakian remarks in her study of the *Heptaméron*, the woman is "in Lévi-Straussian terms . . . both a 'sign' (an object of exchange) and a 'generator of signs' (a speaking subject)." To a great extent in women's writing "this split manifests itself in the disruptive effort to impose a feminine subject on the masculine grammar of narrative desire."[14] Such ideological disruption establishes critical irony and a dialogical relationship between the two terms: counterposing to a viewpoint that sees women as objects one that sees them as subjects.

Interestingly, what is considered the first articulation of feminist theory by a woman occurs in Marie de Gournay's *Le Proumenoir* (1594) as a long digressive critique of a novella. I propose that Gournay derived this critical practice from several of the writers we treat in this study, particularly Christine de Pizan and Marguerite de Navarre.[15] Gournay's feminist digression, which comprised about one-fourth of the original text, was excised from subsequent editions. She later expanded her ideas, however, in *Egalité des hommes et des femmes* (1622). Significantly, in the frame discussion of *Le Proumenoir*, Gournay presents it as a gift to her mentor, Montaigne.

The novella on which Gournay bases her commentary concerns a woman who is used as "an object of exchange, the conqueror's trophy," after the defeat of her country.[16] As Domna Stanton remarks, in Gournay's handling the story, "told by the Daughter . . . is the tale of a Daughter as object of exchange in a world of Fathers and Sons. [It reflects] the dual (and contradictory) vision of a woman as subject and object of exchange" (13). This divided political ontology—being both subject and object for exchange—is what, I believe, occasioned the emergence of a political standpoint, in Lukács's sense of the term, in the women writers of the framed-novelle tradition.

Christine de Pizan's *Livre de la cité des dames (Book of the City of Ladies)* (1405) is the first feminist use of the framed narrative format. While the inset stories are not (with a few notable exceptions) fiction but rather exempla gleaned from classical, Judaic, and Christian myth and history, Christine's work provided a model for subsequent women writers. Her use of the frame for feminist didactic purposes was particularly influential; as can be readily seen in later women writers from Marguerite de Navarre to María de Zayas and Delarivier Manley. (The *Cité des dames* was translated into English in 1521 as the *Boke of the Cyte of Ladyes*).

The explicit purpose of the *Cité des dames* is to refute misogynistic views of women by means of counter examples that illustrate women's strengths and virtues. The frame "plot" consists of a dialogue between the author's persona, "Christine," and three allegorical figures, Reason, Rectitude, and Justice [Raison, Droitture, and Justice]—all of whom are female. The three allegorical women instruct Christine in the ways of the world (in this case the misogynistic ways of a patriarchal world) and suggest to her counter arguments and strategies.

In one section of the *Cité des dames*, Christine uses novellas as the inset stories, thus employing the framed-novelle format. These narratives, which are much longer than the others, include three novellas adapted from Boccaccio's *Decameron* and one, the Griselda story, taken from Petrarch (although the story is also in the *Decameron*). Significantly, Christine chose only novellas that illustrate a feminist thesis. Two—Boccaccio's IV.1 and IV.5—show brutally tyrannical treatment of women by male relatives who disapprove of the women's choice of lovers and punish them by murdering the lovers. In the first of these, the story of Ghismonda, the woman is served her lover's eviscerated heart as punishment for defying her father's orders. Versions of these much recounted tales were picked up by Jeanne Flore (*Comptes amoureux*, novella seven), Marguerite de Navarre (*Heptaméron*, novella forty), and María de Zayas ("El traidor contra su sangre," *Parte segunda*, novella eight).

The third tale that Christine borrowed from Boccaccio (II.9) is the story of Bernabo's wife. Here a woman falsely accused of adultery by her husband and condemned to death acts as her own defense attorney (in male disguise) and wins her case. In Boccaccio's handling, however, the feminist thesis of the tale is undercut by the frame. He juxtaposes it against a misogynist tale (II.10) that illustrates women's fickleness, such that the women listeners in the frame narrative conclude that Bernabo was right not to have trusted his wife.[17] Mihoko Suzuki suggests, indeed, that "the *Decameron's* paradigmatic narrative strategy [is a] juxtaposition of . . . female-directed discourse with stories . . . that function to subjugate the female character to the will of the male protagonist," thereby negating through the frame potentially feminist theses.[18]

Subsequent women writers, starting with Christine de Pizan, restored the feminist thesis of II.9 vitiated by Boccaccio. Indeed, María de Zayas expands the tale considerably in "El juez de su causa" ("The Judge of Her Own Case"), novella nine in the *Novelas amorosas*. Christine de Pizan may thus be said to have pioneered the feminist framed-novelle genre, which was picked up by her successors.

Les Évangiles des quenouilles (ca. 1466–74), which translated means "The Gospels of the Distaffs" or more loosely "The Gospels of Women," is like the other works analyzed in this chapter a framed collection of narrations with a purportedly feminist purpose; in this case the narrated material is not, however, novellas or even historical/mythical biographies such as in the *Cité des dames*. Rather, it is an assemblage of approximately 230 folk beliefs and sententiae, many of them relative to women's lives.

In this work, however, there is an overt clash between the inset materials and the frame, such that the ultimate message of the work remains ambiguous. The inset materials are presented by women narrators who have the expressed feminist desire to preserve matriarchal oral traditions. Since as rural women they are presumably illiterate, they engage a male scribe to write down their stories. He does so but with satiric asides that undercut their presentations.

The women narrate their "gospels" (which are a series of folk aphorisms) while they are working the distaff (the spool used in spinning) during six successive winter evenings in the winter carnival season between Christmas and Candlemas. The frame is thus that of a women's oral culture.

In the prologue of the frame, which is narrated by the male scribe, we learn that he has been charged by the women with putting into writing or recording this oral material. He claims that the work is dedicated to "the honor and glory of women" ["faittes a l'onneur et exaucement des dames"] and presented in order to counter antifeminist derision.[19]

This sentiment is echoed by the first speaker, Ysengrine du Glay, who in a prologue of her own explains her desire to have women's cultural traditions preserved: "it is my opinion . . . that it would be a good idea if with the help of our secretary and friend we put together a little treatise composed of chapters . . . derived from materials of our great, ancestral mothers, which have been found, in order that they not be forgotten" ["il m'est avis . . . que bon seroit que a l'ayde de cestui nostre secretaire et ami, nous feissons un petit traittié des chappitres . . . lesquelz de pieça de noz grandes et anciennes meres ont esté trouvez, affin de les non mettre en oubliance" (80)]. She also is motivated by a concern to counter misogynist views of women, thus harking back to Christine de Pizan: "it is remarkable," she comments, "how men of the present time never cease to write and produce defamatory libels and malicious books which strike at the honor of our sex" ["il est tout notoire comment les hommes du temps present ne cessent de escripre et faire libelles diffamatoires et livres contagieux poignans l'onneur de nostre sexe" (80)]. Each of the women then presides in turn over an evening's recitals of short, folkloric observations, which are usually accompanied by a short (one or two sentence) gloss. The narrative proceeds through six successive days, so the structure of the work is a "hexameron," as editor Madeleine Jeay points out (9).

The scribe, however, does not present the material unambiguously; rather he provides an ironic, parodic perspective that tends to undermine and criticize the authority of the women. He does this mainly through short pejorative descriptions of the story-tellers, which precede each evening's recital. Jeay notes that the composite narrator is an ugly woman, marginalized by her location in a sexual demi-monde (being a prostitute, panderer, or widow), who has special powers and knowledge, especially of herbs, folk remedies, and childbirth. She is in short an examplar of the rural witch-woman suspected of heresy and sorcery who was persecuted during the early modern period (29–30). There is thus a clash between the self-presentation of the women and their culture and the critical perspective of the scribe, who represents the emerging world of rationalism, which ridicules feminine oral folk culture (31). Nevertheless, the women's text remains accessible despite the parodic frame. Jeay maintains that the "ironic treatment by the author takes nothing away from the authenticity of the folkloric material: the two texts coexist side by side" ["le traitment ironique de l'auteur m'entame en rien l'authenticité du donné folklorique: les deux textes se côtoient" (15)].

The inset material in the *Évangiles* is a series of aphoristic folk observations. A few of these have a feminist point (especially those of Ysengrine de Glay on the first day), but most are simply folk superstitions. The feminist "gospel" includes pronouncements such as "the man who inappropriately spends wealth that comes from his wife, without her consent and agreement, will have to explain to God" ["l'omme qui despend indeuement les biens qui lui viennent de par sa femme et sans son gré et congié, il en rendera conte devant Dieu" (82)]. The folk superstitions include such notions as that the sex of a child can be determined by putting salt on the head of a sleeping pregnant woman—if she then says a man's name, the child will be male, and vice versa (84)—or that a crow crying on the chimney of a sick person's house means the person will die (96).

Although the patent silliness of many of these beliefs may tend to reinforce the scribe's satiric intent, the work appears to provide a rare glimpse into rural women's folk culture and clearly illustrates the connection between the framed-narrative genre and women's economic culture (the women characters are engaged in use-value production—spinning—and a gift exchange system) and social culture (orality). It also bespeaks once again the feminist intent of these women authors (here considering the narrators as "authors"). Since the *Évangiles* was very popular and went through many editions (an English translation was made in 1507), it remains an important version of the genre, one that probably influenced later writers.[20]

Jeanne Flore's *Comptes amoureux* (ca. 1537) is another French example of a feminist use of the framed-novelle genre; seven stories are linked by a frame where several women—the stories' narrators—are gathered to tell each other the stories and to comment upon them (an expression of oral culture). The extant text of the *Comptes amoureux* is apparently a pastiche of selections from two original texts: stories number two, three, four, and five being from one source and number one, six, and seven from another.[21] The latter three stories (as well as number three) are unified by the theme of the unhappy young woman married to a jealous older man, with a claim made for her right to happiness and love, which are not provided by the spouse. While some have argued that the *Comptes amoureux*, like *Les Évangiles des quenouilles* and *Les Caquets de l'accouchée* (1622), are misogynist satires or parodies, others contend that it is, on the contrary, the work of "a champion of women's rights."[22] One scholar in fact notes that in Flore's work "the [medieval] misogynist text is negated . . . [and] the theme of the 'mal-mariée' . . . is introduced through the eyes of a woman who presents herself as the spokesperson for her sex," that she is, in short, expressing a feminist standpoint in the on-going *querelle des femmes*.[23]

My hypothesis is that the stories of the first original text may have been intended parodically, but not those of the second, which indeed includes (story seven) the tale of Ghismonda treated by Christine de Pizan and later by Marguerite de Navarre and María de Zayas—all from a feminist point of view. The claim, moreover, that women, as subjects, have legitimate desires and are right not to want to be treated merely as objects for exchange—Flore's main thesis—is certainly feminist.

In the opening epistle to her cousin, the author (first-person narrator) recalls that the stories were recently told "in her company" and that she has written them down in order to present them as a gift to her cousin, an example of writing as a gift-economy practice. "[J]'avois prinse la plume en main pour le vous mettre par escript" (97). While the frame characters are not well developed, Flore extends the frame plot beyond her predecessors' in that Cébille—to whom the stories are told as exempla—appears to learn from them (to respect the power of love). In this Flore anticipates the work of María de Zayas, whose frame women learn from the inset stories and change their lives as a result.

As with Christine de Pizan and Marguerite de Navarre, Jeanne Flore appears to be responding at least in part to the *Decameron*'s antifeminist theses. The *Comptes amoureux* is in fact the first French work modeled on the *Decameron* (Cerrata 251). In her negative critique of young women trapped in arranged marriages with older men Flore seems to be reacting against Boccaccio's depiction of women in such marriages as "sexually insatiable and adulterous" (Suzuki 233). In her commentary on tale number one the narrator, Madame Melibee, points up a counter, feminist thesis: "The young girl Rosemonde was long oppressed by her jealous husband" ["La damoiselle Rosemonde fut longuement opprimée de son jaloux mary" (129)]—thus articulating the voice and point of view of the subordinate, enacting the possibility of Bakhtin's dialogic.

Flore's work may be seen as an intermediary between the *Cité des dames* and the *Heptaméron;* like the former it retains a feminist hypotaxis, or unifying focus, but the frame format and the use of fictional stories point in the direction of Marguerite de Navarre's great work.

In *L'Heptaméron* (1549) Marguerite de Navarre turned the frame in the framed-novelle into a dialogical, "discussion-group" forum in which the stories are interpreted and evaluated by the storytellers. Considering how she expanded and enriched it, many scholars consider her to have invented the discursive frame. In *L'Heptaméron,* the frame comprises approximately one-third of the text, including a prologue and discussions following each of seventy-two novellas. The frame here is much more developed as a work of fiction in its own right than were its predecessors. The frame characters—five women and five men—are distinct (psychologically and ideologically consistent) individuals (as opposed to the generally flat characters in antecedent frames), which has led one critic to see them as "forerunners" of the novel's characters, who are similarly provided with consistent psychological motivation (unlike earlier genres such as the romance and the epic where characters are rarely developed).[24] The frame characters do not act or change their lives as in a novel, however; María de Zayas appears to have been the first woman writer to develop this evolutionary innovation.

Several critics have suggested that Marguerite developed the discursive frame as a way of responding to the misogyny rampant in the Renaissance novella tradition. In this, she was furthering the cultural work of Christine de Pizan, the women of the *Évangiles des quenouilles,* and Jeanne Flore. As Robert Clements and Joseph Gibaldi note in *Anatomy of the Novella,* "With Marguerite de Navarre proving that she could beat her countrymen at their own game and María de Zayas . . . women eventually moved in totally, metamorphosing the once predominantly misogynistic genre into a vehicle for propounding their own strongly feminist ideas" (181, emphasis in original). While Christine de Pizan was not her only source, Marguerite probably owned a manuscript of Christine's, and, in any event, was quite familiar with her work.[25] She also may have known the *Comptes amoureux* (Jourda 1930, 685), and possibly the *Évangiles des quenouilles.*

Each character in the frame has a consistent position in the *querelle des femmes,* which is the issue that dominates the discussions, providing the text's hypotaxis. Unlike the *Cité des dames,* however, the feminist position is but one of many expressed on the subject. The work remains more genuinely dialogical, arguably the first work in Western literature to evince the heteroglossia that Bakhtin heralded in the novel. In the *Heptaméron* the standpoint of women is clearly presented.

In the Prologue, Parlamente—generally considered Marguerite's voice in the text—proposes that the storytellers—the "devisants"—"not write any story that [is] not truthful" ["de n'escripre nulle nouvelle qui ne soit veritable histoire"].[26] And, that none "who studied and were men of letters" (69) ["ceulx qui avoient estudié et estoient gens de lettres" (9)] would be permitted to contribute stories because of a fear that "rhetorical ornament would in part falsify the truth of the account" (69) ["de paour que la beaulté de la rethoricque feit tort en quelque partye à la verité de l'histoire" (9)]. Thus, Marguerite registers a resistance to "learned" rhetoric, undoubtedly meaning a resistance to Latinate hypotactic syntax. Indeed, Marguerite's style is not Latinate, but rather is a "spoken style": she employed "the language which she herself actually spoke, using the simplest terms" (Jourda 927, 967).

While the claim to authenticity was a convention by this time in the novella collection, many of the stories in the *Heptaméron* appear to be based on historical incidents; several purport to come from eye-witnesses and at least twenty are connected in one way or another with the courts of the queen of Navarre or her brother. Late in the work a character observes that "we have sworn not to tell stories from a written source" (512) ["nous avons juré de ne rien mectre icy qui ayt esté escript" (400)]. This puts a slightly different cast on the injunction to be truthful, suggesting a preference for (women's) oral history and a mistrust of (men's) written traditions (perhaps because of their anti-woman bias). The frame discussion group in fact reflects the oral culture of Marguerite's own court where courtiers and ladies-in-waiting participated in a daily ritual of oral discussion during which Marguerite often engaged in needlework (Jourda 291, 294, 1003). The *Heptaméron* is also conceived in the Prologue as a gift to Marguerite, reflecting its gift-economy base.

The call for truthfulness means, however, not just historical verification but allowing the truth of the silenced, in this case women, to be heard. As Cholakian remarks, "'Truth' in the *Heptaméron* does not always mean historical fact. Marguerite de Navarre is telling the truth about gender relations, from a woman's point of view" (77). Indeed, Cholakian argues (a point confirmed by numerous sources) that the *Heptaméron* is "a profoundly autobiographical text" (xiii), that certain incidents happened to Marguerite herself, most notably the rape attempt described in novella number four. Cholakian claims in fact that a primary motivation for the production of the *Heptaméron* was Marguerite's desire to speak out about her own near-victimization and other women's victimization by rape (18). It is a kind of bearing witness. Rape is indeed the central feminist issue in the *Heptaméron*. Several stories point up the ways in which the woman's experience of rape is silenced by the fear of losing her reputation.

As mentioned, these include novella number four, in which a lady-in-waiting warns a noblewoman that if she prosecutes a man who attempted to rape her, "people will say that he *must* have had his way with you. Your honour . . . would be put in doubt wherever this story was heard" (94) ["si courra le bruict partout qu'il aura faict de vous à sa volunté. . . . Et vostre honneur . . . sera mise en dispute en tous les lieux là où cette histoire sera racomptée" (32)]. Another example is novella number ten in which when the woman cries out during the rape attempt and help arrives (in the form of her mother), the rapist denies her accusation implying that the woman is delusory. Since the mother at least provisionally believes him, the victim refuses to speak further about the incident. The issue of women's silence is also raised in stories twenty-two, sixty-two, and seventy.

Novella twenty-two is a classic representation of sexual harassment, in this case of a nun by a prior. He coerces her in nearly every imaginable way; when she screams during a rape attempt he, like the rapist in novella ten, covers himself when help arrives, and promises her that if she keep silent he will reward her with a promotion. When his harassment escalates to the point of forbidding her all outside contact, she manages to write her story down, smuggling it to her mother who in turn relays it to Marguerite, the queen of Navarre, who intervenes, saving the woman and having her promoted to abbess. The story is in some ways a synecdoche for the entire collection, which appears to be an attempt to write down the woman's side of the story in order that women be saved from further persecution.

Many of the other novellas in the *Heptaméron* serve as exempla to illustrate feminist theses. Critics have provided detailed comparative analyses of some of these, showing how Marguerite modified a misogynist source into a feminist statement.[27] In several stories women are not only allowed to speak, they expound lengthy monologues asserting their rights, defending their positions in no uncertain terms (see especially novellas eight, fifteen, twenty-one, and forty-two). Also, novella forty raises the issue of the silencing of the woman's voice in her choice of husband in the marriage-market exchange system (novellas nineteen, twenty-one, and fifty-one implicitly raise the issue, too). This was especially a problem among the nobility, where women were in essence objects for exchange, "goods . . . up for sale . . . by the highest bidder" (186) ["marchandise . . . en vente . . . emportées par les plus offrans et derniers encherisseurs" (114)].

Marguerite de Navarre thus circulates in the *Heptaméron* the voices of women as subjects speaking out against their reification in patriarchal exchange systems. She provided a model for subsequent women writers who continued to use the frame to comment on the inset material from a feminist standpoint, and she may have planted an idea that later found fruition in the English women's writings, of using one's own life experiences as evidence to refute misogynist preconceptions.

Chapter Four

The Women's Framed-Novelle: The Spanish and English Traditions

PROBABLY THE MOST SUCCESSFUL REALIZATION of the feminist potential of the framed-novelle genre was accomplished by Spanish writer María de Zayas y Sotomayor. Her two collections, the *Novelas amorosas y ejemplares* (1637) and its sequel, the *Parte segunda del Sarao y entretenimiento honesto,* popularly called the *Desengaños amorosos* (1647), remain—together with the *Heptaméron,* which was one of Zayas's sources—the finest examples of the genre, and masterpieces in their own right.

While Zayas retained the conventional framed-novelle structure, her innovations, especially in the frame plot, portend the novel, in which the frame plot becomes dominant, subsuming the inset stories. In Zayas's work the stories themselves reflect what one critic has called a "patchwork composition" of sources.[1] Like Marguerite de Navarre she used the "plain style" in prose,[2] and also like her French predecessor Zayas often reshapes the material or uses it as exemplum to point up a feminist thesis.

The *Heptaméron* was clearly a major influence—as a structural model, in its feminist perspective, and in providing plots or parts of plots for at least four of Zayas's novellas. Novella four in the *Novelas amorosas,* "Forewarned but Not Forearmed" ("El prevenido engañado"), which is narrated by a man and is about the untrustworthiness of women, derives a plot episode from the *Heptaméron*'s novella twenty, in which a wealthy woman is discovered having an affair with a stable boy. The eighth story in the *Novelas amorosas,* "Triumph over the Impossible" ("El imposible vencido") also has a plot episode—an improvised ghost appearance—that appears to derive from a similar event in the thirty-ninth story of the *Heptaméron.*[3]

Two of the novellas in the *Parte segunda* are largely based on stories from the *Heptaméron:* number four in the former on number thirty-two in the latter, and number eight in the former on number forty in the latter. The fourth novella in the *Parte segunda,* "Tarde llega el desengaño" ("Too Late for Disillusionment") concerns the gruesome punishment a husband metes out to his wife for alleged adultery: he forces her to drink out of her lover's skull and hangs the latter's skeleton in her boudoir. Zayas's version of this much-recounted tale is by far the most elaborate and complex, and her thesis is the most clearly feminist. In comparing her version with its immediate source, the *Heptaméron,* one may note that Zayas adds a number of episodes, including a lengthy opening section where the protagonist, don Jaime, has an affair with an assertive woman named Lucrecia, who retains control of their relationship and nearly has him killed by assassins after he violates her trust. Soon after, he marries a woman, Elena, who resembles Lucrecia, suggesting a continuity between the two. Later a black servant woman tells him that Elena is having an affair with a cousin. The husband, don Jaime, immediately kills the cousin and proceeds with the punishment described above. As she is dying, the black woman confesses that she has lied because she had been rejected by the cousin and scolded by the lady for suspecting her of an affair. Shortly thereafter Elena dies and don Jaime goes mad.

The narrator in Zayas's version, Filis, gleans a feminist moral from this macabre tale, that

> men are indeed to be feared, for they let themselves be driven by their cruelest instincts. . . . This story also shows likewise that many women, although innocent, endure dire punishments. Let us bear in mind therefore that, contrary to what public opinion would have us believe, not all women deserve to be blamed, as they commonly are [de que en lo que toca a crueldad son los hombres terribles, pues ella misma los arrastra . . . y se ve asimismo que hay mujeres que padecen inocentes, pues no todas han de ser culpadas, como en la común opinión lo son].[4]

In the *Heptaméron,* strangely, both Parlamente and Oisille, her mother, approve of the woman's grotesque punishment (she is assumed guilty in Marguerite's version). There is also in Zayas's version the implicit possibility that don Jaime is really avenging himself on Elena for Lucrecia's rejection of him—at least this has disposed him to believe the false accusations.

This story has a long history. Even before Marguerite de Navarre's version it appeared in the *Gesta Romanorum* (ca. 1340) in Latin. The Italian novelist Matteo Bandello also included it in his 1554 collection of novellas (II.12). William Painter's "A Strange Punishment of Adulterie," novel fifty-seven in Volume I of *The Palace of Pleasure* (1575), brought Marguerite's version into English, where it (or probably a variation by Painter, "Of a Ladie of Thurin," novel forty-three in *The Palace*) became the source for Delarivier Manley's version, "The Husband's Resentment. Example I," in *The Power of Love* (1720). In all of these except Zayas's the wife is assumed guilty.

The eighth novella in the *Parte segunda*, "El traidor contra su sangre" ("A Traitor to His Own Flesh and Blood"), is also based on the *Heptaméron*, novella forty. Both are narrated by women. Loosely, this plot is similar to that seen in the Boccaccio novella (IV.5) adapted by Christine de Pizan in which two brothers kill their sister's forbidden lower-class lover. In the *Heptaméron* version, a tyrannical brother discovers his sister's unauthorized liaison and has the lover killed and the sister imprisoned. The discussion that follows among the frame characters highlights the issue of women's lack of choice in marital arrangements—a concern that dominates this tradition of women's literature. Again Parlamente and Oisille take a conservative position favoring parental control over the marriage choice, while one of the men, Geburon, suggests the brother's behavior was illegal, since the sister was legally of age to make her own choice. Even Hircan, the most resolute antifeminist in the work, agrees that the brother had exceeded his legal authority over the sister.[5]

Another of the men, Dagoucin, offers a political analysis of arranged marriages, that they are made—especially in the upper echelons—for *raisons d'état:* "in order to maintain peace in the state, consideration is given only to the rank of families, the seniority of individuals and the provisions of the law ... in order that the monarchy should not be undermined" (374) ["pour entretenir la chose publicque en paix, l'on ne regard que les degrez des maisons, les aages des personnes et les ordonnances des loix ... afin de ne confondre poinct la monarchye" (280)].

Zayas modifies this tale considerably. First, it is preceded by a feminist preface in which the narrator, Francisca, warns women not to be vulnerable to men's deceits ["Esto es señoras mías, no dejarse engañar" (*Parte segunda* 371)], a point the story, a "desengaño"—which connotes "demystification" or "enlightenment"—is to illustrate. Thus, the novella is conceived, like the others in the collection, as revealing a feminist lesson or message to its women hearers/readers. Here again Zayas's thesis is more straightforward, less problematized, than that presented in the *Heptaméron*.

In Zayas's version, the woman is motivated to engage in the unauthorized liaison largely for feminist reasons: she "thought of the tyrannical way in which her father and brother wanted to deprive her of her freedom in order to cheat her of her inheritance. Overcome by anger" she agrees to a tryst with her suitor ["considerando cuán tiranamente su padre y hermano, por desposeerla de la hacienda, la querían privar de la libertad, desesperada con la pasión"].[6] (The father wants to reserve the estate for his son, and so wants to place the daughter, unmarried, in a convent. Thus she is vulnerable to the "engaño" [romantic deceptions] of the suitor). Another change is that the brother, don Alonso, kills his sister (rather than the lover) when he learns of the liaison. Finally, Zayas adds a denouement in which don Alonso marries, deceives, and kills another woman. He is eventually executed.

Zayas's feminism may also be seen discursively in the prologues to her works and in the frame plots, with the frame characters changing their lives largely as a result of the stories they hear. In the prologue to the *Novelas amorosas,* the author defends her right to publish her work despite her gender: "There will be many who will attribute to folly my audacity in publishing my scribbles because I'm a woman, and women, in the opinion of some fools, are unfit beings" ["habrá muchos que atribuyan a locura esta virtuosa osadía de sacar a luz mis borrones, siendo mujer, que, en opinión de algunos necios, es lo mismo que una cosa incapaz"].[7] She protests women's "cloistered" condition and lack of educational opportunities: "the real reason why women are not learned is not a defect in intelligence but a lack of opportunity. When our parents bring us up if, instead of putting cambric on our sewing cushions and patterns in our embroidery frames, they gave us books and teachers, we would be as fit as men for any job or university professorship" (1–2) ["la verdadera causa de no ser las mujeres doctas no es defecto del caudal, sino falta de la aplicación, porque si en nuestra crianza como nos ponen el cambray, en las almohadillas y los dibuxos en el bastidor, nos dieran libros y preceptores, fuéramos tan aptas para los puestos y para las cátedras como los hombres" (22)]. Zayas proceeds to catalog past learned women, and comments of herself that she is a voracious reader: "The moment I see a book, new or old, I drop my sewing and can't rest until I've read it" (2) ["en viendo cualquiera nuevo o antiguo, dexo la almohadilla y no sosiego hasta que le paso" (22–23)].

Her frame plots, which, as noted, are more developed than her predecessors', are clearly organized around a feminist thesis. In the *Novelas amorosas* interactions occur among six men and six women (five narrators of each gender, as well as a female hostess and another male who tells no story). The plot is that friends of Lisis, a young noble woman who is ill, plan a series of evening entertainments for her during the Christmas season. These festivities include dancing, music, and songs, as well as storytelling (the songs are incorporated into the text). Two stories are narrated each evening. Meanwhile, amorous intrigues occur among the characters during the frame interstices between the stories; the main plot being the competition between don Juan and don Diego for Lisis. By the end of the work she is betrothed to the latter though she loves the former.

In the *Parte segunda*, the *Desengaños amorosos*, the same people are in attendance but four additional women are there and only women narrate stories. It is in many ways more feminist than the *Novelas amorosas*. Many of the stories are about brutal treatment of women by men. After narrating a particularly grisly tale, novella ten, "Estragos que causa el vicio" ("The Ravages of Vice"), Lisis delivers a feminist oration in which she condemns men's poor opinion and ill treatment of women and announces that she is breaking off her engagement and entering a convent, where she is joined by several other women characters. The narrator proposes that "this end is not tragic but rather the happiest that one could have asked for, because she, wanted and desired by many, did not subject herself to anyone" (xvii) ["No es trágico fin, sino el más felice que se pudo dar, pues codiciosa y deseada de muchos, no se sujetó a ninguno" (510–11)]. Thus, the frame has a coherent plot itself, and the characters are influenced to assert themselves as subjects by the feminist message of the stories.

The English women writers of prose fiction in the seventeenth century inherited the framed-novelle genre as the principal women's prose form.[8] The *Heptaméron* had been available in English since 1597, and a selection of Zayas stories—including "The Judge of Her Own Case" ("El juez de su causa," novella nine in *Novelas amorosas*)—was available in English translation in 1665. Unfortunately, however, Zayas's name was elided in the translation process. Paul Scarron had included the above story as "Le Juge de sa propre cause" in his *Roman comique*, part 2 (1657), and three other of her novellas in his *Nouvelles tragi-comiques* (1655–57). A collection of Scarron's novellas (including these four by Zayas) were translated by John Davies as *Scarron's Novels* in 1665. There was also another French translation of several Zayas stories in 1656–57. In addition, three Zayas novellas appeared in a collection of novellas erroneously attributed to Cervantes, *A Week's Entertainment at a Wedding*, in 1710.[9] Thus, scandalously, Zayas was erased from English literary history even though her work was prominently available and clearly influential.

The English women writers of the period, while influenced by Zayas and Marguerite de Navarre, soon, however, began to enact important modifications in the framed-novelle form they inherited from their continental sisters. The ideological currents in favor of individualism were such by mid-century that the English women began to modify the genre in ways that anticipated the novel and its focus on the individual life-story.

An intermediate work, which suggests the reconceptualization occurring in the mid-seventeenth century is *The Case of Madam Mary Carleton* (1663), which is discussed in more detail in chapter five. It is relevant to note here, however, that Mary Carleton conceived of her life-story as a series of Boccaccian novellas unified by an autobiographical frame or hypotaxis: in her preface she asks readers to "cast a favourable eye upon these Novels [novellas] of my life, not much unlike those of Boccace [Boccaccio]."[10] Carleton thus conceives the autobiographical episodes in her life-story as novellas in a framed-novelle, which further suggests how powerful a structural paradigm the framed-novelle genre was at the time.

Similarly, the seventeenth- to eighteenth-century Englishwomen treated in this chapter—Cavendish, Manley, and Barker—were beginning to use autobiographical swatches or women's life-histories as the basis for feminist commentary in the same way that traditional novellas had been used as exempla or cases in earlier works in the genre, by Marguerite de Navarre or María de Zayas for example. In their use of the life-history as case, these women invented a new way to interrogate the ideology of women's subordination, established by their predecessors as the dominant theme of the genre.

A new English translation (by Robert Codrington) of the *Heptaméron* appeared in 1654, while Cavendish was writing *Natures Pictures* (1656). Marguerite de Navarre's influence is apparent, but *Natures Pictures* represents a movement away from the framed-narrative format and toward the novel. The first part of the work, entitled "Her Excellencies Tales in Verse," retains a frame similar to that of the *Heptaméron*, with several aristocratic men and women exchanging stories and comments on the general theme of the *querelle des femmes*. While much less developed than its predecessor, the frame nevertheless contains characteristically pro and antifeminist remarks. Following an essay in verse on women's narcissism, for example, the women auditors threaten to leave, but the men beg them to stay.[11] After a short essay that argues that, for men, the single state is better, a woman responds with a tale to illustrate that "Marriage is to Woman far more worse/Than 'tis to Men, and proves the greater Curse" (57). At one point the women comment critically on the "dispatch" (85) with which the men tell their stories, which aside from its sexual innuendo, suggests an aesthetic preference for a meandering paratactic style. Later a woman claims "the masculine Sex" is obsessed with "vain-glorious foolish amorous love" (87).

But the second and much longer section, "Her Excellencies Comical Tales in Prose," dispenses with the frame altogether. And three of the stories threaten to break out of the collection completely as autonomous works. These three pieces include two novellas—"The Contract" and "Assaulted and Pursued Chastity"—and Cavendish's autobiography (one of the first by a woman), "A True Relation of My Birth, Breeding, and Life."

The novellas, which I focus on here, no longer resemble the short anecdotal tales seen in the classic framed-novelle (the *Decameron*, for example); rather they are extensive treatments of one individual's life-story, unified by feminist explanatory theses. "The Contract" is really in embryo a female novel of manners of the *Evelina* type, and "Assaulted" is a prototypical female picaresque novel. The central issue in the former is the marriage-market economy and the woman character's refusal to be made into an object for exchange, claiming instead the right to choose according to her own inclination or desire. The latter story also provides a critique of the "traffick" in women, and thus similarly exhibits a feminist thesis.

In "The Contract" a young woman is married by contract at the age of seven for economic reasons. Her husband, however, marries another, and she is left with an uncle guardian who is charged with bringing her out in society and educating her in the ways of the (social) world—a set pattern in the female bildungsroman where "bildung" or education means learning how the marriage-market works. The protagonist in this piece (Delitia) resists, however, her uncle's "educational" schemes: "When her Uncle was gone, Lord, said she, what doth my Uncle mean to set me out to shew: sure he means to traffick for a Husband; but Heaven forbid those intentions, for I have no minde to marry" (189). The tale ends happily with Delitia successfully arguing her case in court (which we discuss in the next chapter) and in effect winning the right to live with the man of her choice—a feminist ending her literary foremothers would have approved of.

The other novella of major significance in *Natures Pictures* is the oddly titled "Assaulted and Pursued Chastity." This wildly imaginative story, somewhat similar to her utopian fantasy, *The Description of a New World, called the Blazing-World* (1668), has not received the attention it deserves. In this feminist novella the woman character, variously called Miseria, Affectionata, and Travelia, resists and escapes from the "traffick" in women, by arming, disguising herself as a man, and through various escapades. In one lengthy episode she serves as general of an army, recalling Zayas's "Judge of Her Own Case" (see discussion in chapter five). The "traffick" in this story is not marriage, however, but prostitution. The story opens with Miseria discovering herself in the clutches of a bawd, "which used to marchandize; and trafficked . . . for the riches of beauty" (220). Miseria resists the rape attack of a client, who is a prince, by shooting him with a pistol; he survives, however, and has her imprisoned. Later she escapes by dressing as a male page and jumping ship, where she is adopted by the ship's master. After a shipwreck, they land in a cannibal culture, but as they are about to be sacrificed she shoots and kills the chief priest and henceforth she and the old master are treated as a god's messengers.

After they leave this realm, Miseria and her companion meet up with the prince she had shot earlier who is still after her. She and the old master escape again, arriving in a land ruled by a queen who immediately falls in love with Miseria, now called Travelia. Meanwhile, the prince ends up in a neighboring kingdom, where the king is warring against the queen because she is refusing his seduction attempts. The prince then becomes the king's general, and Travelia becomes the queen's general. After lengthy battle scenes the men are subdued, and all the parties wed—after the lesbian relationship between Travelia and the queen has been artificially resolved. The king tells the prince to court Travelia so as to remove her as his rival for the queen's affection, saying "Dispose of your Mistress some way, for I am jealous . . . although she is a Woman. Sir, said the Prince, I have as much reason to be jealous of the Queen as you have of my mistress, setting her Masculine Habit aside" (267). Travelia finally tells the queen that she "cannot return such love you desire, for you have placed your Affection upon a Woman" (267). Thus, with Cavendish we leave behind the recycled novellas of the classic framed-novelle collection; rather the inset stories are becoming autonomous entities in their own right, more mini-novels than novellas, still, however, unified by a feminist perspective.

Like *Natures Pictures* Delarivier Manley's *Secret Memoirs and Manners of Several Persons of Quality, of Both Sexes from the New Atalantis, an Island in the Mediteranean* [sic] (1709) is a work that is structured in the framed-novelle format but that threatens to break out of that format in new directions. The frame of Manley's work is in fact very similar to Christine de Pizan's *Cité des dames*. Here a Manley persona, Astrea, who lives in a "lunary World" far from earth, decides to revisit the planet in order to better educate a young prince, who is her tutorial charge. She wants to find out "if Humankind were still as defective, as when she in a Disgust forsook it."[12] Astrea is accompanied on her return by two allegorical women figures—Virtue, who is in rags (1:2), and Intelligence. The latter serves as narrator of twenty inset stories and anecdotes that enlighten Astrea about the current state of humankind, which she learns is "universally corrupted" (1:15). Manley's style throughout is similar to Cavendish's, a familiar, gossipy parataxis.

As with its continental predecessors the frame serves a feminist didactic purpose; following several episodes either Virtue, Intelligence, or Astrea point up the often feminist moral of the story. Many of the episodes and characters are only thinly disguised, true stories about members of the English court. Manley's work is thus a proto-roman à clef, although some of the episodes seem to be more or less traditional novellas. (Manley was very familiar with the novella tradition; see chapter seven below.) And, as noted, one of the stories is her own thinly fictionalized autobiography (vol. 2, episode eight). In her use of "true stories" Manley recalls Marguerite de Navarre.

Manley's frame characters sometimes intervene in the stories, however, meeting and influencing the inset characters, so that the frame plot and the inset plots converge at times in a way that is more like the novel than the framed-novelle. In the second volume the first episode, for example, opens with a frame discussion of whether the frame women should go to the aid of a woman they discover groaning by the wayside, or whether they should hear her story first (2:9). Intelligence argues the story should be told in order to expose vice, while Virtue suggests they should dispense with the story and help the woman. Intelligence wins out with her argument that telling the story is an ethical, not simply an aesthetic act (and thus reaffirming the stated moral purpose of the *New Atalantis;* see preface, 2:A5^r). The story is then introduced by Mrs. Nightwork, a midwife, who has delivered numerous illegitimate babies to women of the court, and who has just delivered the woman they heard moaning, who is "Harriat" (ostensibly Lady Henrietta Long), the victim of a rape-seduction plot.

In the third episode (2:59–113) of the same volume the women hear another woman in distress and intervene, scaring off a "spark" who had been attempting to rape her; the woman, the lady Elonora, then tells her story. This tale, though told as a first-person narration from a subjective viewpoint, is in the tradition of the Spanish novella (complete with Spanish names), which suggests a possible Zayas influence. After hearing her story, the frame women decide to rescue Elonora and provide her with protective custody (2:109).

In having her frame characters intervene in the inset stories—significantly, by having the frame women come to the rescue of the women in the inset tales—a feminist gesture—Manley is employing a central device of the novel: protagonists' encountering others who then tell their stories. In cases where those stories remain essentially discrete, connected paratactically, the form remains more of a framed-novelle collection; but where the characters of the frame or central story and the narrators of substories interact and change each others' life-plots, the work becomes a novel. The *New Atalantis* is on the cusp between these two forms but remains in the framed-novelle genre because the life-histories of the frame characters are not developed enough.

One of the stories in the *New Atalantis* is, however, Manley's own: the story of Delia, who at the age of fourteen is seduced and then married bigamously by a cousin-guardian by whom she bears a son (2:185–93). These are all incidents from Manley's life. Like Zayas's frame characters Manley's see the story as a "desengaños" that can help to prevent "Women from *believing*" and "Men from *deceiving*" (2:192).

Perhaps recognizing the potential inherent in the use of autobiographical materials to make a feminist point, Manley went on to write *The Adventures of Rivella,* her thinly fictionalized autobiographical memoir that serves as a feminist *apologia pro vita sua.* Its enunciated thesis is "*If she had been a Man, she had been without Fault:* But the Charter of that Sex being much more confin'd . . . what is not a Crime in Men is scandalous and unpardonable in Woman"[13]—a condemnation of the double standard, which establishes the text's main theme. In this work Manley provided Defoe with an important model for *Moll Flanders* and *Roxana.*

By using the escapades of court figures as her source, Manley was following in the late seventeenth-century French tradition of the scandalous "histories" or "chroniques scandaleuses," written largely by women. These exposés of the sexual indiscretions of powerful men of state were not written simply to titillate; they had a clear political purpose: to undermine the sources of political authority. While Manley has been seen as revealing the affairs of Whigs in order to promote the Tory cause (which indeed was one of her motives), she also and perhaps more insistently exposes masculine betrayals, abuse, and exploitation of women. Indeed, the central pedagogical message that Astrea gleans for her protegé, as enunciated near the end of the second volume, is that he should govern his regime in a way that protects women from abuse: "My prince shall make it Death to those who can be prov'd to have seduc'd a *Virgin.* Since sense of *Shame* and *Reputation* can't with-hold 'em! since *Conscience, Honour,* and what the World calls Principles, can't deter those *Betrayers;* the Laws must, and those shall be Sanguinary. My prince shall adore, and serve the Fair" (2:192) (meaning the "fair sex," i.e., women).

In her preface to the second volume, Manley claims that she has a serious satirical intent, aligning herself with the great satirists of antiquity, Lucian and Varro, who, she insists, targeted specific individuals even as she has done (Manley here is apparently defending herself against criticisms that she should not have personalized her attack on corruption). Her purpose, she claims, is in the end not sensationalist but moral: "the very Soul of Satire, is scourging of Vice, and Exhortation to Virtue" (2:A5r).

Perhaps the most powerful story in the work, and certainly one that well illustrates Manley's feminist satirical purposes, is that of Charlot, a tale that anticipates *Les Liaisons dangereuses* in its exposé of ruthless, cynical manipulation and the corruption of the innocent and powerless by the powerful. The victim here is Charlot, a young female ward of a duke (ostensibly the Duke of Portland, a minister to William III). Her guardian, the duke, "followed the wise Maxims of *Machiavel*" (1:49) to seduce his charge.

Manley manages in this seduction tale to introject a critique of the Machiavellianism of political figures in pursuing *raisons d'état;* it is not just their personal behavior that is corrupt but also their public, political modus operandi. The duke "had a seeming Admiration for *Virtue* . . . but he was a Statesman, and held it incompatible (in an Age like this) with a Mans making his Fortune, *Ambition, desire of Gain, Dissimulation, Cunning,* all these were meritoriously serviceable to him" (52). In preparing for the seduction, the duke "open'd a *Machiavel*" (61), and then has the girl read an Ovidian story about father-daughter incest (63–64). After her ruin, Charlot is advised by a cynical countess that "the first thing a Woman ought to consult was her Interest, . . . ; that Love shou'd be a handle towards it" (73). The duke soon abandons Charlot, who then "dy'd a true Landmark: to warn all believing Virgins" (83), and he marries the countess after she bargains with him for a title (still playing liaisons as an economic, political game).

Manley also wrote an unframed collection of novellas, *The Power of Love* (1720). This work is of interest because it shows how Manley modified novellas she inherited from continental antecedents, including Marguerite de Navarre and María de Zayas, modifications that signify the emergence of realism. Manley's collection of seven novellas is based largely on Painter's *The Palace of Pleasure;* five are adaptations from Painter. But two of these derive from the *Heptaméron* and two were also treated by Zayas (Manley's novella four from the *Heptaméron,* number thirty-two; novella five, from *Heptaméron,* number thirty-six; novella three, though it probably derives from Bandello, is also treated by Zayas in *Novelas amorosas,* number one; and novella four parallels Zayas's number four in the *Parte segunda,* as noted above).

Since I analyze Manley's novella three at length in chapter seven, I will confine myself here to novella five, "The Husband's Resentment. Example II" (novella four, "The Husband's Resentment. Example I," was the skull story described earlier). Manley follows the plot laid out in the *Heptaméron,* but her addition of realistic details in character development shows strikingly what realism was and how its addition made the novel, which Manley closely approximates, so distinct a genre. The plot is that of a Grenoble city-official who discovers that his wife is having an affair with a household clerk. In order to preserve his honor, he acts as if nothing has happened; later, however, he exiles the clerk and secretly poisons the wife. The *Heptaméron* version uses the story as a case to discuss the ethics of the husband's act (we discuss it further in the next chapter). Manley, however, adds to the story a pathetic old woman servant, Mrs. Ursula, who remains loyal to her master, but who becomes a kind of scapegoat, with the master publicly accusing her of lying, when she reveals the affair to him, and then banishing her. In developing this character Manley presents the standpoint of the female underclass, thus providing a new critical perspective that further ironizes the main characters' behavior, such that the novella in her handling is more a novelistic episode than a novella.

Mrs. Ursula had been with the city-official since his birth; she had been his wetnurse and was wholly devoted to him. She considered that he had married below his class, and his wife resented her, often asking him to get rid of her. "She used to tell [him] she loved Faces that were young, and would not shock one as Mrs. *Ursula's* did, with forbidding Wrinkles and antique Head geer, as if she had been fetch'd from out of the Tombs."[14] When Mrs. Ursula tells the husband about his wife's affair, his doubt deeply offends her: "That she should have suckled him, and brought him up, nay, and loved him better than his own Mother, to meet such Returns! She had rather die a Thousand times over than have her Truth suspected!" (278). (Note Manley's use of indirect discourse here.) When, based on Mrs. Ursula's tip, the husband finds the wife in flagrante delicto, he denies what he has seen and blames her: "poor Mrs. *Ursula* thought she came to an absolute Triumph, and flew rather than hobbled at the Sound of her Master's Voice" (282) only to be fired for her troubles. Her weeping departure, cast out with nothing after a lifetime of service, is described in detail. This pathetic character recenters the story away from the adultery issue and onto a kind of class struggle between masters and servants. The gratuitously evil behavior of the master and his wife toward each other (seen in the original novella) is turned into a kind of political evil, wherein the dominant mistreat the dominated. Highlighting the point of view of the oppressed, the marginalized, is, as we have seen, a hallmark of the novel, and Manley does just that in this story.

Like many of the works by Cavendish and Manley, Jane Barker's unjustly neglected *Patch-Work Screen for the Ladies* (1723) is an innovative, protean work that anticipates the novel but is structured in the framed-novelle format. Although labeled in its subtitle, "A Collection of Instructive Novels" (meaning novellas—in English at the time novellas were called *novels,* with the accent on the second syllable), *Patch-Work Screen* is more than a collection; it retains a weighty frame that tends to merge with the main inset story, the autobiographical narrative of the central frame character, Galesia. Thus the focus on one woman's life-story from a feminist point of view—seen emerging in earlier women's writings—becomes the central narrative in *Patch-Work Screen,* thereby anticipating the bildungsroman, which used the fictional life-story as a central unifying device, its hypotaxis. The *Patch-work Screen,* as its title suggests, remains too "patchwork" or paratactic in structure to be considered a novel. It, however, perhaps more than any other work, illustrates the tensions between the conflicting pulls of hypotaxis and parataxis, unity and diffusion, cohesion and eclecticism (or what Bakhtin calls "centripetal" and "centrifugal" forces),[15] which were finally resolved in the novel in favor of a unity of theme and character, subordinating other elements.

That Barker was concerned with the question of unity is suggested in her preface "To the Reader," discussed in the preceding chapter, where she analogizes a patchwork composition first to a "tea-table" discussion and then to the unifying order that operates in the physical cosmos, "*the* Clashing *of* Atoms, *which at last united to compose this glorious Fabrick of the* UNIVERSE."[16] Interestingly, Barker then contrasts her patchwork structure with Defoe's "Histories *at* Large; *viz.* Robinson Crusoe, *and* Moll Flanders" (iv), indicating an awareness on her part of the structural differences between her work and his.

Barker experiments with two structural devices in this work. The first frame she uses is a stagecoach journey where various characters recount stories. This is a variation on the framed-novelle format used successfully by Marie-Catherine le Jumel de Barneville, the Baroness d'Aulnoy, in her *Relations du voyage d'Espagne* (1691) (*The Ingeneous and Diverting Letters of the Lady—Travels into Spain*), which narrated the voyage retrospectively through letters. It was also used by Delarivier Manley in the satirical *Letters Writen* [sic] *by Mrs. Manley* (1696), later retitled *A Stage-Coach Journey to Exeter* (1725) (treated in chapter six).

Barker dispenses with the epistolary format, however, using a third-person narrator to describe a short stagecoach trip north of London in which Galesia, the main character, hears a number of short stories narrated by four other passengers and tells one herself. In her story she alludes to Mademoiselle de Montpensier, suggesting the familiarity of the English women writers with their French counterparts (A8ᵛ). (Also one of the stories is a retake of the *Portuguese Letters* [*Lettres portugaises*], by then a popular French, romantic narrative about a nun and her lover.) At the end of the story-telling the coach collides with another on a bridge and crashes into a river. This accident ushers in the second and main frame that Barker uses in this work, which is that of Galesia helping a noblewoman who has taken her in to construct a patchwork screen. The construction becomes a metaphor for the composition of Barker's fiction; Galesia contributes poems, swatches of autobiographical narrative, novellas, letters, even recipes, which are patched together to make the work. The frame remains that of the two women discussing the merits of the various pieces and deciding where they should be placed in the "screen."

But a new unifying force threatens to take over the *Patch-Work Screen*, and that is the story of Galesia herself, which is itself informed by a feminist perspective. It is feminist on two counts: the first is her resentment, which we have seen in chapter two, at having been deprived of a formal education and for being shunned when she does reveal her autodidactic knowledge: "A Learned Woman [is] . . . like a Forc'd Plant, that never has its due or proper relish" (11); the second, also discussed earlier, is her critique of the marriage market in which she, as a young woman, has been prepared as an object for sale. She also has it in for faithless men, since she has been abandoned by the one suitor she loved. Rejecting that "Beau World" (55) Galesia becomes a·herbal healer and develops renown locally for her skills. "People come to me for Advice in divers sorts of Maladies, and having tolerable good Luck, I began to be pretty much known." She acknowledges that "Pride and Vanity" were "in some Degree" "united to this Beneficence; for I was got to such a Pitch of helping the Sick, that I wrote my *Bills* in *Latin*, with the same manner of *Cyphers* and *Directions* as Doctors do" (55–56). Here we see women's sense of being exiled from the Latin tradition of learning; Galesia uses it mimetically, with no understanding of its meaning, as a means of seizing power. Earlier, as noted, Galesia had apologized for her lack of skill in a classical verse form, the Pindaric ode, wondering whether her "Fingers ought to have been imploy'd rather at the Needle and the Distaff, than to the Pen and Standish, and leave these Enterprizes to the Learned" (7–8).

The Lining of the Patch Work Screen (1726), a sequel to the earlier work, is also organized in the framed-novelle format. I see it in fact as the terminal work in the women's tradition of the framed-novelle. Galesia (now spelled Galecia) is here the central frame character and tacitly gleans from many of the stories a feminist point. What is innovative in the frame is that in at least some of the episodes we see Galesia alone, and some of the inset stories come from books she is reading in solitude, signifying the beginnings of print culture. In one case, for example, a secondary character reads Aphra Behn's "History of the Nun; or the Fair Vow-Breaker" (1689), and that story is then reproduced.[17]

While the effect of these stories on Galecia is not fully developed, many of them point up the feminist conclusions she had reached in *The Patch-Work Screen:* that men are not to be trusted, that young women are often victimized in various marriage-market schemes, and that solitude is preferable to being prey to the "traffick" in women. The work concludes with Galecia's returning to the country, having despaired of urban Machiavellianism and feeling "inexpressible Joy" to be rejoining a woman friend there.[18] Thus, in both *The Patch-Work Screen* and the *Lining,* Barker seems to be torn between using, on the one hand, the format of the framed-novelle tradition, which she inherited, and moving toward a new form in which the central focus is on the "history" and development of the central, female protagonist.

The increasing emphasis on the individual life-story, which came to be the main focus in the novel, was undoubtedly due to numerous social and economic forces, as Ian Watt details in his study. One of these (which Watt does not treat) is the popularization of the theological tradition of casuistry. In *Defoe and Casuistry,* G. A. Starr isolates this tradition as an important source of the novel's dialectics. In the following chapter I will show that women writers' use of casuistry led to an emphasis on the particularized life-story as a further means of articulating a feminist standpoint. By focusing upon the particular details of an individual woman's story, women writers could establish a case for the defense of women. In so doing they contributed to the constitution of the novel as a genre that valorizes the *particular* details of common life, thereby lending the novel one of its defining characteristics.

Chapter Five

Circumstances Alter Cases: Women, Casuistry, and the Novel

CASUISTRY IS A FORM OF LEGAL AND MORAL REASONING that mediates between general rules or maxims and specific circumstances by means of the case history, a short anecdote or story—a "hypothetical"—that points up the contradictions between the circumstances and the law in order to effect accommodation or change. Etymologically, casuistry derives from the Latin *casus* [chance, happening, accident], which itself stems from *cadere* [to happen].

While today casuistry retains the negative connotations earned by the excesses excoriated by Pascal in the *Les Provinciales* (1656–57), it was (and some claim still is) an important mode of moral reasoning, one that in any event by the seventeenth century "was a central instrument in the social construction of reality."[1] The dominance of casuistry as a mode of "practical divinity" emerged after the Fourth Lateran Council (1215), which promulgated the doctrine of required annual confession—a practice whereby the priest applied generalized theological doctrine to the specific case and levied a specific penance on the sinner. The golden age of casuistry was from the early fourteenth through the seventeenth century, reaching a peak from the mid-sixteenth to mid-seventeenth century, during which period more than six hundred collections of "cases of conscience" appeared in print.[2]

Because the case narrative is a fiction, usually posed as a hypothetical example, it only needed the addition of a few fictional details for it to become extrapolated as a separate literary form in and of itself. That form was the novella, which, numerous authorities point out, derived in part from courtly love casuistry.[3]

A good example that illustrates the close kinship between the case as presented in casuistry texts and the literary novella may be seen in novella thirty of Marguerite de Navarre's *Heptaméron*. This novella, which is referred to as a *cas* [case] by a frame character,[4] concerns mother-son incest. The story was widely recounted in various forms during the early modern period, and seized upon by casuists. Joseph Hall, for example, an Anglican casuist, devoted four pages to it in his *Resolutions and Decisions* (1650) in a section entitled "Cases Matrimonial."

> Case III.—"Whether an incestuous marriage, contracted in simplicity of heart, betwixt two persons ignorant of such a defilement, and so far consummate as that children are born in that wedlock, ought to be made known and prosecuted to a dissolution?"
>
> "The case thus: A gentlewoman . . . had her son trained up in her house; who, now having passed the age of puberty, grew up, as in stature, so in wonton desires. . . ."[5]

Hall proceeds to relate how, to stop her son's harassment of a chambermaid, the mother substitutes herself for the maid in a nighttime assignation; however, "the devil so far prevailed . . . that . . . she yielded to the lust of her son, and by him conceived a daughter" (7:410). The story is complicated by the fact that when the two offspring grow up, they unknowingly wed—another incestuous union. Hall resolves that the mother's hiding of the original sin was worse than the incest itself, but that with "all circumstances thoroughly weighed, the penitent mother should . . . secretly make her peace with God" (7:411).

Marguerite de Navarre recounts essentially the same plot as Hall, although in somewhat greater detail, elaborating considerably more the subjective point of view and emotional state of the mother. We learn, for example, that "plunged into a deep sadness and melancholy" (319) ["demoura longuement en grande tristesse et melencolye" (231)], she considered abortion. After the marriage of her children has been consummated, she consults ecclesiastical authorities. These "doctors of theology" (321) ["docteurs en theologie" (233)], undoubtedly casuists, counsel that she should continue to guard her secret but do penance the rest of her life.

As with many of the novellas in the *Heptaméron* this story is treated as a case, which the frame characters rigorously analyze. Interestingly, the gist of their discussion of this story determines that the woman is more guilty of pride—in thinking that she could control her feelings—than of lust. In other words, the woman is seen as exhibiting human failings rather than exemplifying the going misogynist idea that women are inherently promiscuous, "the devil's gateway," as early Christian theologian Tertullian put it. Patricia Cholakian remarks, "What began [in earlier circulations of the story] as a sexist attack on women has been broadened to include the whole human race."[6] Thus, Marguerite de Navarre constructed her novella as an amplified case study of the kind analyzed in casuistry treatises; use of the casuistical format enabled her to refute a misogynist generality about women.

One of the genetic structures of the early novel was that of a series of case/novellas linked together by a frame plot. The tradition of casuistry has been recognized, therefore, as an important component in the constitution of the novel, which, as J. Paul Hunter remarks, "only becomes distinct . . . when it gets down to cases, recording particulars and telling an individual's story."[7] Defoe's conception of the novel as a series of "cases" reflecting moral dilemmas facing his protagonists grows directly out of the casuistical tradition, as G. A. Starr demonstrates in *Defoe and Casuistry* (1971). Indeed, Starr suggests that the episode of Moll Flanders's unwittingly incestuous marriage derives from the casuistical discussions described above, including the *Heptaméron*'s novella thirty.[8]

The novel's focus on the circumstantial and the anomalous gave it the subversive character Mikhail Bakhtin and others have identified as definitional to the genre. For attention to the idiosyncratic inevitably destabilizes the general rule or maxim. In casuistry, case narratives necessarily point up contradictions in the law and thus precipitate a "dispersal of norms."[9] As an "interpretive practice" casuistry "militate[s] against the authority of final answers" (Gallagher 4). Thus, "the hermeneutics of casuistry can be seen as . . . enact[ing] what Bakhtin saw as the signal characteristic of novelistic discourse: . . . the representation of a dialogic . . . orientation. . . . [B]y inhabiting, and eroding, a discourse of power charged with the presence of an authoritative Word, the discourse of conscience [casuistry] articulates the inherent capacity of the 'novelizing' act to serve as a vehicle for political and ideological subversion" (Gallagher 15–17).

Early modern women writers seem to have realized the subversive potential of casuistry and early put it to feminist use. That is, they realized that a focus on the particular circumstances of women's situations would alter the cases, in other words, change the stories, and thereby challenge the ideological norms, rules, and maxims that were misogynistic, or otherwise injurious to women. Significantly, the earliest women writers in the Western tradition—beginning with the women troubadours and amplified by Christine de Pizan—used casuistry for feminist purposes. It appears that the casuistical construction, which permitted the expression of an oppositional viewpoint, enabled the articulation of feminist views. Here I trace the feminist use of casuistry, contending that it allowed women writers to represent a women's standpoint in the continuing *querelle des femmes,* which in turn contributed to the problematization of the "word of the fathers," which Bakhtin saw as integral to the rise of novelistic discourse.

Feminist casuistry takes its place within a more general feminist tradition in the early modern period, whereby women attempted to refute or problematize misogynist maxims and thus to challenge ideological assumptions about women. Writers, of course, operate in an ideological continuum and must deal with its inherited set of assumptions and notions of probability that restrict their representational possibilities. Gérard Genette and Nancy K. Miller have pointed out, for example, how ideological concepts of probability limited critics' understanding of Madame de Lafayette's *La Princesse de Clèves* (1678).[10] I contend, even further, that these ideological maxims were what Madame de Lafayette—like many women writers—was writing against, and that indeed she conceived her novel as a particularized case study intended to controvert misogynist generalities about women.

For example, her protagonist challenges the rule that all women are prey to uncontrollable and violent passion. When the princess finds herself falling for Monsieur de Nemours, she fears that she has become "like other women—I, who was so different from them. . . . I shall be looked upon by everyone as a person who has a mad and violent passion" ["que je me trouve, comme les autres femmes, étant si éloignée de leur ressembler. . . . Je serai bientôt regardée de tout le monde comme une personne qui a une folle et violente passion"].[11] Earlier, in a celebrated deathbed scene, her mother had warned the princess to control her feelings and not to "fall to the level of other women" (39) ["tomber comme les autres femmes" (85–86)]. That the protagonist does control herself, first by admitting her extramarital involvement to her husband and finally by renouncing a liaison with Nemours after her husband dies, establishes her as a unique case whose circumstances challenge the misogynist maxim.

Miller calls the protagonist a "heroine without a maxim," a character "whose behavior is deliberately idiopathic"; she "violate[s] a grammar of motives that describes while prescribing . . . what wives, not to say women, should or should not do" (340). Further, Miller poses the question that "if we were to uncover a feminine 'tradition'—diachronic recurrences—of such ungrammaticalities, would we have the basis for a poetics of women's fiction?" (341).

The tradition of feminist literary casuistry constitutes one vein of diachronic recurrences of such "ungrammaticalities." Its genealogy reaches back to the women troubadours and Christine de Pizan and continues via Marguerite de Navarre and María de Zayas to English writers Margaret Cavendish, Mary Carleton, Delarivier Manley, and Jane Barker.

Courtly love poets appropriated casuistry early on as a means of discussing moral and romantic choices available to lovers in the culture of "fin' amors." This "casuistique d'amour" [love casuistry], as it has been called, was the tradition from which feminist casuistry emerged. Two of the debate genres favored by the Provençal troubadours—the *tenson* and the *joc partit*—exemplify the use of casuistry to explore romantic issues.[12] An early example of how a woman poet seized the opportunity to express a feminist point of view in such a debate may be seen in an early thirteenth-century *tenson* by Gui d'Ussel and Marie de Ventadour, which discusses the balance of power in a love relationship. In response to the question of whether a courted woman must "observe the laws of love" ["los dreitz que tenon l'amador"] as faithfully as the suitor, Marie replies, "she must honor the lover/as a friend and not as a master" ["e dompna deu a son drut far honor/Cum ad amic, mas non cum a seignor"].[13]

Often the *joc partit* or *tenson* was accompanied by a prose *razos*, a commentary or explication that highlights the issues discussed or circumstances of composition. The feminist thesis of the above *tenson* is underscored in an accompanying *razos:* "my lady Maria held the view that the lover should have neither seigneury nor authority."[14]

Significantly, the *razos* were at the time often referred to as *novellas*. Walter Pabst theorizes in his *Novellentheorie und Novellendichtung* that the *razos* was a source for the framed-novelle genre. As noted, in the framed-novelle the enclosed novellas often served as "cases," which were then discussed by the frame storytellers. Boccaccio indeed refers to his novellas as "casi d'amore" [love cases] in his preface to the *Decameron* (Pabst 20).

Christine de Pizan also employed the Provençal debate-forms in several of her long poems, particularly "Le Debat de deux amants," "Le Livre des trois jugemens," and "Le Livre du dit de Poissy."[15] In all of these, "love cases" are presented for debate. The first case in the "Livre des trois jugemens" presents a woman accused of perjury because, after having been abandoned by a lover to whom she had pledged troth, she has taken another. She argues in her own defense that she is not a perjurer ["Vous m'avez dit de m'appeler parjure,/ Car ne le suis . . ."]. Instead she argues casuistically that one is relieved of one's oath if the other party has not lived up to the deal ["Que qui promet pour quelque chose avoir,/ Se il ne l'a, quitte doit estre voir/De son serment"].[16] In other words, rules are not absolute and circumstances alter cases. In arguing her case the woman is effectively challenging the subtextual misogynist maxim embedded in the perjury accusation that women are fickle and untrustworthy. Women writers' use of casuistry frequently follows this model; a woman pleads her side of the case, often in a court or before a legal authority.[17]

Christine uses a similar format in a novella reworked from Boccaccio's *Decameron* in the *Livre de la cité des dames* (1405), the story of Bernabo's wife (*Decameron* II.9). A comparison of Boccaccio's and Christine's versions will help to further distinguish women writers' use of the format.

First, let us note, however, that Boccaccio also introduces a feminist use of casuistry in two other stories (VI.7 and VII.5)—both of which concern women who, like Bernabo's wife, successfully argue their cases by means of casuistry. However, in each situation Boccaccio undercuts the woman plaintiff, thus rendering a potentially feminist assertion ambiguous (see also II.3). Both novellas depict women whose behavior is otherwise so reprehensible it undercuts their forensic success.

In the seventh story of day six, for example, a woman successfully argues that a law mandating that adulterous women be burned alive is inequitable. Madonna Filippa develops her case with a two-fold argument. The first part is an example of syllogistic logic: just laws, the woman claims, "should be equal for both sexes and made with the consent of those who are to obey them" ["le legge deono esser communi e fatte con consentimento di coloro a cui toccano]."[18] This law is unjust ["malvagia"] because it applies only to women, and women did not consult in its passage—a convincing enough argument.

In the second part of her contention, however, Filippa adds a casuistical argument: since she fulfills her husband sexually yet has sexual energy left over, she should not waste it but share it with another man. By using her circumstances, that of being an adulteress, Filippa challenges the concept of adultery as immoral, claiming another "right"—the duty to share her sexual energy. That the idea is obviously facetious—the audience in the court laughs at it—undercuts the serious feminist point Filippa had made in the first part of her argument.

A second example of Boccaccio's use of casuistry occurs in the fifth story of the seventh day. Here a wife tricks an obsessively jealous husband who had impersonated a priest in the confessional in order to determine if she is having an extramarital affair. She recognizes him and confesses to him that she is having an affair with a priest, which is not the case. Later she claims she told the truth because her husband was the "priest" at the time of the confession. This slippery casuistry works to compromise the woman's character, which is further tainted by her continuing deception of her husband (by in fact having an affair). Thus, although the listeners in the *Decameron* support her, her obviously corrupt character undercuts whatever feminist message one might otherwise glean from the tale.

Christine de Pizan chose not to use either of the above novellas in the *Cité des dames;* rather she picked three others, among them Boccaccio's ninth tale of the second day, the story of Bernabo's wife.[19] The plot is this: Bernabo had come to a hasty conclusion, based on fraudulent evidence, that his wife was unfaithful and had ordered a servant to kill her. She, however, survives and is eventually exonerated when she presents her case in a court-like proceeding before a magistrate in which she acts in disguise as her own attorney, disproving the evidence that had earlier convicted her in her husband's eyes. In Christine de Pizan's version the slandered wife displays considerable forensic skills (more so than in Boccaccio's version), requesting the magistrate to rule "according to the merits of the case" ["justement selonc le cas"], and confronting the husband directly for so gullibly accepting false evidence: "You deserve to die for not having sufficient proof!" ["Vous estes digne de mort; car vous n'aviez mie preuve soubffisant"].[20]

The husband has clearly fallen prey to a misogynist generality about women—that all wives are easy lays and untrustworthy—which the woman disproves by bearing witness to the particular details of her particular case. The story thus, as a case study that works to contradict and destabilize a misogynist maxim, exemplifies a feminist use of casuistry.

Boccaccio, although recounting essentially the same tale, undercuts the message by following it with a counter example, the story of an elderly judge (II.10) whose wife abandons him for a pirate who sexually satisfies her better. The women listeners in the *Decameron* determine from this exemplum that "Bernabo was a fool" (167) ["Bernabò era stato una bestia" (157)] (to have repented of his distrust of his wife)—thereby reinscribing the misogynist maxim that women are sexually voracious, fickle, and irrational. Thus, while Boccaccio anticipates a feminist use of casuistry in three of his tales, he negates the message in the ways indicated.

Succeeding women writers restored, however, Boccaccio's vitiated feminist message. Spanish writer María de Zayas in fact picked up and elaborated considerably the story of Bernabo's wife in her *Novelas amorosas y ejemplares* (1637). "El juez de su causa" ("The Judge of Her Own Case") adds a number of escapades to the Boccaccio/Pizan version, including having the woman (here named Estela) serve in male disguise in the military. She is rewarded by the emperor for her service with a judicial position. In this capacity she serves as judge of her former lover, who has been wrongly accused of kidnapping and murdering her. In the course of the trial the lover reveals, however, that he has nevertheless falsely held misogynistic views about Estela, considering her fickle and inconstant. Upon hearing these the judge Estela roundly condemns him for jumping to conclusions, revealing herself finally, as in the earlier versions, as the ultimate proof of her own truth; the particular details of her story prove her case, demolishing misogynist maxims (such as that women are untrustworthy) in the process, another example of a feminist use of casuistry.

Probably the most extensive and significant appropriation of casuistry for feminist purposes in early modern literature remains in the *Heptaméron* (1549) by Marguerite de Navarre.[21] We have noted that by her time the framed-novelle genre had become a vehicle for the expression of virulent misogyny, especially in the French tradition, and it is apparent that her extension of the frame discussions (generally recognized as her contribution to the genre) was at least in part to counter this misogyny. Although modeled on the *Decameron,* Marguerite's opus greatly extends the casuistical frame analysis of the novellas, nearly one-fourth of which are explicitly designated "cases," and nearly all of which present case-like moral dilemmas. This extensive use of casuistry in the *Heptaméron* has not received scholarly attention.

Marguerite de Navarre was, as a member of a royal family, well educated, especially in Christian doctrine. One of her early teachers, François Demoulin, wrote a penitential manual for her; it used the dialogue format of the casuistry treatises and undoubtedly reflects their influence.[22] Marguerite was surely familiar as well with many of these treatises, and, although clearly critical of the excesses of casuistry, appropriated its methodology in the *Heptaméron.* Moreover, and perhaps more relevant, Marguerite was quite familiar with courtly love casuistry.[23] Indeed, her immediate entourage would often spend time discussing in salon-like fashion "a case of romantic casuistry," according to her biographer, Pierre Jourda (291). Jourda further proposes that the *Heptaméron's* originality lies in its moral study of the "case of conscience," where earlier exemplars of the genre largely described amoral escapades only for entertainment purposes (960). Significantly, a seventeenth-century English translator of the *Heptaméron,* Robert Codrington, writing during the heyday of English casuistry, remarks in his preface, "The Canonists also, and the Casuists, will here have enough, in many passages, on which with admiration to reflect."[24]

Those novellas that exemplify Marguerite's use of casuistry for feminist purposes are of particular interest to this study. Several of these follow Christine de Pizan's model of the woman speaking out in her own defense. (As noted, Marguerite was familiar with her predecessor's work—she probably owned a Christine de Pizan manuscript—according to Jourda, 518, 534, 1288). And like Christine's characters, Marguerite's women display impressive rhetorical and forensic skills (I am not proposing Christine de Pizan as her only model, of course, but she was probably an influence).

In three of the novellas, numbers fifteen, twenty-one, and sixty-one, women act as their own defense attorneys, as if in a court of law, arguing casuistically that the crimes they are accused of are not really sins and/or that they were justified in their commission. Significantly (and this is another aspect of the *Heptaméron* that has not received attention), in each of these novellas the frame discussion pointedly ignores the subversive implications of the women characters' antinomian positions. Perhaps this was because Marguerite did not want to highlight the radical feminism embedded in these stories; she had already antagonized Church authorities with her *Miroir de l'âme pécheresse* (1531), which had been condemned by the Sorbonne as heretical in 1533. In those days heresy was of course a serious matter; a reformer connected to Marguerite's circle, Louis de Berquin, had been executed for heresy in 1529.[25]

Nevertheless, while the subversive character of the women's positions is not accentuated in the frame discussion, it is manifest in the women's declamations. The situation in novella fifteen is that a woman, long ignored by her philandering husband, takes a platonic lover in courtly love fashion. The husband then exerts his authority, forbidding her to see the lover, whereupon she bursts forth with a lengthy speech damning the double standard in sins: Why is what is regarded a major crime for a woman considered a minor peccadillo for a man? Confronting her husband, she protests, "Now, Monsieur, do you intend . . . to take revenge on me for the very kind of thing you yourself have been guilty for years . . . ?" ["Et vous, monsieur . . . vouldriez-vous prendre vengeance d'un oeuvre, dont si, long temps a, vous m'avez donné exemple . . . ?"][26] She concludes by using the casuistical formula of the Provençal love debate: "Well, then, judge without bias. Which of the two of us most deserves to be punished, and which of us most deserves to be excused?" (197) ["Or, jugez sans faveur lequel de nous deux est le plus punissable ou excusable . . . ?" (123)]. Thus, with the realities of the case laid forth, and the woman's point of view given clear expression, the authority of "the law of men [which] attaches dishonour to women who fall in love" extramaritally (196) ["la loy des hommes (qui) donne grand deshonneur aux femmes qui ayment autres que leurs mariz" (123)] is challenged. By using a case that points up the moral contradiction of the double standard, Marguerite effectively critiques that rule.

More seriously heretical is the position of Rolandine in novella twenty-one, who argues her case before royal authority, contending that she and her lover were morally justified in marrying outside the Church and in opposition to royal decree (marriage had been forbidden because the lover was a bastard and penniless). In her defense she claims that what she has done is not a sin: "If it were the case that I had sinned against God, the King, [the Queen], my parents and my own conscience, then indeed I would be obdurate not to weep tears of repentance" (248) ["Quant je aurois offensé Dieu, le Roy, (la Reyne), mes parens et ma conscience, je serois bien obstinée si, de grande repentance, je ne pleurois" (170)].

A similar position is argued by the main character in novella sixty-one, who has abandoned her husband and lived in an essentially bigamous but happy second alliance for fourteen or fifteen years. In defending herself, the woman claims that she had not sinned against God, and that it would indeed be a sin to take her away from her second "spouse" and return her to the first. "Let no one imagine that my way of life contradicts the will of God. . . . [W]e live . . . without either of us ever uttering a word of disagreement. . . . And it would be a sin to make us part, for [he] is nearly eighty years old, while I am only forty-five, and he would not live for long without me!" (482). ["Et, s'il ne fault point que l'on pense que je vive contre la volunté de Dieu, car . . . [nous] vivons . . . sans que jamais entre nous deux y eut eu parolle. . . . Et, qui nous separera fera grand peché, car le bon homme, qui a bien près de quatre vingtz ans, ne vivra pas longuement sans moy, qui en ay quarante cinq" (375)]. Thus, by invoking the particulars of her case, which suggest the possibilities of another moral rule, the woman is able to raise questions about the patriarchal law that makes her her husband's possession.[27]

Other *Heptaméron* novellas are similarly presented as cases for casuistical discussion. The most significant of these are numbers twelve, thirty-six, and forty (and number thirty, as noted above). Novella twelve, which is discussed as a case by the frame characters, concerns a conflict between two moral imperatives: the claims of loyalty versus the claims of honor. A nobleman, chief servant to a duke, is asked by the latter to procure for him his sister. The nobleman is thus torn between loyalty to his master and the obligation to defend his sister's (and family's) honor. He chooses the latter course and assassinates the duke to protect his sister. In the frame discussions the women consider that he acted properly; the men do not (162/95).

Novella thirty-six also concerns a murder and whether it is justifiable. In this case a city official discovers his wife's adultery and eventually poisons her as punishment. (This story was the one retold and reworked by Delarivier Manley as "The Husband's Resentment. Example II" in *The Power of Love* [1720], discussed in chapter four.) The frame discussion is a characteristic casuistical analysis of whether the murder was a sin, the issue hinging on the question of the husband's state of mind, with some contending that a violent act committed in the heat of passion is not so grevious as a coldly premeditated act (this was a standard issue in the casuistry manuals).[28] In this case the husband had delayed his revenge for several months. One of the discussants observes that if "he had killed her out of anger, . . . the learned doctors say that such a sin is remissable" (356) ["il l'eust tuée en sa collere . . . les docteurs dient que le peché est remissible" (264)]. Others consider that his anger might have lasted that long.

Another of the discussants engages in the kind of casuistical reasoning that has given it a bad name, in arguing that since it was love that drove the man to murder it should only be considered a venial sin, because it is by "passing up the ladder of worldly love" that one reaches God (357) ["c'est ung degré pour monter à l'amour parfaict de luy" (265)]. This is an ironically perverse reworking of Marguerite's own platonic theory, and is put down immediately in the text.

Novella forty, while it may, like much of the *Heptaméron,* have a basis in historical fact (see François, p. 480, nn. 589, 591), recounts a story that was oft told—that of the sister who defies patriarchal authority (a brother who has acceded to family sovereignty because of the father's death) by marrying or consorting with a forbidden lover.[29] The brother responds by killing the lover. In addition, in the *Heptaméron* version, the woman is imprisoned for life.

The frame characters discuss the story as a case (the word *cas* [case] is used twice [279]). Their discussion focuses on the issue of familial control of marriage choice, with two characters questioning whether the brother legally had authority over the sister because he was neither husband nor father, and she was no longer a minor ["qu'elle estoit en l'aage que les loys permectent aux filles d'eulx marier sans leur volunté" (278)]. The issue of daughters having free choice of marriage partner, which the frame characters further debate, was a hot one in casuistry treatises, which generally supported at least the daughter's right to veto a parental choice (see Starr 40, n. 75). The issue continued to be a major one in women's literature.

Undoubtedly under the influence of Marguerite de Navarre, María de Zayas continued the feminist use of casuistry in her two framed-novelle collections, the *Novelas amorosas* and the *Parte segunda,* the *Desengaños amorosos.* Significantly, in her preface to the reader of the *Novelas amorosas,* which, as we have seen, presents a lengthy defense of women's right to write and a plea for women's education, Zayas suggests that it was by reading casuistry treatises in the vernacular that women became literate: "there were the . . . *Summas morales* in the vernacular so that women and lay people could become literate" (*Enchantments* 2) ["hay . . . *Sumas morales* en romance, los seglares y las mujeres pueden ser letrados" (*Novelas amorosas* 22)]. Zayas may be referring to the *Summa Moralis alphabetice per casus digesta* by Gabriel Saint-Vincent (officially published in 1668, it probably circulated earlier). In any event, there were numerous works of casuistry available in Spanish by Zayas's time, including what is considered to be one of the most important works of high casuistry, the *Enchiridion sive manuale confessariorum et poenitentium* (1569) by Martin Azpilcueta, the "Doctor of Navarre."

Like the *Heptaméron,* Zayas's works include a continuing frame discussion of the *querelle des femmes.* The stories in the *Novelas amorosas* told by women (five are told by men and five by women) have a feminist point, and all the stories in the *Desengaños,* which are all told by women, concern feminist issues. Indeed, we have noted that the narratives in the *Desengaños* are intended to be "case histories" ["casos verdaderos"], which are designed to "enlighten, or disenchant, women about men's deceptions" (*Enchantments* xvii) ["y que tuviesen nombre de desengaños" (*Parte segunda* 118)]. The stories are also to be "in defense of women's name" (xvii) ["por la fama de las mujeres" (118)]. The concept of *desengaños* or disenchantment, central to Spanish literature of the period, means that the stories are to disabuse women of any illusions they may have about men and romance. In this sense, the novellas thus have the feminist moral purpose of "consciousness-raising." And, indeed, all of the "cases" in the *Desengaños* portray brutal abuse of women from a feminist standpoint.

Feminist casuistry remained a central rhetorical mode in the writings of seventeenth- and early eighteenth-century English women. Margaret Cavendish continues the tradition in *Natures Pictures* (1656), her framed-novelle, which was also modeled on the *Heptaméron.* Two stories—"The Contract" and "The She-Anchoret"—are particularly relevant. The latter sets up a woman (a Cavendish persona) as a casuistical divine to whom various people pose questions. The question-answer format is that of a casuistry text (333–44). The She-Anchoret is clearly a kind of intermediary between the theological casuist and the popular casuistical advice-giver of late seventeenth-century journalism, which Starr sees as an important source for Defoe's use of casuistry in the early novel.

One of the first English periodicals for women, the *Athenian Mercury* (1690–97), specialized in fact in this kind of popular casuistry. Its original title was significantly *The Athenian Gazette: or, Casuisticall Mercury* (Starr 9). A subtitle, "resolving all the most nice and curious questions proposed by the ingenious" was expanded after the first volume (in 1691) to include "of either sex."[30] Bertha-Monica Stearnes notes that casuistical issues (of the type discussed by the She-Anchoret), such as "whether it be lawful to look with pleasure on another woman than one's wife?," were staple topics. Increasingly, the issue "whether it be proper for women to be learned"—a perennial concern of early modern women writers—was discussed (47). The editor, John Dunton, realizing the potential market of female readers, established regular special issues for "ladies." In these issues, according to Stearnes, the "cases became more elaborate in detail and if not actually short-stories, certainly offered plot material" (51).

G. A. Starr notes, the *Athenian Mercury*, to which Defoe contributed pieces, was "an important link between Defoe and the earlier casuistry" (9). He suggests that the episodic, paratactic structure of Defoe's plots probably derives from casuistry.

> In Dunton's periodical, highly diverse ethical dilemmas are resolved through detailed consideration of the relevant circumstances . . . each case of conscience becomes something of an episode. . . . [T]he casuistical method tends to dissolve narrative into a series of discrete episodes. . . . [T]he paratactic structure of such books as *Moll Flanders* . . . is in part ascribable to Defoe's habit of approaching experience casuistically, case by case. (32)

Another important source for Defoe's use of casuistry was, however, the writings of several women writers whose contribution I outline in the remainder of this chapter. Margaret Cavendish, for example, enlarges the tradition of women arguing their own cases in "The Contract" (the novella in *Natures Pictures* discussed in chapter three). The story is an important (if neglected) forerunner of the female bildungsroman, anticipating Fanny Burney's *Evelina* by over a century, but in its complex, casuistical plot harking back to the novella. It revolves around the issue of which of two marriages a bigamous duke has contracted is valid; it ends with a court hearing in which all the parties present their cases.

In the process, however, Cavendish develops the subjective point of view of a woman—the first wife, Delitia—to a much greater extent than generally seen heretofore in literature. Her standpoint presents a clear critique of the marriage-market system. She resists, as we have seen, her guardian's efforts "to traffick for a Husband" (*Natures Pictures* 189).

Her situation is complicated by the fact that she is already married, having been contracted in an arranged marriage at the age of seven. Her husband, however, later bigamously married another. Upon meeting again as adults (he not knowing who she is) they fall in love. The uncle-guardian, however, wants her to marry an older and wealthier man. After they have a lengthy casuistical debate on the subject, the uncle warns her "not to use Rhetorick against your self, and overthrow a good Fortune" (197).

In the court hearing over the validity of the marriages Delitia argues that her contracted marriage is valid, urging the judges to "cast aside your Canon Law . . . and judge it by the Common Law" (210). Here Delitia (and thus Cavendish) shows her knowledge of theological casuistry. Canon law generally favored marriages made with free consent of the parties, and opposed the arranged marriage of minors. Canon law would thus hold the husband's second marriage valid.

However, in Joseph Hall's casuistry text, *Resolution and Decisions* (1650), a treatise Cavendish as an Anglican might well have consulted, case number ten (7:398) in the section "Cases Matrimonial" advises that a second marriage should be dissolved in the case of a first marriage with a living spouse—obviously Delitia's case. The judges rule in her favor. By means, therefore, of clever casuistical subtleties Cavendish provides an ironic portrait of marriage-market "trafficking" from a feminist point of view: the woman only succeeds in "choosing" her spouse, who happens to be her husband, because of the ironically coincidental circumstances of her case (and because of her knowledge of casuistry).

The feminist use of casuistry took a significant turn in the latter seventeenth century, when women writers began to construe their life-histories as cases in order to challenge laws or ideological norms (encoded as maxims) that were pejorative to women. Exemplifying the life-as-case construction are *The Case of Madam Mary Carleton* (1663), *The Adventures of Rivella* (1714), and *A Patch-Work Screen for the Ladies* (1723). Defoe picked up on this construction in both *Moll Flanders* (1722) and *Roxana* (1724). We have already seen an anticipation of this construction in *La Princesse de Clèves* (1678) by Madame de Lafayette.

The Case of Madam Mary Carleton (1663), which has been designated as part of "a missing chapter in the history of the English novel,"[31] is the autobiographical defense written by Mary Carleton, who was a somewhat notorious figure tried for bigamy and eventually executed as a thief, and about whom circulated a series of narratives that debated her guilt or innocence.[32] She maintains her innocence in *The Case of Madam Mary Carleton,* arguing in the process that the *feme covert* laws, which deprived wives of legal standing and ownership of property, were unjust.[33]

As noted in chapter four, in her preface Carleton refers to her life as a series of novellas, asking her readers to "cast a favourable eye upon these Novels of my life, not much unlike those of Boccace [Boccaccio], but that they are more serious and tragical" (A4ᵛ). Indeed, the escapades in the *Case* do read like novellas, and early commentators considered it fiction (see especially C. F. Main and Ernest Bernbaum). If that is true, Carleton should be considered the first woman novelist, combining as she does the novella tradition with an autobiographical frame and a first-person narration—central formal components of the first novels.

Like the other women writers in this study, Carleton uses casuistry to argue her case—an aspect of her work that has not received attention. In relating her amusingly deceitful courtship (where both she and her suitor are pretending to wealth and status that neither has), Carleton argues casuistically that "*to deceive the deceiver, is no deceit*" (46), which she claims is "a received principle of Justice" (46). In fact, it was a received principle in casuistry, one that was analyzed in the *Athenian Mercury* (11.20.10) and picked up by Defoe; in *Moll Flanders* one episode, as Starr notes, is "built around a case of conscience . . . namely, the question of whether it is legitimate to deceive a deceiver" (Starr 128; also n.26). Carleton proceeds to act successfully as her own defense attorney in court against a charge of bigamy (the *Case* includes a purported transcript of the trial).

Ernest Bernbaum convincingly argues that the Mary Carleton narratives, particularly as they were synthesized in Francis Kirkman's fictionalized *The Counterfeit Lady Unveiled* (1673), were important progenitors of the novel. In particular, the "curious parallelism between the careers of Moll Carleton and Moll Flanders with their frequent marriages, their thefts, and their transportation" is noteworthy (89), leading Bernbaum to see *Counterfeit Lady* as "an early link in the chain of realistic novels" (90). His view is corroborated by the dean of authorities on the "rise of the novel," Ian Watt, who notes, "the closest seventeenth-century analogue to Moll Flanders" is Mary Carleton (101 n.1).

In *The Adventures of Rivella,* Delarivier Manley extrapolates from the feminist defenses seen in earlier works, particularly *The Case of Mary Carleton,* to construct a novel-length autobiographical defense of her life. In other words, Manley here makes her life a case in the ongoing debate about women, and thus takes her place in the continuing feminist use of casuistry. Manley had first explored the possibility of making her life a case in the *New Atalantis* (1709) in the story of Delia who at the age of fourteen was seduced and then married bigamously by a cousin-guardian by whom she bore a son—all of which are incidents from Manley's own life (2:185–93). The frame characters interpret the story like many others in the *New Atalantis* as a "desengaños" that raises the question of how to prevent "Women from *believing*" and "Men from *deceiving*" (2:192).

Manley's knowledge of casuistry is apparent elsewhere in the *New Atalantis* where she shows how men use it to deceive women: for example, in the Charlot episode (1:45–84), in which Portland legitimizes his seduction of a ward casuistically, which is refuted by Astrea, a frame character, in the frame discussion. In a similar episode another guardian seduces his charge by persuading her of the legitimacy of bigamy—indeed polygamy. The narrator acidly ironizes his position as follows: "she could admit of *Poligamy,* but would not hear a word of *Concubinage;* whether the difference be so material I leave to the *Casuists*" (1:226).

But it is in the Delia episode that we can best see how the *New Atalantis* is a transitional link between the novella-case seen in earlier works and the more extended representation of women's side of the case seen in *The Adventures of Rivella*, itself an immediate forerunner of the novel. In the latter work the frame consists of two men; one, an acquaintance of Rivella's, tells her story to another. Her "case" is used to damn the double standard:

> Her vertues are her own, her vices occasion'd by her Misfortunes; and yet as I have often heard her say, *If she had been a Man, she had been without Fault:* But the Charter of that Sex being much more confin'd than ours, what is not a Crime in Men is scandalous and unpardonable in Woman, as she herself has very well observ'd in divers Places, throughout her own Writings. (7–8, emphasis in original)

Rivella is an autobiographical defense; the events of Rivella's life being closely modeled on Manley's own, which was troubled by scandal, gossip, and social ostracism. She clearly wrote *Rivella* to present her side of these personal stories or cases. For example, in one episode Rivella serves as a companion to a wealthy, flighty duchess, Hilaria, who soon tires of her, dismissing Rivella with false charges that she has been having an affair with Hilaria's son. Rivella, who knew that Hilaria "always blasted the Character of those whom she was grown weary of" (35), denies the accusation as if in a court proceeding. When Hilaria says, "I saw [my son] to Day kiss you as he lead you thro' the dark Drawing-Room down to Dinner," Rivella retorts, "Your Ladyship may have seen him attempt it . . . and seen me refuse the Honour" (38).

Rivella, whose reputation has already been ruined by the bigamy of her cousin (the Delia episode in *New Atalantis*), is learning the truth of a warning imparted to her earlier by a neighbor, about "the Ill-nature of the World, that wou'd never restore a Woman's Reputation, how innocent soever she really were, if Appearances prov'd to be against her" (32). Since in the seventeenth century a woman's reputation (for chastity) was the primary component in her value as a commodity in the marriage-market exchange system, it was crucial that she maintain that reputation. Once it was destroyed and she was labeled a fallen woman, her value was lost. It was thus imperative that she contest damaging allegations by presenting exonerating specifics—her side of the case, as Manley attempts to do here. In *The Adventures of Rivella* Manley conveys the specific circumstances of Rivella's particular story in order to challenge the generality "fallen woman" that had been attached to her. It is a casuistical process.

Defoe adapted women writers' feminist casuistry—especially, conceiving the life-history as a case or series of cases—in *Moll Flanders* and *Roxana*. Both protagonists bear considerable resemblance to Mary Carleton and Rivella, suggesting direct influences. All are victims of circumstance, all are touched by scandal, and all manage to survive by engaging in questionable moral behavior. Indeed, Roxana at one point acknowledges her resemblance to Mary Carleton, noting "I might as well have been the *German Princess.*"[34]

The differences between Defoe's use of feminist casuistry and the women writers' are, however, significant. For, like Boccaccio, and unlike the women, Defoe establishes an ironical frame that tends to undercut the feminist message or at least render it ambiguous.[35] For example, Roxana articulates one of the strongest feminist defenses in early modern literature in her denunciation of the slave-like status of the wife, choosing herself to remain a whore, and thus retaining her independence. "The very Nature of the Marriage-Contract was," she said, "in short, nothing but giving up Liberty, Estate, Authority, and every-thing to the Man, and the Woman was indeed . . . a Slave" (148).

Yet the statement is ironized both by the context—Roxana soon repents of the vanity and "ambitious Mind" (161) that led her to such an opinion—and by her character. Her behavior, after all, like Moll Flanders's, is that of an unmitigated reprobate. Thus, as Starr notes, one can easily construe Defoe's heroines' use of casuistry as serving "to confirm rather than qualify their guilt" (186). That ironical context or frame is not present in *The Case of Mary Carleton* (it was added, however, by others in subsequent versions of her life, including Kirkman's), nor in *Rivella* or *Patch-Work Screen*. One might in fact hypothesize that the frames used by Manley (of a sympathetic male narrator) and by Barker (of a sympathetic female narrator) were developed to forestall ironical readings of their "cases," such as is invited in the Defoe works. In short, however, it is clear that the women writers' use of casuistry—in particular the idea of the life as a case or series of cases—contributed importantly to Defoe's conception of the novel.

Jane Barker continued the feminist use of casuistry in several of her works, although like her women predecessors, to different purposes than Defoe. *Exilius* (1715), Barker's first work of prose fiction, is clearly constructed as a series of cases. It is modeled on the French heroic romance, particularly Madeleine de Scudéry's *Clélie* (1654).[36] The French romances derived from the courtly love tradition and carried on its "casuistique d'amour," though in somewhat frivolous form, considering questions like "whether a fair and merry mistress be more amiable than a fair and melancholy."[37] Indeed, a seventeenth-century English critic of the romance warned of the influence its casuistry could have on the young woman reader: "those Authors are subtil Casuists for all difficult cases that may occur in it, will instruct in the necessary Artifices of deluding Parents and Friends and put her ruine perfectly in her own power."[38]

Barker presents case-studies in *Exilius* that reflect familiar casuistry concerns. Is a marriage contracted for minors valid (that between Jemella and Marcellus)?[39] Jemella compares another woman's case to hers in that both are disobeying their father's choice of husbands (2:71–72), thus critiquing the marriage-market. Another figure, Clarintha, resists her father's attempt to marry her to his bastard son, which would be incest. But the son, Valerius, offers "Casuistical by-ways" to try to persuade her it would be a legitimate union (1:41).

Other cases include that of a queen of Egypt who decides to annul her incestuous marriage to her brother (1:118–57). Cordiala, another character, learns circumstances about her birth—that she is the adopted daughter of a wetnurse—that alter her case. "And now, Madam," she is told, "that you know the Case" (2:7), it is hoped she will wed the person her mother has chosen. Cordiala resists, however, in a vignette that recalls Cavendish's "Assaulted and Pursued Chastity," fleeing in disguise as a man, in which situation she and another woman fall in love, presenting another case-dilemma (2:15).

And, in one of the more intriguing stories Galecia (probably a Barker persona), a princess, kills her lover in defending another man from the lover's jealous attack. Since no one can believe a woman could do such a thing, they hold the other man guilty: "the Princess . . . was believ'd on no Side; which shews, that Men credit what they fancy" (2:41). Galecia's story thus is another case-example that refutes stereotypical assumptions about women. The situation is further complicated by the fact that the dispatched lover is the head of a neighboring kingdom that wants revenge. A character asks, "I beg you to consider what is to be done in this Case" (2:44). The story is resolved artificially but it illustrates once again women writers' use of casuistry for feminist purposes.

In *A Patch-Work Screen for the Ladies* (1723) Barker picks up on the idea of using a woman's life history as a case. In this complex modification of the framed-novelle the main inset story, as we have seen, is the autobiographical narrative of one of the frame women, Galesia, another Barker persona. Her story functions overall as a case that argues for women's education, warns of the treacheries of men, and most importantly, critiques the marriage-market exchange of women. The work includes several other case studies that articulate Galesia's feminist theses. There is, for example, the story of a seduced-and-abandoned woman who

has venereal disease (52); "The Story of Belinda" (74–79), another seduced-and-abandoned victim, who narrates her own account; "The History of Lysander" (81–90), another suitor whose interest in Galesia turns
out to be entirely financial. Other suitors similarly are found to be treacherous (Bellair [31–38], for example, who deceives Galesia's parents, is later
revealed as a fraud and executed for theft).

Discouraged by these "Beau Rakes" (37), Galesia soon finds herself
similarly nauseated by the beau monde of the London marriage market,
in which as a country girl she finds "the *Assemblèes* [sic], *Ombre,* and *Bas-
set-Tables,* were all *Greek* to me" (43); and "at the *Toilet,* I was as ignorant
a Spectator as a Lady is an Auditor at an *Act-Sermon* in the University,
which is always in *Latin;* for I was not capable to distinguish which Dress
became which Face; or whether the *Italian, Spanish,* or *Portugal* Red, best
suited such or such Features" (44–45). Interestingly, here Galesia presents
herself as an outsider to two traditions, that of Latin rhetoric and that of
self-marketing for a husband—thereby ironically undercutting both of
these patriarchal institutions.

Preferring solitude and study to "those gaudy Pleasures of the Town,
which intangle and intoxicate the greater Part of Woman-kind" (47), Galesia becomes an herbal pharmacist of some repute—an accomplishment in
which she takes some pride. "Thus . . . *I celebrated my own Praise . . . for
want of good Neighbours to do it for me*" (59). These words could stand as
the catch phrase for these women writers' use of casuistry—voicing their
own particularized and truthful case as a means of refuting ideological assumptions about women's nature and place.

Barker also conceives the sequel to *A Patch-Work Screen, The Lining of
the Patch Work Screen* (1726) as a series of case-novellas held together in
a framed-novelle format. In "The Story of Philinda," for example, we find
a reappropriation of the woman arguing her own case. Here a wife, falsely
arrested for inadvertently being in a house of prostitution, debates how to
exonerate herself to her husband: "thus she weigh'd every thing but could
pitch upon nothing that had any Face of probability. . . . At last, she resolv'd on the plain Truth" and tells her husband "the true State of the
Case" (55–56).

From the women troubadours to Jane Barker we find a series of
women writers using casuistry to present "the true state of the case" from
a woman's point of view. This feminist use of casuistry allowed women
writers to represent women's circumstances in detail and thus to alter
people's understanding of women's situations. It enabled the articulation
of a women's standpoint and thus contributed to the cultural work of ideological transformation in the early modern period, destablizing the
"word of the fathers." It also provided a major organizational idea—the

notion of the life as a case or series of cases—that contributed importantly to the conceptualization of the early novel. Male writers like
Defoe—and later Samuel Richardson—seem to have responded to these
new representations and to have incorporated (however ambiguously)
women's cases in many of their works.

Feminist casuistry thus provided a point of resistance to misogynist
generalities about women that pervaded the early modern period. Voicing
the women's side of the case complicated the picture and problematized
ideological assumptions; in this way feminist casuistry contributed importantly to the constitution of the critical, ironical, dialogical, and subversive mentality we associate with the rise of the novel.

Chapter Six

The Nineties Generation:
A Feminist Prosaics

WHILE THE REALIST TRADITION IN ENGLISH WOMEN'S PROSE fiction really began in the mid-seventeenth century with Margaret Cavendish, it was not until later in the century that a continuing tradition of realist prose fiction by women could be said to have developed. In the last two decades of the century and into the early eighteenth century such a tradition emerged. Pioneered by Delarivier Manley, Catherine Trotter, and to a lesser extent, Aphra Behn, it was most fully developed by the unfortunately neglected Irish woman, Mary Davys, and culminated in the works of Jane Barker. These women invented women's realism in English literature, a realism that did much to establish the character of the English novel. In their works the woman of sense (as opposed to sensibility) takes charge, and she expresses the viewpoint of feminist critical irony, by then firmly established by the women writers of the framed-novelle tradition. What these British writers add is a kind of commonsensical, comical perspective wherein the woman of sense serves as *eiron* to the *alazon* of romantic sensibility. More often than not her (and the author's) critical perspective undermines generic stereotypes of women, offering instead a feminist prosaics wherein the specific realities of women's lives are treated with serious attention.

This 1690s generation of English women writers constitutes an important "wave" in women's literary history that has not been recognized. They were undoubtedly influenced by the rising tide of rationalism that was sweeping intellectual discourse of the period and by the feminist theoretical treatises that had been appearing with some regularity since early in the seventeenth century. These included works by French theorists Marie de Gournay (1622) and Poulain de la Barre (1673; English translation 1677); Dutch writer Anna Van Schurman (1641; English translation 1659); and English writers Rachel Speght (1617), Margaret Cavendish, and Bathsua Makin (1673).[1] Moreover, numerous women of the period engaged in serious intellectual correspondence with some of the leading male philosophers of the day—such as Descartes, Hobbes, and Locke—establishing a kind of blue stocking image that necessarily challenged notions of female intellectual inferiority and demonstrated that women could be rational and speak with "sense."[2]

Probably the most important of these theorists in promoting the doctrine of feminist rationalism, which so influenced the women writers of the nineties generation, was Mary Astell. Her "Serious Proposal to the Ladies" (1694) and "Some Reflections upon Marriage" (1700) formally articulated a feminist critique of marriage and faulty female education. "For since GOD has given women as well as men intelligent souls," Astell argued in her first essay, "why should they be forbidden to improve them?"[3] Like many women writers Astell criticized romances and urged that instead of wasting their time "reading idle *novels* and *romances*" women should study philosophy (121).

"Some Reflections upon Marriage" critiques arranged marriages and analogizes the patriarchal family to a monarchy in which the husband rules (this being somewhat of a theoretical commonplace at the time).[4] While Astell does not go so far as to advocate equality in marriage or the abolition of the institution, she does suggest that women might well choose to avoid it, since it is an "absolute sovereignty" (139): "For if arbitrary power is evil in itself, and an improper method of governing rational and free agents, it ought not to be practiced anywhere; nor is it less, but rather more mischievous in families than in kingdoms, by how much 100,000 tyrants are worse than one" (140). Astell concludes the essay with this ringing cry, "If *all men are born free,* how is it that all women are born slaves?" (140). With such ideas in the air it is not surprising that women writers of the nineties generation adopted an anti-romantic, rationalist thematic and created women characters of sense.

While Astell and others undoubtedly encouraged these thematic inclinations, probably the most important immediate fictional influence on the nineties generation of English women writers was Madame d'Aulnoy's *Relation du voyage d'Espagne* (1691; *The Ingenious and Diverting Letters of the Lady—Travels into Spain,* English translation 1691), an enormously popular work that went through ten editions in England by 1735.[5] Characterized as "a kind of Heptameron-cum-guide book" by Bridget MacCarthy,[6] it is indeed a variant of the framed-novelle. Several novellas

and other short narratives are embedded within a frame, which is a journey allegedly taken by the author in 1679–80 from Bayonne in southern
France to Madrid. The journey is recounted retrospectively in fifteen
dated letters to a cousin in France.

The author's preface "To the Reader" is an important realist manifesto
in which she claims to have verified the factual truth of her contents and
to have fabricated nothing: "I write nothing but what I have seen, or heard
from persons of unquestionable credit . . . you have here no novel, or
story, devised at pleasure; but an exact and most true account of . . . my
travels" ["Je n'ay écrit que ce que j'ay vû, ou ce que j'ay appris par des personnes d'une probité incontestable . . . —ce que l'on trouvera dans cette
Relation, est très-exacte et très-conforme à la verité"].[7] D'Aulnoy challenges the by-then standard probability criterion saying that anomalous
incidents must not be considered false simply because they do not fit into
preconceived expectations. Because "things . . . must . . . seem probable,
to gain belief" (3), some "will accuse me of hyperbolizing, and compos-
ing romances" (3) ["qu'il faille encore que [les choses] soient vrayes-
semblables pour les faire croire. . . . Je ne doute point qu'il n'y en ait . . .
qui ne m'accusent d'avoir mis icy des Hyperboles" (154)]. But, she retorts,
"A fact must not be presently condemned as false because it is not public
or may not hit every man's fancy" (3) ["Un fait n'est point faux, parce qu'il
n'est past rendu public, ou parce qu'il n'agrée point à quelque particulier"
(155)]. In other words, that a fact does not fit within public ideological
expectations does not mean it is not true. Here d'Aulnoy is valorizing the
kind of particularized and subversive realism—a prosaics—that Bakhtin
considered so important to the constitution of the novel. She is willing to
present—indeed is interested in—details that controvert generalities that
go against the conventional grain. In this she is similar to her sister Gallic
writer Madame de Lafayette (whose subversion of ideological givens was
discussed in chapter four).

D'Aulnoy's claim to be presenting an eyewitness account is, however,
false. Percy G. Adams asserts that she never took this trip to Spain and that
her *Travels into Spain* is a fiction; she was able to provide realistic description by reading travel narratives.[8] As we have noted, by this time it
had become routine for authors to claim veracity for their stories. In
d'Aulnoy's case, it appears that while some of the "local color" material is
geographically and historically accurate (and thus true), the four embedded stories in volume I are simply recycled novellas. So the work is an interesting and original combination of a realistic frame and conventional
novellas.

The central frame character is of course the author-narrator herself,
whose personality is considerably particularized, which adds much to the

work's appeal. And her environment is rendered in realistic detail. After arriving in Irun, a town just over the border, the narrator notes, "I had a great supper . . . but all was so full of garlic, saffron and spice that I could eat nothing" (14) ["un grand souper . . . mais tout étoit si plein d'ail, de safran et d'épice, que je ne pûs manger de rient" (167)]. On another evening, in St. Sebastian, she remarks, "I betook my self to bed after a good supper, for, my dear Cousin, I am none of those romantic ladies that never eat" (20) ["je me couchay après avoir bien soupé; car, ma chere cousine, je ne suis pas une Heroïne de Roman, qui ne mange pas" (175)]. Such comments establish her as a woman of sense, whose perspective undercuts romantic stereotypes about women.

Local customs and people are described, sometimes comically, sometimes with apparent embellishment. For example, in "Letter I," a group of Spaniards are described as wearing "periwigs, one of which had enough hair for four, and so frizzled, as made them look as if they were frighted" (14) ["des Perruques où il y a plus de Cheveux qu'il n'en faut pour en faire quatre autres bien faites, et ces Cheveux sont plus frisez que du crin boüilly" (167)]. On another occasion she encounters a group of "Amazons" (18) who run boats in the River of Andaye. "I was told these wenches swim like fishes, and suffer neither women nor men among them. This is a kind of republic" (16) ["L'on me dit que ces Filles au Piedmarin nâgeoient comme des poissons et qu'elles ne souffroient entre-elles ni femmes ni hommes; c'est une espece de petite Republique" (170)].

When the narrator's cook makes the mistake of molesting one of these women, "She being not used to this sort of plain dealing without any words broke his head with her oar" (17) ["elle n'entendit point de raillerie, et sans autre compliment, elle luy cassa la tête avec un Aviron armé d'un Croc" (170)]. In fright she then jumps overboard but several of her sister oarswomen swim after and rescue her. Later on land "we saw this wench which was saved out of the water making up towards us with near fifty others, each with an oar on their shoulder, marching in battle array, with fife and drum" (17) ["nous vîmes cette Fille que l'on avoit sauvée bien à propos. . . . Elle venoit à nôtre rencontre avec plus de cinquante autres, chacune ayant une Rame sur l'épaule; elles marchoient sur deux longues files, et il y en avoit trois à la tête qui jouoient parfaitement bien du Tambour de Basque" (171)], demanding reparation for damage to the assaulted woman's clothing. They then "fell loudly beating their drums, and the rest of their Amazons set up a holloaing, leaping and dancing and fencing with their oars in a most astonishing manner" (18) ["commencerent à les fraper plus fort; elles pousserent de hauts cris, et ces belles Pyrates firent l'Exercise de la Rame, en sautant et dançant avec beaucoup de disposition et de bonne grace" (171)]. While this episode may have had some basis in fact, it rather resembles something out of Margaret Cavendish's feminist fantasies, "Assaulted and Pursued Chastity" or *Blazing-World.*

D'Aulnoy's *Travels into Spain* had an immediate and perceptible influence on three significant works by British women, and thus helped to establish the English women's literary tradition of the nineties. These are: Catherine Trotter's *Olinda's Adventures* (1693), Delarivier Manley's *Letters Writen* [sic] *by Mrs. Manley* (1696), and Mary Davys's *The Fugitive* (1705), later revised as *The Merry Wanderer* (1725). All of these follow d'Aulnoy's *Travels into Spain* in using a modified framed-novelle format, offering realistic and often comic details, and providing sensible female protagonists. Where they improve upon d'Aulnoy from a feminist point of view is in their use of satire and the critical perspective they bring to bear on marriage-market machinations. Since the d'Aulnoy influence on Manley's *Letters* is explicit (the author alludes directly to the *Travels into Spain* as a point of comparison),[9] I start with it.

Like d'Aulnoy's, Manley's narrative is told in a series of letters (eight here, as opposed to fifteen in d'Aulnoy's work), all of which are dated (as were d'Aulnoy's) from June 24, 1694, to March 15, 1695. In them Manley recounts a journey by stagecoach she presumably took from London to Exeter. Embedded within this frame are three novella-like stories (I say "novella-like" because although the plots are somewhat conventional, the characters and settings in at least two of the stories are located historically and geographically more precisely than they would be in the traditional novella).

Like d'Aulnoy, Manley presents specific details about food and fellow travelers that are often comic and satirical. A landlord at an inn is described as "a Master in the Trade of Foppery" (7). Indeed, the work concludes with a document Manley claims to have found, a sequel to the *Portuguese Letters.* This item, "A Second Letter from a supposed Nun in Portugal," is in fact a burlesque of the French romance the *Portuguese Letters* (*Lettres portugaises*), exuding the same breathless anguished desperation that made the original so popular (see further discussion in chapter eight, "Women Against Romance").

Meanwhile, a frame plot develops wherein Manley rejects the continual advances of a baronet's son she meets in the coach, thus providing an ironic critique of sexual harassment and marriage-marketing. The initial encounter between them establishes the tone of the relationship. Upon arriving at an inn the would-be suitor changes his

Travelling Suit, for a Coat and Vest, design'd to dazzle the Curate and all his Congregation. The way I took to mortifie his Foppery, was, not to speak a

Word of the Change; which made him extream uneasie: At length, out of all
Patience, he desired my Opinion, If his Taylor had used him well? . . . And
recommended to my Curiosity the exquisite Workmanship of the
Loops. . . . I answer'd him, That Finery was lost upon me. (8–9)

Manley disassociates herself from a women's use-value craft, sewing, insofar as it is employed to construct clothing that is used aesthetically to
market a marriage product—an interesting early example of the connection between feminist critical irony and use-value production.

The encounter between the author and the suitor continues when, un-
invited, he recounts to her his story, the first of the embedded novellas.
Manley breaks her "Splenetick Silence, and . . . laugh[s] heartily" (24) at
the denouement (where he has discovered his lover in bed with another),
thus effectively undercutting his romantic earnestness.

She finally arrives in Exeter, having warded off this unwanted beau, determined to enjoy solitude and reflection, though she confesses she misses
the social life of London (64–65). Manley had apparently taken this journey after being dismissed by the duchess of Cleveland (Hilaria), the
episode in *The Adventures of Rivella* discussed in chapter five. Robert Day
estimates Manley's *Letters* (later retitled *A Stage-Coach Journey to Exeter*
[1725]) one of the most "vivid and authentic" descriptions of English
"provincial life and manners" of the period, and "one of the liveliest pieces
of fiction writing before Fielding."[10]

Equally important and engaging as the Manley work is Catherine Trotter's *Olinda's Adventures* (1693).[11] Of it Day notes, "such criteria of the
'modern novel' as those proposed by Ian Watt are all modestly but ade-
quately met" in this work, which anticipates "the English domestic and realistic novel" by several decades.[12] Trotter was herself a philosopher and
published various treatises, including "A Defense of Mr. Locke's Essay of
Human Understanding" in 1699.[13] Her philosophical bent is evident in
Olinda's Adventures.

While the work is divided into eight letters and thus uses the epistolary
format of D'Aulnoy's *Travels* (and earlier Cavendish's *Sociable Letters*), it
is really a short autobiographical novel, written by the subject, who is thir-
teen when the work begins. As a kind of autobiographical defense, it represents another use of the life as case, recalling *The Case of Madam Mary
Carleton* and *The Adventures of Rivella.*

As in Cavendish's "The Contract" and numerous subsequent novels of
manners, the plot concerns marriage-marketing: Olinda's mother is trying to market her for a husband, a process Olinda observes with caustic
irony. The story is structured on eight suitors whose stories are thus embedded within the frame plot as in a framed-novelle. Olinda dismisses all

but one of these with biting sarcasm. The description of the courtship of Beronthus in "Letter I" is characteristic:

> *Beronthus* . . . tells her [the mother] he's stark staring mad in Love with her Daughter: The next thing they talk of is Joynture, and Settlement, etc. . . . So I am call'd for, and commanded to look upon this Spark as one that must shortly be my Husband. . . . I had a firm Resolution never to Marry him; but I found my Mother so much set upon it, that I durst not let it be known.[14]

Similar to the scene in Barker's *Patch-Work Screen* in which Galesia over-hears herself haggled over, the daughter's exchange, here being negotiated by parent and courter, is overheard by the subject, who is being objecti-fied as goods in the transaction, which is principally an economic matter involving such issues as "jointure" and "settlement." Note how Olinda first presents herself in the third person, as the daughter, an object, and then switches to the first, a subject.

Olinda eventually settles for a rather unorthodox arrangement with the suitor she favors, Cloridon, in which he is to support her without see-ing her until his wife dies whereupon they are to wed. This agreement ap-parently raised eyebrows, and Delarivier Manley, who had been a friend of Trotter's, became one of her principal accusers. Applying her *vraisem-blance* criterion (enunciated in the preface to *Queen Zarah*) to *Olinda's Adventures*, Manley declared it fraudulent and its author a hypocrite. In the *New Atalantis*, Manley's roman à clef, she accuses Trotter/Olinda of "an Air of *Virtue pretended*" (2:55) and makes a similar point in *The Ad-ventures of Rivella* (66).

In the *New Atalantis* Manley also connects Trotter to a "Lesbian Cabal," a group of women romantically involved with one another who shared property and engaged in other separatist practices (2:52–56). Trotter was in fact known to have what were probably lesbian relationships with sev-eral women.[15] It may well be then that we have in *Olinda's Adventures* one of the first expressions of a lesbian feminist standpoint, if Olinda's resis-tance to male suitors is rooted in her preference for women.

Olinda does discuss her relationship with two women, Ambrisia and Clarinda, in "Letter III." The latter has betrayed her, which, she says, might have led her to accept misogynist generalities about women's untrustwor-thiness had she not met Ambrisia, who provided her with a refuting counter-example. Of Clarinda she notes:

> I involv'd the whole Sex in her Faults, and with *Aristotle* . . . Repented that I had ever Trusted a Woman. I don't know whether I forgot I was one, or

whether I had the Vanity to think my self more perfect than the rest; but I resolv'd none of the Sex was capable of Friendship . . . till I knew *Ambrisia,* who . . . is just *Clarinda*'s Antipodes. (150)

Trotter's rhetorical construction is an interesting variation of the feminist use of casuistry, with a case example being used to refute a misogynist generality. But the discussion also indicates Olinda's (and presumably Trotter's) intense involvement with female friends. (It is likely, however, that her falling out with Manley was not over the issues of lesbianism or virtue but rather over politics: Manley was a staunch Tory and Trotter a Whig.)[16] There are two other important uses of casuistry in *Olinda's Adventures.* In the first Olinda indicates that she is writing her "adventures" as a kind of defense of her reputation. In other words, like Mary Carleton and (ironically) Delarivier Manley, she is offering the circumstances of her case in order to refute scandalous assumptions. Writing to her friend Cleander she explains she is "giving [him] a *particular* account of all that has happen'd to me in my Life . . . that the kindness of a Friend mayn't find out something in the *Circumstances* of the Story to Excuse" (my emphasis). Olinda goes on to admit that "tho' perhaps I have not always been so nicely cautious as a Woman in strictness ought, I have never gone beyond the bounds of solid Virtue" (134).

The second example of casuistry is also of considerable interest. In this Olinda explores the behavior of her friend Ambrisia to Cleander, who is courting her. Olinda uses Ambrisia's case to particularize a stereotype and thereby refute a misogynist assumption. Cleander is worried about Ambrisia's shyness, considering that it means she is not interested in him. Olinda responds:

> Trust me, she loves you and only puts on the usual Disguises of Women as sincere as she is; and give me leave *to justifie her, and the rest of our Sex in that Case:* You [men] have learn'd so well to feign Love, when you have none, that tis' very hard to discern Art from Nature; and 'tis but reasonable we should be allow'd the less Guilty part of concealing ours, till we can know whether you are sincere. (183; my emphasis)

Thus, by exploring Ambrisia's motivations, Olinda refutes the misogynist maxim that women are fickle and deceptive (saying no, for example, when they mean yes). She thereby voices the woman's point of view— which is that such coyness is not a crime but rather a defense strategy developed by women in response to men's betrayals. Since women suffer more, one might add, by abandonment (when they are often pregnant out of wedlock and thus lose their reputations), they have had to adopt cautionary strategies. Not only does such a particularization allow for the representation of the woman's viewpoint, it also deepens the character of Ambrisia and makes her behavior more complex. Such casuistical explorations are certainly a major reason *Olinda's Adventures* meets Watt's criteria for the realist novel.

Mary Davys's *The Fugitive* (1705), later revised as *The Merry Wanderer* (1725), is another extremely important (but still almost entirely neglected) early work in the British women's tradition. It too bears the influence of D'Aulnoy's *Travels* in that it is structured as a framed-novelle with the frame being a journey taken by the author-narrator, in this case through southern England.

The frame protagonist is like d'Aulnoy, Manley, and Trotter's, a sensible woman whose own life-story is well developed; inherent in that story is a feminist critique of the marriage-market. Embedded in the frame-journey are a series of eleven novellas, which are told to the author by the various people she encounters. These stories are then often discussed by the author-narrator and other characters, as in the framed-novelle. The author's viewpoint is generally that of critical irony and many of the stories serve as cases. Somewhat modifying d'Aulnoy, however, Davys acknowledges that there may be some fabrication in her narrative: "I will not say that every Circumstance of the Book is true to a tittle, but the Ground and Foundation of almost every Story is matter of Fact, and what I have not taken upon Credit from any Body, but have been a witness to the greatest part of my self."[17]

What is particularly interesting about this work is that not only is a woman's viewpoint established but also an Irish standpoint. Indeed, the opening section is one of the clearest examples in early modern literature of the positing of a regional or ethnic standpoint, which is used to critique prejudiced attitudes toward the group. Davys opens *The Fugitive* by noting how Ireland is "a place very much despis'd by those that know it not" (2). In *The Merry Wanderer* Davys expatiates with an apology to the reader, admitting that as she is Irish she must deflect anticipated disparagement of her work: "To tell the Reader I was born in *Ireland* is to bespeak a general Dislike to all I write, and he will, likely, be surprized, if every Paragraph does not end with a Bull."[18]

The first episode in *The Fugitive* well illustrates English prejudice against the Irish; Davys uses herself in an attempt to refute these misconceptions. After settling in at an inn near the English-Welsh border, the narrator hears a man outside who wants to see "some of the wild *Irish*" he had heard were staying there. He offers a shilling to a servant to let him see them: "the Wench, who happen'd to have a little more Wit than he, came in with the Jest, to see how far we would encourage it" (3).

The narrator proposes playing along with his expectations: "for my part I was mightily pleas'd at the fancy. . . . Now, said I, does this Fellow think that we have Horns and Hoofs . . . but I shall be so far from striving to change his opinion, that I am resolved to do all I can to confirm him in it" (3–4).

The humorous encounter proceeds:

> By this time he came staring in with Eyes, Ears and Mouth open. . . . Come Friend, said I, you have a mind, I hear, to see some of the wild *Irish*. *Yes, Forsooth*, said he, *an yo pleasen, but pray ye where are thay;* why, said I, I am one of them; *noa, noa*, said he, *forsooth yo looken laik one of us; but those Foke that I mean are Foke we long Tails, that have no Cloaths on, but are cover'd laik my brown Caw a whome, with their own Hair.* Come, said I, sit you down, and I'll tell you all . . . when I was three years old, I was just such a Creature as you speak of, and one day I went a little farther than I should have done, and was taken in a Net with some other Vermin, which the *English* had spread on purpose for us, and when they had me, they cut off my Tail, and scalded off my Hair, and ever since I have been like one of you. (4–5)

He then asks her if she could speak before she was captured. She says, "Speak . . . no, I could make a Gapeing in articulate Noise, as the rest of my fellow Beasts did, and went upon my Hands as well as Feet, in imitation of them; but for any other Knowledge, I had it not till I got into *English* hands" (5). He replies, wonderingly, "*yo may bless the day that ever yo met with that same Net b'r Lady. I have often heard of the waild* Irish *but I never saw any of them before*" (5). She tells him to go and tell his neighbors what he has seen. "Thus this poor Soul went away full of Wonder, to spread the Lye all over the Country, and left us full of Mirth, as he was of Folly" (6).

The point of view or standpoint here is clearly that of an ethnic group rejecting or ironizing their objectification—in this case as animals— thereby establishing themselves as human subjects. The author uses herself, obviously a human being to the reader, to undercut and refute the Englishman's racist misconceptions about the Irish.

The kind of comic irony used on behalf of the Irish in this section is manifested on behalf of women in several episodes where the narrator herself has to contend with being objectified as a woman in marriage-market rituals. After attending a Christening the author-narrator is "accosted by a Gentleman . . . [who made] violent Court to me" (129). He turns out to be a man with whom she had engaged in a *querelle des femmes* debate at the event. While he is a person of "good Estate" (129), the narrator soon realizes that "his Designs were mercenary" (134), hav-

ing discovered that she has a brother abroad "of very good Circumstances" from whom she expects a "Bounty" (133). The narrator laments
friends who encourage her to marry for money, thinking "that alone sufficient to make a Woman happy, tho' it came attended with all the Circumstances of a Coxcomb" (131). So she decides to get rid of him by
showing him up for what he is, a fortune-hunter. "I thought if I made my
self a little Sport with him, it would be but a just return for his under-
hand-dealing with me" (135). Her "Scheme" is to masquerade as a finan-
cially attractive woman, an episode that is nearly identical to one in
Olinda's Adventures (147–48), which suggests Trotter's influence on
Davys. The narrator first writes a pseudo love letter from an imaginary
admirer—a burlesque of the romantic epistle:

> SIR, LAST Summer . . . it was my fortune to see a Gentleman . . . whose
> Person made such an Impression in my Heart, that I immediately found my
> self in the greatest Disorder. . . . I have ever since endeavour'd to stiffle my
> growing Folly, but finding it too strong for me, I am forced to . . . apply my
> self to you for Cure. My Person is noway to be despis'd, my Fortune and
> Family are above your Wishes. (136–37)

The narrator then disguises herself as this admirer and in a secret rendezvous gets the suitor to admit that he is only after her fortune (137–48).
Learning that "there is . . . Money in the case," as Davys put it in *The Merry
Wanderer* revision (227), makes him willing to renounce the narrator and
to engage sight unseen (she is still masked) with his newly discovered admirer. The narrator ruefully reflects, "Thus did poor I sit and hear myself
despised, for one, who for ought he knew might have had the Face of a
Bear" (*Merry Wanderer* 227). She then pulls off her mask, revealing him to
be a crass fortune-hunter and effectively getting rid of him as a suitor.

The Fugitive ends with similar parodies of romantic courtship cum
fortune-hunting. After a series of stories told by guests at a dinner, the
narrator tells a tale of her own about an ale-wife, which in *The Merry
Wanderer* version she admits is "not a parallel case" (engaging in the terminology of casuistry) to the preceding tale (246). A *Heptaméron*-like discussion ensues in which one guest complains that her story is a non
sequitur to its predecessor. The narrator says she offered it for diversity,
thus proposing another aesthetic principle: "I hope . . . you don't think I
could be guilty of so much absurdity, to tire the company with the same
Thing over again: No, my Business is to divert the Subject, and bring in
something novel" (*Fugitive* 188). This exchange suggests Davys's concerns
about maintaining unity in a text and her awareness of classical aesthetic
theory, which we discuss further in chapter nine.

Several days after this confrontation, the narrator receives an anonymous threatening letter telling her she has been uppety in her argumentative outspokenness: "*the whole Country takes notice of your Pride; with how much Insolence you usurp a Superiority over those, who know how to talk, and behave themselves as much to advantage as you do*" (191–92). Far from being chastened or silenced by this epistle, the narrator invokes the muse "Spight" (in *The Merry Wanderer* 249) and responds with biting sarcasm: "I fancy you inveigh against Wit, for the same reason that the Mob rail at Grandure, and fine cloaths, because they are out of their reach" (*Fugitive* 194). The narrator soon discovers the correspondent to be the man (Mr. Watts) who had protested her story. In a parody of the Spanish novella, the narrator's cousin immediately vows to avenge the insult to her, challenging Watts to a duel. All is resolved peacefully, however, with Watts marrying the cousin's sister.

The final episode in the work concerns an instant courtship proposed in a happenstance encounter between a young female traveling companion and a horseman who accosts her and the narrator. Without knowing her he latches on mindlessly nevertheless, enacting the courtship ritual mechanistically. The young woman turns the tables on him, however, by requiring him to go through a series of comical trials (179–204), a further parody of courtly love ritual.

The other significant fiction Davys wrote at this time (1700) was *The Amours of Alcippus and Lucippe* (published 1704; revised as *The Lady's Tale* in 1725). A transitional work between the romance novella and the realist novel, it has an interesting frame in which the female protagonist Abaliza (Lucippe was so renamed in *The Lady's Tale*), tells her story to a woman friend whom she hasn't seen in four years. The friend occasionally interjects comments but Abaliza cuts her off saying, "If you interrupt me . . . I shall forget where I left off, and make a Botch of my Story."[19] This comment reveals Davys's sensitivity to issues of narrative control and reflects the transition then occurring from the framed-novelle to the novel.

The plot is another critique of arranged marriages, but Davys's touch is uniquely satirical, enlivening a pedestrian plot with the delightful comic realism seen in all her works. Abaliza, for example, describes a man she thinks her parents have chosen for her husband as "a Something, which was, I fancy'd, design'd for a Man, tho' Nature, to shew us some diversion, and to let us see she can be merry over her own Compositions, had made the thing look like a Creature engender'd betwixt a Monkey and a *Dutch Mastiff*. His Eyes were red and very small . . . his Mouth was wide, his Teeth black, his Chaps thin and wrinkled" (126).

Like the other women protagonists in this tradition, Abaliza is a take-charge character, unlike the wishy-washy heroines of the traditional romance. When Alcipus, her lover, mistakenly assumes an uncle of Abaliza's is a rival and leaves the country in despair (an incident similar to one in Aphra Behn's "The Unhappy Mistake" [1698]), Abaliza persists in tracking him down, eventually finding him in Holland and chastizing him for his lack of faith. "[M]y business," she says majestically, "is first to reproach, and then abjure you for ever" (187). Alcipus faints twice in the course of this encounter. With Abaliza's honor thus revindicated, the two reconcile and are wed.

Before discussing the rest of Davys's works, which appeared in the second decade of the eighteenth century and thus are contemporaneous with Jane Barker's main works, I would like to consider Aphra Behn's contribution to the English women's realist tradition of the later seventeenth century. Behn has until recently been considered *the* premiere woman writer of her day and indeed the first professional woman writer in English. Many remember Virginia Woolf's celebrated paean in *A Room of One's Own:* "All women together ought to let flowers fall upon the tomb of Aphra Behn . . . for it was she who earned them the right to speak their minds."[20]

Behn was certainly a pioneer, but her contribution to the tradition of women's literary realism that I am treating in this chapter was not so great as the other writers I consider. In part, this is because she preceded them chronologically. Most of her works were written or published in the 1680's and thus before a solid tradition of realism began to emerge. Behn's work in fact generally hovers on the cusp between the romantic novella and the realist novel but retains more of the former than it pioneers of the latter. In addition, she lacks the comic perspective seen in the other writers of this early women's tradition. Her best-known work, *Oroonoko* (1688), for example, while having interesting touches of realism, remains a romantic work, its principal characters and the plot are stereotypical of the romance. Similarly, her *Love-Letters between a Nobleman and His Sister* (1684–87), which has been heralded as the first English novel, remains largely in the vein of the *chronique scandaleuse,* despite its subversive critique of political Machiavellianism.[21]

Several Behn stories are, however, relevant to this study; in particular, "The Fair Jilt" (1688), which may be Behn's first work (possibly having appeared as early as 1678);[22] "The Adventures of the Black Lady" (1681–83); "The Wandering Beauty" (1687; published 1698); "The History of the Nun" (1689); and "The Unfortunate Happy Lady" (1700) exhibit important sallies into realism.

"The Fair Jilt; Or, the Amours of Prince Tarquin and Miranda" is an interesting pastiche of two sources: one, a Bandello-like novella and the other, a contemporary news story. The author claims an eyewitness status and, as in *Oroonoko,* occasionally interjects personal comment. The arrival of one character, for example, is dated as occurring in Antwerp "about the time of my being sent thither by King Charles."[23] Behn had served as a spy in Holland for Charles II in 1665 during the English-Dutch War.

The novella part of the story concerns a conniving mendacious woman who persuades her husband to kill her sister in order that she receive the sister's inheritance. He fails in this project but is caught and sentenced to beheading. The execution is described in realistic detail that suggests eye-witness observation. Indeed, it has been discovered that Behn based this episode on an actual event, which was reported in *The London Gazette* of 28 May to 31 May, 1666, in which a beheading was aborted because the executioner's sword missed the neck and hit the shoulder blade. So the story, largely a somewhat lurid novella, introduces a new kind of factual realism, portending the realist tradition in prose fiction that was soon to emerge.[24]

"The Adventures of the Black Lady," which may be Behn's first story (if "The Fair Jilt" is not), is also of considerable interest, opening with an "as near as I can remember" claim to authentic reportage.[25] The story is a realistic portrayal of an unwed mother's plight and provides a pointed critique of parish handling of such cases. Accurate London street names are used and financial transactions are specified (she had to pay £30 for church shelter), signaling a decided departure from the traditional novella.

"The Wandering Beauty" and "The Unfortunate Happy Lady" are both realistic explorations of a young woman's struggle with male relatives (a father in the former and a brother in the latter) over control of their lives, marital fortunes, and economic resources. In the former story (which is introduced as a true story that the author-narrator had been told in her youth), Arabella runs away from home after learning her father had engaged her to a sixty-year-old wealthy friend, which she calls an "almost unnatural Proposition."[26] Her perambulations through the countryside give a realistic description of provincial life and manners, and constitute a success story as well, for Arabella is able to support herself as a governess, eventually marrying a man "of quality."

"The Unfortunate Happy Lady: A True History" is also a success story where the female protagonist, Philadelphia, triumphs over a brother who had placed her in a brothel in order to get her inheritance. After numerous escapades and two marriages, Philadelphia is wealthy and powerful enough in the end to take pity on the dissipated brother, who has in the meantime been imprisoned for debt. This story, if expanded, could certainly stand as a realist novel. It continues the women's revenge plot seen in the novella tradition (the genealogy of which we consider more fully in

chapter seven)[27] and further enlarges the conception of the woman protagonist who is the subject, rather than the object, of the plot. It also has
more comedic touches than usually seen in Behn. Interestingly, both this
story and "The Wandering Beauty" were used by Jane Barker in *The Lining of the Patch Work Screen:* the former in "The History of Malhurissa"
(147–57) and the latter in the "Lady Gypsie" story (82–102). As noted,
Barker also picked up what is perhaps Behn's most famous story, "The
History of the Nun; or the Fair Vow-Breaker" (1689), in *The Lining.*

We conclude this chapter with Mary Davys's late novels, which, together with Barker's works, culminate this early tradition in women's realism. These include the *Familiar Letters, Betwixt a Gentleman and a Lady,
The Cousins,* and *The Reform'd Coquet*—all published in the *Works*
(1725)—and *The Accomplished Rake; Or, Modern Fine Gentlemen* (1727).

The *Familiar Letters,* which was likely written several years before 1725,
is indeed a work "of exceptional merit," as Robert Day observed in *Told in
Letters* (190). Clearly influenced by *Olinda's Adventures,* it wittily portrays
a growing and inadvertent attachment between two correspondents who
start out as determined opponents of love and marriage. The work is
structured in a series of twenty-two letters dated from November 1 to Jan-
uary 25. The two correspondents are opposites in certain respects, which
heightens the drama of their discussions. (Berinda is a Whig; Artander, a
Tory. She prefers the city; he, the country.)

Berinda is a rationalist free-thinker, who is opposed to religious fa-
naticism (she catalogs the atrocities of Cromwell's suppression of the Irish
Rebellion in 1649) and favors a limited monarchy.[28] She is a champion of
liberty and rejects institutions or experiences that limit it. Of marriage she
says, "I hate a Yoke that galls for life" (270). And love, which she says goes
"so much against my grain," is a "base Imposture" (289): the "God of
Love . . . makes mere Idiots of Mankind" (297). When she becomes aware
that Artander is falling for her, she begs him to resist the power of Cupid:
"pull out the Dart" (303), she says.

Marriage and love are seen by Berinda as tyrannies that limit one's liberty. In a passage that suggests the influence of Mary Astell, Berinda
analogizes marriage to a monarchy with the husband as king. Like Astell
she does not contest that women should be subordinate, but she does resist entering the institution (and perhaps for that reason) (303). Love is
similarly a tyranny and she castigates those who "instead of fighting for
their own Liberty and Property . . . tamely yield to an arbitrary Power. . . .
For shame, *Artander,* shake off your Chains. . . . Remember your Liberty
lies at stake" (303).

The Cousins picks up from Behn's "The Lucky Mistake" (1688) and
"The Wandering Beauty" (1687) (and, of course, numerous antecedents

in the continental novella) on the theme of the young girl pledged to an older (in this case lecherous) parental friend. The work includes two embedded novellas, which connect to the arranged marriage theme. William McBurney considers the work may be a burlesque of the continental novella.[29] There is nothing to distinguish *The Cousins* from other English examples of the genre (Behn's, for example), but it may be that these were all intended as burlesques. Certainly, Davys's propensity for comedy would support such an interpretation, in her case at least.

Davys's final (and best-known) works, *The Reform'd Coquet* and *The Accomplished Rake*, are companion pieces, the one designed to show the moral education of a young woman, Amoranda, and the other recounting the moral reform of a young man, Galliard. *The Reform'd Coquet* follows in the female bildungsroman tradition of Cavendish's "The Contract," which leads to Jane Austen's *Emma* and *Pride and Prejudice*. While Jane Spencer, among others, has criticized the novel for its conformist message and condescending attitude toward the heroine,[30] there is much that is positive in the character of Amoranda, and the work has many redeeming comic incidents that must distinguish it from the priggish didacticism of other novels of this type. Amoranda indeed is a fairly forceful character—at least in the first half of the work—and she exhibits a clever juridic intelligence that puts her in the league of the feminist casuists discussed earlier. Note, for example, her rigorous interrogation of Lord Lofty, whom she and her guardian trick into marrying a woman he had seduced and abandoned.[31] Similarly, in *The Accomplished Rake*, the male protagonist, Galliard, is finally bested when foiled by one of his would-be victims, Belinda. She is another example of the witty, argumentative woman who controls her own destiny. From a structural point of view this work is truly a novel; the embedded stories are really subplots that connect directly to the main action. This, together with Davys's comic realism, make the epithet "forerunner of Fielding," which McBurney attached to her, an accurate label. Unfortunately, however, for reasons discussed in the next chapter, the women's tradition of feminist realism described in this chapter came to an end (at least temporarily) with Barker and Davys. It was superceded by a tradition of sentimentalist didacticism that lasted for over a century.

Chapter Seven

The Case of Violenta

THE TRANSITIONS IN WOMEN'S LITERARY HISTORY proposed at the end of the last chapter can be illustrated by tracing the genealogy of a novella—which I call the Violenta novella—from its sources in the early Renaissance to its reproduction by Delarivier Manley in her collection of novellas, *The Power of Love* (1720) and Eliza Haywood's similar collection, *Love in Its Variety* (1727). It has been proposed that a peak of feminist realism was reached in the 1720s, but it was soon superceded by a sentimentalist tradition that many have seen as a capitulation to patriarchal interests, a backing away from the feminist literary wave that began cresting in the 1690s and early eighteenth century.

Whether this backing away was due to the palpable backlash women writers experienced during the early 1700s, or whether it reflects more basic economic transitions remains a matter for conjecture.[1] A number of theorists, building on the still respected Alice Clark thesis enunciated in 1919, have proposed that women's status declined during the period of the transition to modern capitalism because their economic value lessened with the shift toward commodity exchange and the attendant marginalization of production for use. As this process intensified through the eighteenth century, the theory goes, women's political status and cultural authority were also eclipsed.[2]

One may observe a weakening of feminist authority in women writers of the eighteenth century after the first two decades—a process Jane Spencer has detailed in her *Rise of the Woman Novelist* (1986) (see pp. 11–15, 91–92, 118–22). By mid-century Spencer proposes,

> women writers, no longer seeing themselves as men's antagonists, had
> dropped the battle imagery in which their predecessors characterized their

writing as an attack on male domination. . . . Women's writing . . . seems to have been limited in various ways by masculine approval, which many were so anxious not to lose that they became very careful to write in the way that men found acceptably feminine. (92)

Spencer selects Eliza Haywood as a pivotal figure in this capitulation, a conclusion that is supported by my analysis of the historical permutations of the Violenta novella, which serves as a case-study of the historical transitions here proposed.

A popular Renaissance tale, which had numerous retellings and variants, was that of Violenta, a seduced and abandoned lower-middle-class woman who avenges herself by killing her treacherous aristocratic lover. Unlike the sentimentalist "heroine's text," an important tradition in eighteenth-century fiction, in which the betrayed woman dies in disgrace, here the woman has her moment of triumph, in which she takes, many of these writers assert, a feminist stand against exploitation. A comparative study of the genealogy of this novella from sixteenth-century Italy to eighteenth-century England helps to establish important new theoretical formulations about women's literary history of the early modern period.

The primary plot is laid out in Matteo Bandello's *Novelle* (1554), vol. 1, novella 42. Pierre Boaistuau presented a French variant in his loose adaptation of Bandello, the *Histoires tragiques* (1559). The first version by a woman is in the *Novelas amorosas* (1637) by María de Zayas. Her novella, "La burlada Aminta y venganza del honor" (I.2) ("Aminta Deceived and Honor's Revenge") is like Bandello's a feminist revenge story. Zayas used a variant of the same tale in her second volume of novellas, the *Desengaños amorosos* (1647), in a tale entitled "La más infame venganza" (II.2) ("A Shameful Revenge").

English versions of the tale include William Painter's "Didaco and Violenta," a translation of Boaistuau's adaptation of Bandello's I.42 in his *Palace of Pleasure* (1575); Manley's "The Wife's Resentment," "novel 3," in her *The Power of Love* (1720); and Eliza Haywood's "Female Revenge; or, the Happy Exchange" in *Love in Its Variety* (1727).[3]

Bandello, Zayas, and Manley present the heroine sympathetically and see her act in political, feminist terms as expressing an admirable class solidarity with other exploited lower-class women, suggesting that her upper-class lover may have to some extent deserved his fate. Boaistuau and Painter eliminate the feminist thesis, with Boaistuau introducing a misogynist preface (which Painter eliminates), and both weaken the character of Violenta; while Haywood's version condemns the woman outright, casting her lover as innocent victim.

I theorize that Zayas and Manley (and to some extent Bandello) belonged to a continuing feminist tradition in the novella, one that originated principally with Marguerite de Navarre, although she did not treat this story. All three were heavily influenced by Marguerite and in several instances borrowed or reworked material from the *Heptaméron*.[4] This feminist tradition in women's literature appears to end, however, with Eliza Haywood.

While I trace the genealogy of the novella from Bandello to Zayas and Painter and then to Manley and Haywood, I place a special focus on the latter two, whose versions have particular relevance to theorizing about women's contributions to the genesis of the novel. In addition to reinstating the feminist thesis, Manley expands upon Painter, her source, by amplifying economic and social factors—the elements of classic realism that Ian Watt has seen as constituent to the "rise of the [realist] novel." In her version Haywood lays the groundwork for the other major type of novel that dominated the eighteenth century, the sentimentalist.

Haywood's sentimentalist domestication of the novella marks, I believe, a pivotal transformation in women's literary history. She eliminates the feminist import of the tale by changing the central female character from a powerful Medean agent of revenge into an object of contempt; into what soon became the staple of the "heroine's text," the disgraced victim. Despite its title (which in her handling becomes ironic) Haywood's "Female Revenge" in fact bears considerable resemblance to what one may consider the archetype of the sentimentalist genre, Susanna Rowson's *Charlotte: A Tale of Truth* (1791) (better known today as *Charlotte Temple*).That Haywood's version of attenuated female agency superceded that drawn by Manley (and earlier Bandello and Zayas) signifies, I propose, the capitulation noted above.

Matteo Bandello (1480–1561) was a Dominican monk who produced more than two hundred novelle; he is best known to English speakers for having supplied several plots for Shakespeare (notably for *Romeo and Juliet, Twelfth Night,* and *Much Ado about Nothing*—probably mediated through the French *Histoires tragiques*). Bandello's principal audience was that of courtly women—many of his patrons were from this class—and he dedicated his stories to various of them. It is perhaps for this reason that Bandello generally went against the misogynist grain of the novella tradition. Like his contemporary Marguerite de Navarre—a writer who as we have seen transformed the novella even more into a feminist vehicle—Bandello maintained his stories were true. In the epistolary preface to novella forty-two, he claims to have heard the story from a woman who was told it by someone who had traveled in Spain and heard it there. Thus, a kind of oral history is posited for the novella that follows. The story is brought up in the context of a feminist discussion between two noble women of how often men take advantage of "simple" women and how therefore "one should not be surprised if occasionally women retaliate with a vengeance" ["Perciò non si deveno meravigliare se tavolta le donne gli rendono a doppio la pariglia"].[5]

Bandello's novella forty-two is entitled "Signor Didaco Centiglia marries a young woman and then no longer wants her and is killed by her" ("Il signor Didaco Centiglia sposa una giovane e poi non la vuole e da lei è ammazzato" [496]). The basic plot is that Didaco, a wealthy young gentleman (he is twenty-three) becomes enamored of Violante, a twenty-year-old, who is "of low lineage but very beautiful" ["di basso legnaggio, ma molto bella" (496)]. Her father is dead, but she has a mother and two brothers who are goldsmiths, and she herself does beautiful stitchwork.

Violante resists Didaco's improper attentions, until he finally realizes he will have to marry her to achieve his desires. This he determines to do "even if she was of a lower class" ["se bena era di bassa schiatta" (497)], a status she is well aware of. Beforehand he tries to bribe her and her mother with money and a promise of a substantial dowry (for her to marry another), but Violante rejects these, saying she would "rather die than lose her integrity/chastity" ["di prima voler morire che perder la sua onestá" (497)]. Didaco then provides a priest for the ceremony to which the only witnesses are her family and his servant—all of whom he charges to keep the marriage secret.

After about a year, Didaco, in part because he is becoming "ashamed of her low social status" ["che del basso sangue di Violante si vergognasse" (499)], decides to wed a more socially prominent woman, the daughter of Signor Ramiro Vigliaracuta, one of the most eminent families of Valencia. The narrator notes that other factors may have impelled his decision, and that he may simply have "become satiated" with Violante ["di lei fosse sazio" (499)].

When Violante learns of Didaco's betrayal she vows vengeance: in part this is to avenge her honor but it is also to help prevent other poor women from being so easily deceived in the future ["a ciò che per l'avvenire gli uomini non fossero cosí facili ad ingannar le povere donne" (500)]. She thus has an avowed feminist purpose, in that she is identifying with other women as a class that is victimized and is acting to change their situation. The vendetta is carried out by Violante and a loyal African slave named Giannica; the occasion is an assignation that Didaco had arranged with Violante shortly after his new marriage, thinking that because of her deceptively cheerful behavior he could keep her as his mistress: "he thought he could have her cheaply" ["si pensò averne buon mercato" (501)]. He claims that he still loves her and that he had to marry the second wife in order to keep the two houses (his and the Vigliaracuta) at peace. Violante does not buy this, however, and after he falls asleep, she proceeds to avenge herself with a veritable orgy of torture and dismemberment. First, she and Giannica bind him and gag him, preparing knives and other implements "as when a butcher in a slaughterhouse wants to skin an ox or other animal" ["come fa il beccaio quando nel macello vuol scorticare un bue od altra bestia" (503)]. Then she twists his tongue with a pair of pliers, castigating him for pledging false words, and claiming that she is conducting this vendetta to make him an example so that in the future humble people and unsuspecting young girls will no longer be exploited ["a ciò che di beffar le semplici ed incaute fanciulle debbiano guardarsi" (503)].

She then cuts off the tongue in pieces, after which she clips off his fingers and gouges out his eyes, each time addressing him with violent rage, concluding with further dismemberment and a few final stabs to the heart. After he finally dies, Violante tries to persuade Giannica to flee for Africa, giving her sufficient money and jewels, but the slave wishes to stay with her mistress, whom she had raised from girlhood, accompanying her eventually to the scaffold. Violante is soon brought before a local magistrate where she redeems her honor by having her marriage publicly confirmed and by unflinchingly acknowledging her crime and accepting the punishment. Her demeanor is proud and forceful: she responded to questions, the narrator tells us, "not like a sorrowful or timid woman but in a spirited and courageous way . . ." ["la giovane alora non come dolente o timida femina, ma come allegra e valorosa . . ." (506)]. She notes that Didaco's propositioning her after the second marriage particularly galled her: treating me "as if I were his prostitute and whore" ["come se io sua putta e bagascia stata fossi" (507)].

Violante concludes her defense by saying: "I want . . . to defend my reputation so that if anyone in the past has had a low opinion of me, s/he will know for certain that I am the true wife" of Didaco "and not a whore. It is enough for me that my honor is saved" ["Voglio adunque . . . diffendar la fama mia, a ciò che se nessuno per il passato ha di me sinistra openione avuta, sappia ora certissimamente che io del signor Didaco Centiglia moglie vera sono stata e non bagascia. Mi basta che l'onor mio sia salvo" (507)]. Violante is then adjudged guilty and executed along with Giannica.

In María de Zayas's version of the story, "Aminta Deceived and Honor's Revenge" ("La burlada Aminta y venganza del honor"), which is narrated by a woman, the details differ considerably from Bandello, who was apparently her main source,[6] but the character of Violante remains true to the original, and the essence of the plot is similar.

The Violante character is named Aminta in Zayas's telling, and her treacherous lover is don Jacinto. Aminta is younger than Bandello's Violante and is socially and economically well off (so class is not an issue here). Aminta is pledged in an arranged betrothal to her cousin. Jacinto is well-born, handsome, and around thirty. But, unlike Bandello's Didaco, he is already married, and he has a mistress, Flora, who travels with him pretending to be his sister. She operates as the pander in Zayas's version, thinking she will ingratiate herself with him by arranging what she thinks (correctly) will be a passing affair. Aminta and Jacinto are then wed, but during the ceremony her emerald ring splits prophetically and a piece strikes him in the face. After the wedding night—once "the flame of his passion had been assuaged" (*Enchantments* 60) ["que aplacado el fuego de su apetito" (*Novelas amorosas* 100)], he realized he must soon leave town, so he deposits Aminta with an acquaintance and flees the city with Flora. Aminta is soon informed by her hostess that Jacinto is a fraud: his name is don Francisco, he is already married, and Flora is his mistress not his sister.

Aminta is distressed and enraged: "the strength and force of her grievance turned her love for don Jacinto into a desire for harsh vengeance" (65) ["la gala y la fuerza de sus agravios, la iba trocando el amor de don Jacinto en cruel venganza" (106)]. Meanwhile, her hostess's son, don Martin, has fallen in love with her, and offers to avenge her honor. But she refuses him, saying, "I am the one offended, not you, and I alone must avenge my honor" ["porque supuesto que yo he sido ofendida, y no vos, yo sola he de vengarme" (108)]. She promises to marry don Martin but only after she has "killed that traitor" (66) ["hasta que yo quite la vida a este traidor" (108)]. Martin agrees to assist her.

Aminta's assumption of female agency—her determination to carry out her own revenge—must be seen as especially assertive when considered in the context of contemporaneous Spanish mores. As H. Patsy Boyer points out in her introduction to her translation of the *Novelas amorosas* (*The Enchantments of Love*), Zayas reversed the traditional notion of honor wherein women are but pawns in men's agonistic struggles to defend their reputations. Zayas recognizes that "honor represents women's vulnerability, that which gives men power over them" (xvi). If, for example, a woman's chastity is violated, it is a matter of honor among the men involved (her brother or father must take revenge against the perpetrator): she has no role to play. But Zayas challenged this assumption; she believed, according to Boyer, "that women [should] assume responsibility for their own honor, to such a degree that they should be trained in swordsmanship so they can properly defend themselves and women's good name" (xvi). Aminta, then, like many of Zayas's characters, Boyer notes, bears a "resoundingly modern feminist message" (xxiv).

To carry out her vendetta Aminta puts on men's clothes and cuts her hair; then, together, dressed as muleteers, she and Martin pursue Francisco and Flora. When they find them, Aminta in disguise manages to get herself hired as their servant, though they are suspicious of her strong resemblance to Aminta. (She even calls herself Jacinto, which stretches credulity even farther. It should be noted, however, that this kind of improbable disguise is a familiar convention in the novella genre.) Once installed in the household, Aminta carries out her revenge by herself: she stabs Francisco in the heart "two or three times" (73) as he sleeps, and then also kills Flora by knifing her in the throat and breast. She then escapes with Martin as lady and gentleman to Madrid where they wed and live happily thereafter. Thus, Zayas retains the central motif of the woman perpetrating her own revenge but varies the details.

In her other version—"La más infame venganza" ("A Shameful Revenge"), which is more explicitly feminist, having numerous anti-male asides by the woman narrator—Zayas has the revenge accomplished by the victim's brother. The narrator strongly approves of the idea of a woman taking revenge (even though she condemns the method). "And for every woman who seeks, as Octavia did, to revenge herself for the wrongs she has suffered, there are a thousand who of themselves will do nothing. I am sure that if they were all to seek revenge, fewer women would be duped and insulted" ["y que por una procura venganza, hay mil que no la toman de sí misma; que yo aseguro que si todas vengaran las ofensas que reciben, como Octavia hizo, no hubiera tantas burladas y ofendidas"].[7] Thus, as in Bandello, the woman's action is seen as a kind of feminist gesture done to help other women. The revenge method, however, is condemned by the narrator as another "piece of treachery" (65) ["una traición" (190)]; for the brother decides to avenge his sister by raping the wife of the Didaco figure (named Carlos). Here the focus shifts to this woman's suffering—she castigates herself by wearing a hair shirt thereafter, and her husband banishes and eventually poisons her. Thus, the vengeance backfires when the original victim delegates the revenge of her honor to a man: two women end up destroyed and the men remain unpunished.[8]

William Painter's version of the novella, "Didaco and Violenta," in *The Palace of Pleasure* is the main conduit of the tale to later English writers, notably Manley and Haywood. Some of Zayas's stories had been translated into English by the late seventeenth century, as we have noted, but the two stories described above do not appear to have been among them. "La burlada Aminta" had, however, been translated into French by the mid-seventeenth century, and it is conceivable that Manley and/or Haywood may have read it in that translation.[9] But their main source was Painter's tale.

Painter's novella is an almost verbatim translation of Pierre Boaistuau's adaptation of Bandello. As Laura Tortonese points out, Boaistuau made a number of changes in his treatment of the tale. Specifically, he heightened the class issue, seeing Didaco and Violente's relationship as a *mésalliance;* and he increased the role of the slave (named Janique in the French version). In Boaistuau's rendition it is she who proposes the revenge plan, partly out of mercenary interests and a desire for freedom, as well as out of loyalty to her mistress. And in his version Janique escapes Violente's fate, by fleeing to Africa with funds supplied by Violente. Finally, Boaistuau softens the cruelty of the murder, having Violente kill Didaco before dismembering him (in Bandello, as we have seen, she dismembers him alive and then kills him).[10]

Painter follows Boaistuau and Bandello in stressing the class issue: Violenta is seen as being "of base birth," as the daughter of a goldsmith. Ianique (here a servant, however, rather than a slave) acknowledges the class disparity when she lures Didaco to his final fatal rendezvous.[11] The plot follows the outlines laid down in Bandello, although the class situation of Violenta's family is thus stressed more in Painter than in Bandello. When Violenta's mother and brothers find out about Didaco's betrayal, they realize that as lower-class people they have no chance for reparations. "And these poore miserable creatures, not knowing to whom to make their complainte . . . bicause they knew not the priest which did solempnise their mariage . . . they durst not prosecute the lawe against two of the greatest lordes of their citie" (212).

In another detail added by Boaistuau and used by Painter, Violenta writes Didaco a deceptive letter, luring him to his fate, which Ianique delivers, adding her own disingenuous persuasions. When Didaco arrives on the fateful day, he tells Violenta he had been pressured into marriage with the other woman out of financial need, but that he plans to poison his new wife in time and meanwhile to keep Violenta as his mistress. Violenta, "which had her wittes to well sharpened to be twise taken in one trap" (219), pretends to go along with him, saying she is grateful to be allowed to remain as his lover (220). After he falls asleep the two women tie him to the bed and Violenta proceeds to stab him first in the throat, then adding ten or twelve more "mortall woundes" (221). Carried away in her frenzy, Violenta begins dismembering the body, starting with his eyes: "Then shee played the bocher uppon those insensible members" (221). Ianique watches "this pageant" "with great terrour" (222). They then throw all the pieces out the window; Violenta pays off Ianique who flees to Africa; and she herself is apprehended, tried, and executed.

In Painter's version Violenta appears less majestic than in Bandello's, and more pitiful. The class impotence of her and her family is stressed, and, as in Boaistuau, economic motives are proposed for the servant Ianique, which weakens the noble sense of cross-race, cross-class solidarity between the two women that we find in Bandello, and which is restored in Manley. Ianique indeed takes the upper hand in Painter: "Maistres, if you will be ruled by mee . . ." (214). In addition, the fact that the women deceitfully lure Didaco to his fateful rendezvous casts a sinister shadow on their behavior. In Bandello, recall, it is Didaco who arranges the postnuptial assignation with Violante, which she then uses for her own purposes. Violenta's letter to Didaco is not only deceitful, it is lugubriously self-pitying, which further weakens her as a character. Finally, and most importantly, Painter, following Boaistuau, eliminates the feminist motivations; his Violenta says nothing about making Didaco an example to save future poor women from similar exploitation.

Writing in the early eighteenth century, Delarivier Manley modifies Painter's novella considerably by adding social, economic, and psychological detail, by further developing Violenta as a subject (in part through the addition of letters written by her), by making the suitor considerably more obnoxious and thus more deserving of her revenge, and by interjecting occasional feminist comment. The plot follows its sources.

Didaco is renamed Roderigo but Violenta remains Violenta. As in Painter she is literate (not the case in Bandello), "an Accomplishment," Manley tells us, "which, in those Days, few Ladies aim'd at, since they believed all inferior Knowledge, as well as the Sciences, was reserv'd for the other Sex."[12] Violenta is "a poor Orphan, kept by her Mother . . . a Widow, her Husband no better than a Goldsmith," who also "left two Sons, who follow'd his Trade in great Obscurity" (180). Manley thus stresses her lower-middle-class status.

Roderigo presses his courtship, sending her a gift of bracelets, which she returns with a letter cited in the text (Manley's addition) in which she makes it clear that her honor is at stake: "That which Courage is to your Sex, Chastity is to ours" (181). In a second letter Violenta reiterates, "I must perish if I prove otherwise: Since I know it will be impossible for me to live after the loss of my Honour." She concludes: "I would see the whole World in a Conflagration, and my self in the middle of it, before I could be brought to do any thing contrary to the Rules of Modesty" (183)— which serves to indicate the extremity of her temperament (thus establishing aspects of her psychology). Roderigo continues his harassment, however, and although "the Disparity between them was so great he had no Notion of Wedlock," "she [resolved] he should never have Favours of her without it" (184). It becomes a battle of wills. He continues, however, to feel that "he could not bring himself . . . to debase his Blood so far as to mingle by Marriage with one of her low Degree" (186).

As in the sources, Roderigo next tries to bribe the mother. While this scene is very brief in Painter, Manley extends it and adds a touch of humor. Significantly, the scene between Roderigo and the mother is presented in indirect discourse by Manley. This stylistic technique is, as we have noted, particularly congenial to feminist irony, which is quite apparent in this passage. Having failed to win Violente by direct courtship, Roderigo

> resolv'd to change his Battery, and knowing they were pretty poor, he made [the mother] a Visit . . . in which he confess'd his Passion for her Daughter. . . . The old Gentlewoman, to whom this was no great news, tho' she affected to be ignorant, answer'd, That *Violenta* was highly honour'd . . . but that she was a Maid unskill'd in Courts, rude of Fashion, and not us'd to the Conversation of Persons of his Quality. (188)

Roderigo then offers a thousand ducats for her dowry; the mother "let him know, with all Regard to his Quality, that she was offended . . . that her House was no place to purchase Vertue in" (189). The subtle sarcasm of the mother is unmistakable; both her and her daughter's characters are particularized in this scene far beyond anything in the sources.

Manley also adds a prophetic dream in which Roderigo sees Violenta strike a daggar in his heart, telling him (in indirect discourse) "That was the Reward of Treachery and Inconstancy" (190). The next morning Roderigo finds Violenta sewing peacefully—an ironic juxtaposition of scenes. He notes that "she was always employ'd," thus following an old adage "*A vertuous Lady can never be idle*" (190), a touch of comic irony, given the plot.

Violenta finally acknowledges, amidst much blushing and many tears, that she loves Roderigo. These have their effect and Roderigo finally determines he will marry her. At this announcement Manley indulges in mock heroics—an obvious parody of the French romance: "As we have often beheld the Sun break out with sudden Glory, in the midst of Clouds and Rain, so darted from *Violenta's* Eyes, Rays of Light" (193). He then produces a diamond ring "and then, and not 'till then, had he ever presumed to kiss her" (194). The author here extrapolates from Violenta's exemplum of modesty to urge that all girls should be similarly restrained; she set "a Pattern worthy the Imitation of young Virgins" (194). The fact that Violenta ends up as a notorious Medean murderess ironizes this image of decorum and suggests a subtle casuistry on Manley's part: she is using Violenta (perhaps unconsciously) to undermine decorous rules and expectations about female behavior. As in other feminist uses of casuistry, the case of Violenta destabilizes, indeed demolishes, the generality that women should be tame, docile, and dependent.

The wedding ceremony takes place as in the sources with Roderigo providing a country priest, and with the mother, the two brothers, his valet, and her slave, Ianthe, as witnesses. Violenta's immediate family basks in the experience, "as Persons suddenly raised from Poverty to Wealth, or from a mean Degree to an exalted State of Honour" (196). As in Boaistuau and Painter (but not in Bandello), Violenta becomes obsequious after the wedding, "ambitious to please him in whatever he desired, as the poorest Slave" (196). He became "*the Lord of her Idolatry*" (199), a phrase taken from *Romeo and Juliet* (II.ii.114). Tortonese suggests that this slavish worship diminishes Violenta as a character, but it does serve to heighten her sense of abasement after his betrayal and thus helps to motivate the rage she expresses in the dismemberment orgy. As in the sources, the marriage is kept a secret, and thus neighbors talk about his regular visits. This slanderous gossip horrifies the proud Violenta but she comforts herself with the idea that eventually she will be vindicated when the marriage is publicly announced (198). After about a year, as her love intensifies, his fades: "he grew from Cool to more Cold, from Frost to Ice, from Ice to Aversion, and a Hatred of his own Folly for so unworthily matching himself with the Lees of the People" (200). He contracts a marriage with a more socially eminent woman and begins to look on Violenta with contempt as "a little Mistress with whom he condescended to squander away some superfluous Hours of Youth" (202). Again, Manley adds a touch of contempt here that helps to motivate Violenta's passionate revenge.

Manley's most telling addition to her sources is her treatment of the family's reaction to the news of Roderigo's betrayal. First, she has Roderigo reflect that he need fear no retaliation from the brothers, "those Mechanicks . . . who dreamt of no other Notions of Honour but what they expected to find in their Customers." And as for the mother, "he looked upon [her] as a Piece of old Houshold-Stuff quite out of Date" (203). As Roderigo correctly predicted, the brothers remain true to their petit bourgeois class attitudes: "their Souls were of a Piece with their Profession, they did not dream of Honour and Revenge, provided they could Sell their Plate" (203). To buy them off, indeed, Roderigo purchases the silver and gold tableware for his new household from the brothers. The mother chastizes them but soon realizes they are "such Stocks, and Stones" that they will not live up to the Spanish code of honor and avenge their sister (204). She also realizes she is impotent, not knowing the name of the priest who officiated at her daughter's wedding.

In Manley's conception of the brothers as petit bourgeois we see the beginnings of a critique that dominated the realist novel—indeed, as

some (Lucien Goldmann, for example) have argued, provided its principal ethical perspective. The brothers operate, not according to principled
honor as Violenta does, but according to mercenary or "exchange-value"
considerations: what matters to them is selling their product. Where the
mother and Violenta had earlier refused a bribe, the brothers are easily
bought off. One could argue that the women are operating in terms of an
aristocratic sense of honor (despite their lower class status); the clash between aristocratic principles and bourgeois commercialism is indeed a
prime drama in the realist novel. Or, one could argue that they are operating in terms of a "use-value" ethic, that which is associated with the
home, with products that are made for use, not exchange (and therefore
valued for their personal, emotional character); it is a personalist ethic
that involves commitment to individuals as ends not means. When the
mother says "that her House was no place to purchase Vertue in" (189),
she is articulating a use-value ethic, resisting the commodification of her
daughter as a sex object. Manley here continues the important thematic
of women's fiction, the rejection of the sexual commodification of
women, but she conceives it more clearly in economic terms than do earlier treatments of sexual exploitation.

Manley's Violenta is much more motivated, as well, by class consciousness than in the sources. The sentiment expressed by the family in
Painter's version that they cannot hope to obtain justice against such powerful class enemies, is here expressed by Violenta herself. "Too well I know
there is but little Redress for so mean a Person as I am, to expect by Law,
against two of the most potent Families in *Valentia*" (210). Violenta also
expresses intensely bitter class resentment in recalling that Roderigo had
jokingly but contemptuously said

> That Maids of my base Birth had no Pretensions to Honour, what had we
> to do with such fantastick Notions? Vertue and Chastity were pretty Names
> indeed for Boors to play with! As if Courage were only appropriated to Men
> of Quality, or Modesty to Noble Women. (210)

Thus, Manley more fully explains Violenta's psychological state, in particular her resentment of Roderigo's class contempt, than do her sources
(although the idea is implicit in Bandello). Violenta's relationship with
Ianthe is here somewhat more assertive than in Painter, which tends to el-
evate her stature. As in the sources, she asks the slave for her help but says
if that is denied, she will do the deed alone (210). But she does offer Ianthe
2,000 ducats and jewels for her assistance.

Ianthe, a servant in Painter's version, is once again a slave in Manley's
reconception, and her psychology is further developed. She is motivated

partly by affection for her mistress and partly out of "Covetousness and the desire of Liberty, by which she should gain so great a Reward; with which she meant to fly away to her own Land, and seek her Kindred and Parents, if they were yet alive or to be found" (211). Thus, Ianthe's desire for freedom and repatriation, and reunion with her African kin, supercede greed in Manley's sketch of her character, differentiating her from Boaistuau's otherwise similar portrait. Manley also fills in more details about her life and her relationship with Violenta: "This poor Creature had from her Childhood, when she was first made a Slave, been bred up by *Donna Camilla* [the mother]. The Slave had brought up *Violenta,* and so tenderly lov'd her, that she would have done any thing for her Relief" (208).

Ianthe proceeds to lay out the murder plan, which from here on follows the sources with little variation: Roderigo is cleverly lured to the assignation by Ianthe; he tells Violenta he plans to poison his wife and return to her, his true love. This declaration is presented as deliberately deceptive by Manley (more clearly so than in the sources): "He concluded this Discourse which was only fram'd to appease her, with Protestations of his Love, and ten Thousand Vows of Constancy, which easily sworn by those who intend only to deceive" (217). But he retains a secret contempt for Violenta; Manley explains his inner thoughts: "The Count was very well satisfied that he found *Violenta* so well appeased; he thought he need not give himself much Trouble about that little Maid, a Creature of no Consequence, whom he might use as he pleased" (218). Thus, Roderigo is set up as much more offensive a character than he is in the sources, and thus much more deserving of his fate. Manley's sympathies are clearly with the woman.

The murder scene is vividly described. Violenta first stabs him in the throat, and, while Ianthe holds him down, Violenta "like another *Medea,* mad with Rage and Fury, redoubled her Stroke," inflicting several further mortal wounds (219). Then, addressing each member in turn ("Ah trayterous Eyes" [220]), she proceeds to carve up the corpse. This scene is more drawn out in Manley than in Painter. Ianthe watches in horror, and when Violenta is through, they throw the remains out the window. Violenta gives Ianthe her reward, and she escapes to Africa. Violenta is brought to trial and her honor is restored; however, despite townspeoples' sympathy, she is condemned to death because she "had presumed to punish [Roderigo's] Offense by her own Hand" (228) and because of the barbarity of the dismemberment. Like Painter, Manley concludes by citing various sources, including "Bandwell" (Bandello).

Eliza Haywood's version of the novella, "Female Revenge; or, the Happy Exchange," appeared in 1727, just seven years after Manley's.

Haywood claims in her subtitle to the collection *Love in Its Variety* that it is but a translation of Bandello. The subtitle reads: "*Being a Collection of Select Novels; Written in Spanish by Signior Michael Bandello. Made English by Mrs. Eliza Haywood.*" Bandello, of course, did not write in Spanish; it seems likely that Haywood was not just being sloppy here, but rather that her sources were probably not the original Bandello but instead Manley and Painter (of course, she might have been familiar with the Zayas version). Robert Day suggests that none of the novellas in *Love in Its Variety* are translations of Bandello but were "almost certainly original."[13] This particular tale, "Female Revenge; or the Happy Exchange," was hardly original by this time, but Haywood does give it an original twist; she transforms it into a prototype of the sentimentalist "heroine's text" of the seduced-and-abandoned victim.

While the setting remains Spain, the Didaco character is made an English gentleman, Sir William Bellcourt, who, orphaned at fourteen, has been taken in by a rich uncle who lives in Spain. At the age of twenty Bellcourt falls for a lower-class woman, Climene. Realizing that his uncle will never condone "such a Match," Bellcourt agrees to "a private Marriage," and determines to keep it secret from his uncle lest he be disinherited.[14] Climene has a mother and two sisters; it is they who persuade Bellcourt to adopt this course. Indeed, the mother clinches his decision by forbidding him to see her unless they wed. Thus, Bellcourt is considerably milder in Haywood's version: his behavior is coerced by his uncle and by her mother, and he expresses no class contempt nor does he attempt to bribe the mother. Climene is really an object of others' determinations throughout the first part of the novella; indeed she does not speak (in direct discourse) at all in the work—in sharp contrast to the sources.

After the secret wedding, as in the sources, gossiping neighbors begin to talk about Bellcourt's frequent visits to Climene's home, and someone tells the uncle about them. The uncle warns Bellcourt against marriage with her, threatening to cut him off, but also cautioning him against ruining the reputation of a virtuous maiden. Bellcourt deceitfully assures his uncle in no uncertain terms that he would never marry her: "had *Climene* a Fortune equal to what your Bounty has confer'd on me, I wou'd not marry her," and he offers to swear "the deepest and most solemn" oath to this effect (109).

Meanwhile, he continues to see Climene privately and after two years they have two sons. Fortune begins to turn, however, when the mother, whose "Prudence and Cunning" (110) had successfully managed the affair, dies. The uncle also soon dies, leaving his estate to Bellcourt but in his dying moments "charging him . . . to marry *Julia*" (112), "the daughter of a rich Merchant" (110). Bellcourt, however, disobeys his uncle and after

his death publicly announces his marriage to Climene. Bellcourt continues thus (unlike his prototypes in the sources) to behave honorably. In a
complicated plot twist, however, Bellcourt soon falls in love with Julia, his
uncle's choice for his spouse. Julia, however, refuses to engage in a flirta-
tion in view of his marriage. So he contents himself with a "*Platonick
friendship*" (131).

When Climene learns of Bellcourt's infatuation with Julia, she manifests "the extremest Flame of raging Jealousy" (133). He ignores her out-
burst, which "put her beyond all patience and she grew more like a Fury
than a Woman" (133). Thus, Climene approaches the level of wrath of her
counterparts in earlier versions of the novella. At this point Bellcourt feels
the aversion his counterparts had felt earlier (they were motivated solely
by a cooling of passion; he, however, is repulsed by her resentful behavior). "He hated to be near her, took all opportunities of avoiding her
Company" (133).

Climene proceeds to carry out her revenge but it is not murder; rather
she has an affair with Octavio, a friend of Bellcourt's. This is precisely the
kind of revenge the feminist narrator in María de Zayas's "A Shameful Revenge" warned against: "I am sure that if [women] were all to seek revenge, fewer women would be duped and insulted, but there are many
women with such low minds that their idea of revenge, if they are deceived by a man, is to deceive another man in their turn" (*Shameful Revenge* 64) ["que yo aseguro que si todas vengaran las ofensas que
reciben . . . no hubiera tantas burladas y ofendidas. Mas hay tantas mujeres de tan común estilo, que la venganza que toman es, si las engaña uno,
engañarse ellas con otro (*Parte segunda* 189)]. Climene's character is further discredited when Haywood explains that she had married Bellcourt
"more out of a Principle of [economic] Interest than Love" (134).

Bellcourt feels compelled upon learning of their affair to challenge Octavio to a duel. The latter is wounded and Bellcourt discovers a letter from
Climene to Octavio in which she says of Bellcourt, "*I hate and despise the
Wretch*" (136). Haywood's sympathies are by now entirely with Bellcourt;
it is his point of view that prevails: "Whoever is a Husband, may easily
conceive the Shock a Letter such as this must give *Bellcourt*" (137)—
ignoring the fact that it is he who first betrayed Climene. In response,
Bellcourt divorces Climene and marries Julia. Octavio, recovered, leaves
for Constantinople, after rejecting Climene "with Scorn and Derision."
She, then, burdened by "the Grief" of that abandonment "together with
the Shame which her Disgrace had brought upon her" commits suicide by
taking poison (139).

The Didaco-Violante plot is thus drastically transformed in Haywood's
hands. Didaco is turned into a romantic, sentimental hero, exonerated

because all his actions are motivated by sentiment. Violante is robbed of her dignity and stature and turned into a conniving self-seeker who deserves her fate. The elements of economic realism that Manley introduced are gone. Instead we are left with a prototype of the sentimentalist seduced-and-abandoned novel, seen in a work like *Charlotte Temple.* Even some of the characters' names are the same: Belcour is the name of an evil procurer in *Charlotte Temple* and Julia is the woman the male protagonist marries after abandoning Charlotte with child. The differences are also worth noting, however. Where Climene is portrayed with little sympathy, Charlotte is designed to wrench the hardest heart; and where Bellcourt is presented positively, Montraville, his counterpart, is portrayed by Rowson as at least flawed and clearly exploitative of Charlotte. Thus, curiously, Haywood lays out the sentimentalist plot but unlike most later sentimentalist authors whose sympathy is with the victimized female, Haywood sides with the man. Indeed, the central focus in Haywood's novella is on the man rather than the woman. Bellcourt is the principal actor; Climene says nothing and does little—she is largely in the shadows; and Julia, though she has a few lines, is a passive conformist.

Haywood tames a powerful story of female agency and feminist revenge, turning it into a misogynist tale of male ascendancy and female powerlessness, disgrace, and death. That her version of the novella accords with the changing ideological climate of the time, in which women's economic and social power was in eclipse, suggests a reason for Haywood's capitulation.

The successive versions of the Violenta novella thus provide an interesting comparative case study wherein are inscribed changing ideological climates, as well as individual authors' preoccupations. Bandello, writing in the midst of the *querelle des femmes,* seized the feminist import of the tale. In his treatment Violante acts for all poor women as well as on her own behalf. María de Zayas, who wrote from a consciously feminist perspective, conceives her character Aminta as justly carrying out her own socially-mandated vengeance rather than depending on a man to do it for her. Painter, following Boaistuau, eliminates the feminist message, conceiving the story primarily as bizarre entertainment. Manley restores the feminist thesis and adds important socio-economic details that link her work to the emerging realist novel. Finally, Haywood sentimentalized the novella; gone is the forceful subject of female agency seen in earlier versions; gone is the contemptuous aristocratic harasser of lower-class women. Instead the story is recast in terms of a male supremacist ideology: the man is seen as sincere, morally pure, innocent, and the women are dichotomized. One, Climene, is presented as a self-interested operator who violates the patriarchal rules of the marriage-market exchange system and is thus victimized, abandoned, and doomed. The other, Julia, conforms to the system and is thus rewarded with love and marriage. These are the classic dysphoric and euphoric endings available to female characters in the sentimentalist plot, the "heroine's text," which came to dominate women's literature for the next century.[15]

Chapter Eight

Women against Romance

DESPITE THE APPARENT SUBMERGENCE AND ECLIPSE of feminist critical re-alism by the sentimentalist heroine's text after the first two decades of the eighteenth century, an anti-romance undercurrent continued to circulate in the English women's literary tradition throughout the century. While women have long been popularly associated with the ro-mance, both as writers and readers, the female anti-romance tradition that I trace in this chapter suggests that the anti-romance was at least as important in women's literary culture as the romance.

Many critics and literary historians have, however, overlooked women writers' connection with the anti-romance. Indeed, many as-sume that it was an inherently masculine tradition to which women were not attracted. Charles Mish, for example, speaking of a series of late seventeenth-century "anti-romantic love stories, ironic rather than passionate," says they "seem [for this reason] intended for a masculine rather than a feminine audience."[1] In a 1977 article, "Serious Reflections on *The Rise of the Novel*," which revises his theory of the novel, Ian Watt contends that the novel of manners, exemplified in Jane Austen, reflects a "contradiction between Augustan values on the one hand, and femi-nine and youthful values on the other."[2] By "Augustan values" Watt means "masculine and adult values" (102), rationalist norms of sense, as opposed to romantic sensibility. But Watt's association of sense with masculinity is contradicted by the scores of sensible women characters in women's literature who put down excesses of sensibility as injurious to women's survival interests. As early as Mary Astell feminist rational-ists were warning against the cultivation of excessively romantic sensi-tivities in women.

In *The Anatomy of Satire* (1962), a classic work on the subject, Gilbert Highet goes so far as to say "very few [women] have ever written, or even enjoyed, satire, although," he acknowledges, "they have often been its victims."[3] Even Northrup Frye in *Anatomy of Criticism* (1957), another classic study, erroneously claims, "the female *alazon* is rare."[4] In fact, the clash between a female *alazon* and a female *eiron*—in the shape of the woman of sensibility (sometimes cast as a female quixote) versus the woman of sense—is at the heart of the women's bildungsroman and novel of manners. There are scores of female *alazons,* who figure prominently in numerous novels. The assumption, therefore, that women as subjects are absent in the literary traditions of satire and the anti-romance is simply incorrect.

There is no disputing, however, the importance of the anti-romance to the constitution of the novel, and so it is highly relevant to establish women's contribution to the anti-romance tradition. Probably the most cogent theory of the novel as an anti-romance is proposed by Maurice Shroder in his classic article, "The Novel as a Genre" (1969). Definitionally, Shroder claims, the novel enacts a process of "demythification," by which he means something very similar to the *desengaños* proposed by María de Zayas as a central purpose of her fiction. Zayas, recall, said that she wrote her stories in order to "enlighten or disenchant women about men's deceptions" ["y que tuviesen nombre de desengaños"].[5] (See chapter five.)

The novel, according to Shroder, is concerned with disabusing gullible innocents of illusions they hold about the world, illusions that compromise their ability to survive in the world as it really is. All novels are therefore in a sense bildungsromane, he says, dealing with the education of the protagonist, which means stripping her or him of false, usually romantic, ideas or ideals.[6] Shroder's theory is congruent with the conception of the novel laid out in chapter one, that it is an inherently anti-theoretistic genre. For the false ideals or illusions of the disabused protagonist equate to the abstract theories and reified ideologies that are inevitably undermined by the novel's particularistic realism, according to Bakhtin and other theorists noted in the first chapter. It is in fact by means of the experiential process of disillusionment or disenchantment that the novel debunks such theoretistic notions.

That debunking is done by means of irony. As noted in chapter two, Shroder sees the *alazon-eiron* confrontation as at the heart of the novelistic process of *desengaños.* The archetypal *alazon-eiron* couple is Don Quixote, with his romantic illusions, and Sancho, who continually undercuts them. Irony is therefore crucial to the demythification process because, as one critic notes, irony "resists enchantment."[7] We have already noted the critical irony and attendant *desengaños* women writers have brought to bear on ideologies and institutions that wrought harm to women, such as marriage-marketing courtship rituals.

Mikhail Bakhtin also insists on the centrality of the anti-romance in the formation of the novel. In *The Dialogic Imagination,* Bakhtin maintains that the novel performs "a comical operation of dismemberment"[8] by exposing heroic pieties to ridicule. "[I]n popular laughter, the authentic folkloric roots of the novel are to be sought . . . [, where] flourish parody and travesty of all high genres and of all lofty models embodied in national myth" (21). Parody of "official" genres—for example, of the medieval chivalric romance—was an essential gesture of the early novel (6), and thus because of its antiestablishmentarianism, the novel in its origins was anti-romantic to the core. Such irreverence Bakhtin traces back to antiquity, to Socratic irony and the Menippean satire, whose sole purpose was "to put to the test and to expose ideas and idealogues" (26).

In *Rabelais and His World,* Bakhtin extends his discussion of novelesque parody focusing on the carnivalian antiauthoritarianism in Rabelais's *Gargantua et Pantagruel.* In this work Bakhtin touches on what is most problematic for a feminist in the men's parodic tradition, its virulent misogyny. Bakhtin acknowledges that there is a manifestly "negative attitude toward women" in "'the Gallic tradition.'"[9] However, he argues that one must distinguish between the folk representation of women and Church misogyny. The former he claims is healthy, as opposed to the latter. In the former women operate as earthy *eirons* to male pretentiousness: "She represents in person the undoing of pretentiousness, of all that is finished, completed, and exhausted. She is the inexhaustible vessel of conception, which dooms all that is old and terminated" (240). In short, as a representation of the earthly, woman embodies the comic spirit of rebirth. While the first part of Bakhtin's thesis—that women may operate as *eirons* to male pretentiousness—can certainly be appropriated to the women's comic anti-romance tradition, the reduction of women to earthly avatars merely reifies women into fixed roles, which contravenes the purportedly anti-theoretistic spirit of parody. Throughout his work Bakhtin is in fact surprisingly blind to women as individuals and fails to incorporate their voices, as Wayne Booth has noted, in his heteroglossal ideal.[10]

Bakhtin sanitizes the misogyny in Rabelais's work, where, as Booth notes, we are often asked "to laugh at women *because* they are women and hence inferior" (160). The implied reader is male, and "not only . . . are [there] no significant female characters; it is that even the passages most favorable to women are spoken by and addressed to men who are the sole arbiters of the question" (164). "The truth is," Booth concludes, that nowhere in Rabelais does one find any hint of an effort to imagine any woman's point of view or to incorporate women into a dialogue. And nowhere in Bakhtin does one discover any suggestion that he sees the importance of this kind of monologue, not even when he discusses Rabelais' attitude toward women. (165–66)

Rabelais was not alone in exemplifying how men's parodic satire—particularly of the courtly love tradition with its idealization of women—often slipped into a most brutal misogyny. Indeed, there is a long tradition of misogynist satires, beginning with Juvenal's Sixth Satire (Highet 39, 224–28). That tradition seemed to become especially virulent in the fourteenth to the mid-sixteenth century. Erich Auerbach notes a "pronounced contempt for women" ["eine entscheidene Frauenverachtung"] in the literature of the period.[11] Patricia Cholakian observes that Gallic wit in the early French novella "was practically synonymous with obscenities directed at women" (105), a point echoed by Ferrier (5) and Clements and Gibaldi (78).

Jean de Meung's section of the *Roman de la rose* (ca. 1275) was one of the first to parody courtly love at the expense of women. One of the first feminist responses to this kind of misogynistic representation of women (that they are sexually opportunistic, amoral, grotesquely physical beings—in other words, the opposite of the chaste virginal courtly love ideal) was Christine de Pizan's *Epistres sur le Roman de la rose* (1400) and *Epistre au dieu d'amours* (1399). In the latter she argues that if women were writing the texts, the women characters would be different, "for they well know they have been wrongly blamed" ["Mais se femmes eussent les livres fait/Je sçay de vray qu'autrement fust du fait,/Car bien scevent qu'a tort sont encoulpées"].[12] Christine's critique initiated the *querelle des femmes* that continued for centuries and out of which emerged the first tradition of women's prose fiction, also initiated by her, the women's framed-novelle, which eventually produced a comic thematic of its own.

In order to better situate the women's anti-romance it is necessary to briefly trace the men's version of the genre. By the mid-seventeenth century, that tradition, which derived largely from Cervantes's *Don Quixote*, was a dominant form. Considerably more benign than the misogynistic comedy of the Rabelaisian type, it was much more amenable to adaptation by women writers. The works in this tradition purported to be strictly parodic burlesques of the romance, but, as Paul Salzman points out in a section entitled "Anti-Romance" of his *English Prose Fiction 1558–1700* (1985), they often moved beyond their original satiric intent, especially in French literature, engaging in a new kind of social realism.[13] While Salzman claims the English anti-romances tended to remain burlesques rather than works of comic realism, that is not true of women writers in the English tradition, such as Manley, Trotter, and Davys, as we saw in chapter six.

One of the earliest anti-romances (after the originator of the genre, *Don Quixote*) was Charles Sorel's *Le Berger extravagant* (1627), which Bakhtin highlights as an important proto-novel in *The Dialogic Imagination* (6). *Le Berger extravagant* parodied the popular pastoral romance, in particular Honoré D'Urfé's 5,000-plus page *l'Astrée* (1607–27). Sorel picked up the reading thematic from *Don Quixote;* his main character is an educated Parisian who reads one too many romances about shepherds, begins to see the world in pastoral terms, and attempts to lead such a life himself. Sorel's novel was translated into English by John Davies in 1653 as *The Extravagant Shepherd* with the significant subtitle *The Anti-Romance; Or, The History of the Shepherd Lysis.*

Sorel's perpetuation of the quixote whose vision is warped by his or her reading laid the basis for the "female quixote" who becomes a stock figure in the women's anti-romance tradition. The first appearance of this character (to my knowledge) is in Adrien Thomas Perdou de Subligny, *La Fausse Clélie* (1670), translated into English (with another significant subtitle) as *The Mock Clelia, or, Madam Quixote: Being a Comical History of French Gallantries and Novels, In Imitation of Don Quixote* (1678). Here the main character has read Madeleine de Scudéry's lengthy romance, *Clélie,* and begins behaving "in imitation of Clelia whom she believed herself to be."[14]

The other branch of the anti-romance tradition included works that were not so much direct parodies of specific works (as *La Fausse Clélie* of *Clélie*) but rather comic and anti-romantic by virtue of their realistically mundane bourgeois setting, their unromantic characters, and their social satire. Probably the most significant of these works are Paul Scarron's *Le Roman comique* (part one, 1651; part two, 1657), translated as *The Comical Romance* (1665); and Antoine Furetière's *Le Roman bourgeois* (1666), translated as *Scarron's City Romance* (1671).

As indicated in chapter four, Scarron incorporated four María de Zayas novellas in his *Roman comique* and in his *Nouvelles tragi-comiques* (1655); these were included in the John Davies 1665 translation, which was entitled *Scarron's Novels.* The Zayas novellas clearly influenced the British women writers, but Scarron's comical frame story in the *Roman comique* undoubtedly had an important effect on them as well. Jane Barker in fact acknowledges in her preface to *The Lining of the Patch Work Screen* (1726) that she "hunt *Scaron* [Scarron] through all his Mazes, to find out something to deck this my Epistle, till I made it as fine as a *May day* Milk Pail."[15]

The *Roman comique* has a travel frame and focuses on a troop of come-
dians who go from town to town encountering various people and adventures. The setting and manners are described in realistic detail, but the
adventures are largely slapstick buffoonery. The anti-romantic opening sentence burlesques the pseudoclassical personification of the sun, seen in
many romance openings, and sets the novel's satirical tone. That tone is
what writers like Catherine Trotter, Mary Davys, Delarivier Manley, and
Jane Barker appear to have picked up, but their satire was more pointedly
focused, as we have seen, on the marriage-market. Unlike Scarron, in other
words, whose humor is largely farcical, theirs has a precise political message.

The women's anti-romance tradition has in fact two components: one
the satire of male-serving, marriage-market rituals we have touched on in
earlier chapters; the other, a kind of subdivision of the first, is the female
quixote tradition, in which a mystified female *alazon* is disabused of her
illusions by a sensible sister *eiron*. Both have as their principal purpose the
desengaños or demythification that Shroder posited as the essential action
of the novel.

As early as the women troubadours noted in chapter five, women critiqued the unreality of courtly love notions, especially the idealistic conception of women therein. There are also a number of sarcastic
anti-romantic comments made by the frame characters in the *Heptaméron*. Parlamente, for example, debunks the idea that one can actually die from unconsummated desire—a commonplace of courtly love
ideology—putting down the idea as a male ploy often used in seduction
schemes (95; 164). This kind of demasking satire is the governing point
of view in Zayas's works, as it is in Christine de Pizan and many subsequent women writers.

One of the first extended comical treatments of marriage-market rituals appears in *Les Nouvelles françaises* (1656), written, according to Joan
DeJean, by Anne-Marie-Louise-Henriette d'Orléans, the duchess of
Montpensier, known as the "Grande Mademoiselle" because of her military exploits in the Fronde, an uprising against Louis XIV (1648–53).[16] *Les
Nouvelles françaises*, a minor work in the women's framed-novelle tradition, has a frame of several noble women in exile who tell one another stories, which are transcribed (somewhat on the order of *Les Évangiles des
quenouilles*) by a male scribe, Jean Segrais. Segrais is in fact usually given
as the author. While most of the inset novellas are flat stereotypical examples of the genre, one replicates the comic realism emerging in Scarron
and others at the time. (There are also several theoretical discussions of
realism that are of some significance.)[17]

"Honorine" concerns a woman who is seeking a husband who is intelligent, noble, and rich. She finds three men, but each has only one of

the characteristics, and it is canceled out by the lack of the others (the rich man is stupid, etc.). She ends up in a convent. What is new about this story is its everyday realism and the realistic description of the characters. Honorine is described satirically as being "of passable looks; she was small but well proportioned for her size. She was white and blond, and being a woman of quality and rich was more than enough to assure her a husband. . . . But she was so conceited and full of amour-propre that she thought no man could look at her without being immediately struck by her" ["Elle était médiocrement belle; elle était petite, mais assez bien faite en sa taille; elle était blanche et blonde, et, étant de qualité et riche, cela ne suffisait que trop pour lui donner un mari. . . . Mais elle avait tant de bonne opinion de soi-même et tant d'amour-propre qu'elle ne croyait pas qu'un homme pût la regarder sans en être aussitot épris" [202]). We are not far here from the satirical novel of manners.

In England the women's anti-romantic tradition was initiated by Margaret Cavendish, if one excludes *The Countesse of Montgomeries Urania* (1621) by Lady Mary Wroth, which, although it is in many ways critical of romance conventions, nevertheless itself remains within the genre of the sophisticated political romance (to some extent a roman à clef *chronique scandaleuse*). We have seen that in a philosophical allegory in *Natures Pictures* Cavendish had Jove order all romances thrown out of Heaven's library (see chapter one), excepting *Don Quixote* "by reason he hath so wittily abused all other Romances, wherefore he shall be kept, and also have his Books writ in golden letters" (360).

In her 1671 preface to *Natures Pictures,* Cavendish emphatically rejects the romance, saying, "I would not be thought to delight in Romances, having never read a whole one in my life; and if I did believe that these Tales . . . could create Amorous thoughts in idle brains, as Romances do, I would never suffer them to be printed."[18]

Among the numerous anti-romance comments in the *Sociable Letters* (1664) is this adumbration of the female quixote articulated in a critique of women's failings: "the truth is, the chief study of our Sex is Romances, wherein reading, they fall in love with the feign'd Heroes and Carpet-Knights, with whom their Thoughts secretly commit Adultery, and in their Conversation and manner, or forms or phrases of Speech, they imitate the Romancy-Ladies."[19] In her preface to the *Sociable Letters,* Cavendish says she abjured the use of a romantic style, noting that she has not "written in a Mode-style, that is, in a Complementing, and Romancical way, with High Words, and Mystical Expressions"; rather "I have Endeavoured . . . to Express the Humors of Mankind" (C2[r]). In other words, she is opting not for romance but social satire.

Cavendish's genius at satiric realism is displayed throughout. This vignette description of a woman who prays too much is representative. "I can hardly believe," the writer exclaims, that "God can be Pleased with so many Words, for what shall we need to Speak so many Words to God, who knows our Thoughts, Minds and Souls better than we our selves?" Far better, she concludes, are "Good Deeds . . . than Good Words. . . . Indeed every Good Deed is a Prayer" (121).

We have seen that Delarivier Manley and Mary Davys wrote two of the most important early modern critiques of the romance and defenses of realism (Manley in her 1705 preface to *Queen Zarah* and Davys in the 1725 preface to her works; see chapters one and six above). And we have noted how the writers of the nineties generation furthered anti-romantic realism through their use of feminist critical irony, creating a feminist prosaics. In her dedication to *The Fugitive* in 1705 Davys explicitly states, "I had a Mind to make an Experiment, whether it was not possible to divert the Town with Real Events, just as they happen'd, without running into Romance,"[20] thus following in the footsteps of Scarron and d'Aulnoy. By the mid-eighteenth century, however, this tradition had been largely eclipsed by the sentimentalist novel. For in the 1730s and 1740s writings by and about women began to adhere to what Nancy K. Miller labeled the "heroine's text," a sentimentalist form "crucially dependent," she notes, "upon the uses and abuses of [the heroine's] chastity."[21] In fact, these novels are as well crucially concerned with the heroine's economic situation, her chastity being her ticket to economic security. If she loses it, her market value on the marriage exchange plummets, and her chances of survival similarly plunge. Scores of novels, beginning with Marivaux's *La Vie de Marianne* (1731–41), replicated the basic pattern: an orphaned girl, who is disinherited and/or abused by a series of guardians and/or suitors, finally recovers her father and patrimony or marries, thus establishing her economic security. If, however, she is raped, she loses her market value, as well as her honor, and she must die. The former plot, seen, for example, in *Pamela* (1740–42) by Samuel Richardson, is labeled "euphoric" by Miller; and the latter "dysphoric" (xi). Richardson's *Clarissa* (1747–48) is a good example of the latter. This sentimentalist tradition continued unabated into the early twentieth century and included, as noted, one of the first American novels, *Charlotte: A Tale of Truth* (1791 in England; reprinted in the United States in 1794), later known as *Charlotte Temple*. It and later American examples of the genre were extremely popular.

In this sentimentalist tradition the woman protagonist—the "heroine"—is really a victim, a passive object, whose subjective decisions or opinions count for little. We have seen this kind of character in Haywood's Climene in her novella "Female Revenge," discussed in the last chapter. Charlotte Temple, for example, is almost entirely at the mercy of others' wills. She is manipulated, coerced, kidnapped, raped, abandoned pregnant, and dies without ever expressing a coherent opinion or exercising even a modicum of will power. She represents an unfortunate opposite to the active, assertive, satirical women characters created by the realist women writers of the late seventeenth and early eighteenth centuries.

That realist tradition, with its inherent social satire and anti-romantic bent, did, however, continue through the eighteenth century in an almost subterranean stream, largely overshadowed by the dominant sentimentalist genre. But even the realist tradition, seen most significantly in the works by Sarah Fielding, Charlotte Lennox, and Maria Edgeworth discussed below, became crucially focused on the issue of women's economic survival. Since, realistically, this meant for most women attracting an economically stable mate, these mid- to late-century works are less critical of the marriage-market as a system than was the case with the earlier writers. These (and other) women writers of the period nevertheless paved the way for the great women novelists of the nineteenth century.

Margaret Doody has noted that while the period from the death of Richardson to Jane Austen has (until recently) been considered a "dead period" in English literary history, in fact it was a period in which "the paradigm for women's fiction of the nineteenth century" was being prepared; "to this enterprise . . . Jane Austen, Charlotte Brontë, and George Eliot are deeply indebted."[22] This paradigm is that of a woman of sense who is economically deprived, who seeks to establish her economic security—but not at any cost. She is usually paired with a more conventional female foil, often a sister, who is more of a flirtatious "belle" or coquette and/or who is a silly romantic, a girl of "sensibility" as opposed to sense. Jane Austen's title Sense and Sensibility (1811) highlights this contrast with two sisters, Elinor and Marianne Dashwood, representing sense and sensibility, respectively. While sensible characters like Elinor (and Elizabeth Bennet in Pride and Prejudice [1813]) make tart and ironic observations about various aspects of courtship mores, the marriage-market system itself remains the norm within which characters operate. "Sense" thus has become the facility of knowing how to operate in the system, how not to take risks, how to avoid becoming prey to rakes who would ruin one's marketability. Hyper-romantic heroines are criticized because their fantasies make them vulnerable to would-be rakes, blinding them to economic reality, a knowledge of which was crucial for their survival. Thus, while the Austenian novel of manners resembles the sentimentalist heroine's text in that both are concerned with the female protagonist's economic survival, it differs in that it has absorbed (in somewhat muted form) the active, satirical woman of sense created by the realist writers of the late seventeenth century. It also differs in other significant ways that I will not pursue here, such as being more secular in outlook (whereas the sentimentalist text inscribes uncritically a Christian world-view) and in using a comparatively plain style (the sentimentalists used a highly emotional, hyperbolic rhetoric).

Jane Spencer is right therefore to highlight Mary Davys's *Reform'd Coquet* (1724) as a harbinger of the Austenian novel of manners. The female protagonist is transformed in that work from being a silly coquet, blinded by romantic illusions and thus easily gulled by enterprising rakes, to a woman of sense. Once disabused of her wrongheaded notions she can marry a sensible husband, and thus her economic well-being is secure. (In her case, since she is already well-off, it is principally a matter of making sure that an inappropriate fortune-hunter not get her wealth.) The boisterous satire of marriage-marketing seen, however in Davys (particularly in her other works) and the other women writers of her era is no longer present in Austen, indeed is no longer prevalent after the 1720s.

It does, however, continue in selected works by Fielding, Lennox, and Edgeworth, whose versions of the women's anti-romance kept the tradition alive, if not flourishing. I have argued elsewhere that these women writers became an important source for the first significant American women's tradition, itself anti-romantic and realist, so their eclipse by sentimentalism was by no means total or permanent.[23]

Sarah Fielding's *The Adventures of David Simple* (1744), while largely a work of sentimentalist didacticism, includes an important woman of sense in Cynthia, who harks back to Jane Barker's Galesia. She provides a feminist critical perspective on women's lot. Like Barker and other predecessors, Fielding uses indirect discourse for ironic effect, as in the following autobiographical passage.

> I loved reading, and had a great Desire of attaining Knowledge; but whenever I asked questions of any kind whatsover, I was always told, *such Things are not proper for Girls of my age to know. If I was pleased with any Book above the most silly Story or Romance, it was taken from me. For Miss must not enquire too far into things, it would turn her Brain; she had better mind her Needlework, and such Things as were useful for Women; reading and poring on Books would never get me a Husband.*[24]

Cynthia especially resents the fact that her brother "hated reading to such a degree, that he had a perfect Aversion to the very Sight of a Book; and he must be cajoled or whipp'd into Learning, while it was denied me, who had the utmost Eagerness for it" (102). She had a close female friend who also loved reading but Cynthia's mother forbade them to spend too much time together. "My Mother was frighten'd out of her Wits, to think what would become of us, if we were much together. I verily believe, she thought we should draw *Circles*, and turn *Conjurers*" (107).

David Simple continues (via Cynthia) the extended critiques of the marriage-market rituals established as the dominant theme in the earlier women's realist tradition. When Cynthia's father decides she should be married, she remarks sarcastically that she hopes she will get to see her husband-to-be "at least an Hour before-hand" (107). When the selected future husband informs her that he and her father had agreed to the match, she retorts, "I did not know my Father . . . had any Goods to dispose of" (108). When the suitor reveals that he has a traditional concept of wifedom—she must keep house, etc.—she responds that she had "no Ambition to be his *upper Servant*" (109) and calls such an arrangement "*Prostitution.*" She also rejects the use of the wife as a status symbol, analogizing her to a "Horse who wears *gaudy Trappings* only to gratify his *Master's Vanity*" (110). Cynthia is punished for her rebelliousness. Her father disinherits her, and after he dies she must make her own way in the world. After various misfortunes, however, she finally inherits some money and marries the brother (Valentine) of her old friend Camilla, whom David, the novel's protagonist, marries.

Henrietta (1758) by Charlotte Lennox is another important novel (surprisingly neglected, however) whose "heroine" is a woman of sense struggling to survive economically and morally in a world where she is beset at every turn by conniving operators. Henrietta is contrasted to a female quixote type, Miss Woodby. Significantly, the satirized woman of sensibility is upper-class, which connects to the historical link between romance as a genre and the aristocracy. The novel as anti-romance has indeed been seen as reflecting a class clash between the emerging bourgeoisie and the aristocracy. Don Quixote in his adopted identity as knight is of the nobility, whereas Sancho is of the lower middle class and expresses its characteristically anti-romantic realism. In *Henrietta* a class distinction between the romantic figure (the woman of sensibility, Miss Woodby) and the realist cohort (the woman of sense, Henrietta) is evident.

When Henrietta first meets Miss Woodby in a stagecoach, the gentlewoman immediately perceives their relationship in terms of the literary romance. They must, she suggests, call each other Clelia and Celinda and consider that they have "contracted a violent friendship." Henrietta responds, "Call me what you please . . . but my name is Courtenay." Miss Woodby hopes aloud that her new friend does not have an "odious vulgar christian name; such as Molly, or Betty, or the like."[25] Later they discuss shepherds and shepherdesses, stock articles in the pastoral romance.

Henrietta acknowledges that when she was fourteen she had hoped to see one "in a fine green habit, all bedizened with ribbons" (1:72). The reality she found, however, was that "the shepherd was an old man in a ragged waistcoat . . . the shepherdess looked like a witch" (1:73).

Henrietta's sensible realism contrasts to Miss Woodby's sensibility; the latter trait proves to be so impractical as to be treacherous, and Henrietta learns that hardheaded perseverance is the primary means to survival. In the course of her trials Henrietta is reduced to working as a servant, perceived as a fate almost worse than death. Nevertheless, Henrietta has chosen a servant's life in preference to others even more disagreeable—being married to an evil rake or being confined in a convent—and therefore her voluntary servitude gives evidence of her basic integrity, as well as her fortitude. Her spirit of independence is seen in her proud comment: "since I have learned not to fear poverty, my happiness will never depend upon others" (2:123). And in her rejection of a disagreeable suitor, "if you had worlds to bestow on me, I would not be your wife" (2:158), Henrietta is another direct descendent of Galesia.

The first book-length satire of the "female quixote" was presented in Lennox's 1752 work of that title. This novel satirizes the seventeenth-century romances by de Scudéry and La Calprenède in much the same way that Cervantes had ridiculed *Amadís de Gaula* in *Don Quixote*. As in other quixote burlesques, the heroine, Arabella, steeped in the romances she has been reading, comes to see the world in their terms. She expects all men to behave as the heroes of romances, to contract "violent passion" for her, to write her secret gallant letters, to carve her initials on trees, etc. An assistant gardener, for example, is taken by Arabella to be a "Person of Quality" who has dressed up as a gardener in order to be near her. "She often wondered . . . that she did not find her Name carved on the trees . . . that he was never discovered lying along the Side of one of the little Rivulets, increasing the Stream with his Tears."[26]

Lennox's novel is especially important because its influence may be traced in a direct line to the American women's literary tradition. Its successor is Tabitha Tenney's *Female Quixotism* (1801), a popular American novel. This rollicking work recaptures the carnivalesque exuberance seen in the writings of the nineties generation.[27] The anti-romance mood is early established by the narrator:

> Now I suppose it will be expected that, in imitation of sister novel writers (for the ladies of late seem to have almost appropriated this department of writing) I should describe [Dorcasina, the heroine] as distinguished by the elegant form, delicately turned limbs, auburn hair, alabaster skin, heavenly languishing eyes, silken eyelashes, rosy cheeks, aquiline nose, ruby lips,

dimpled chin, and azure veins, with which almost all our heroines of romance are indiscriminately decorated. In truth she possessed few of those
beauties. . . . She was of a middling stature. . . . Her complexion was rather
dark; her skin somewhat rough; and features remarkable neither for beauty
nor deformity.[28]

Like other female quixotes Dorcasina shapes the world according to the
romance ideology she has imbibed from reading novels, and is slowly disabused of her fantasies by various sensible characters (including her servant Betty) and adventures.

Lennox also had a direct influence on Irish writer Maria Edgeworth,
who herself was perhaps the most important influence on American
women writers of the first half of the nineteenth century. As with her Irish
predecessor Mary Davys, the leverage point for Edgeworth's critical irony
is an ethnic Irish standpoint. In Edgeworth's case that standpoint merges
with a lower-class position and with a feminist viewpoint to provide a critique of upper-class English attitudes, mores, and behavior, which are
seen as pretentious, artificial, and destructive. The English—often absentee landlords—serve thus as *alazons* to the Irish *eirons*.

The latter role is taken by Thady Quirk, an "illiterate old steward," who
narrates *Castle Rackrent* (1800), Edgeworth's first and probably greatest
novel.[29] Thady speaks in a "vernacular idiom" (11) and from the point of
view of the Irish underclass in this satirical critique of the landlords (in
Ireland "rackrent" meant land rent paid to absentee landlords, a colonial
economic system). Thady is in fact a kind of Irish Sancho Panza who
ironizes the behavior of the dominant class, thus demythifying their pretenses at nobility and legitimacy.

Sandra Gilbert and Susan Gubar have suggested that *Castle Rackrent*
entails "a subversive critique of patriarchy."[30] Indeed, at times Thady does
express a kind of feminist critical irony; in particular in the satirical description of Miss Isabella Moneygawls, a pretentious sentimentalist, who
becomes the wife of Sir Connolly Rackrent. She is a reincarnation of the
female quixote, who threatens to faint at every step, wears a veil, uses pre-
cious sentimental language, and of course reads romances (*The Sorrows of
Young Werther* in her case).

Edgeworth also followed the anti-romance female quixote tradition in
her moral tale "Angelina; or l'Amie Inconnue." Here again the heroine imbibes romances to the point where she functions in their terms. Here as
well a contrast is drawn between a common-sense world, peopled by
provincials who speak in dialect and do not act like heroes in romances,
and those who engage in romantic pretenses. The climax is the meeting
between Angelina and Araminta, a woman she has known only through

gallant correspondence. Araminta turns out to be an unromantic, "coarse, masculine, brandy-loving creature, engaged to an equally coarse, vulgar man, Nat Gazebo," whose epistolary name had been Orlando. An aunt rescues Angelina from her folly and has her read *The Female Quixote* as penance.[31]

Edgeworth's debunking of romance preciosity, which she sees as English and upper-class, continues in *The Absentee* (1812). In this novel the upper-class establishment world of London society is satirized from the standpoint of the Irish outsider. The novel revolves around the figure of Lady Clonbrony, who has convinced her family to live in England, leaving behind their Irish homeland (and hence operating as "absentees") and denying their Irish heritage. Lady Clonbrony affects an English *haut monde* accent; one observer notes facetiously, "you *cawnt* conceive the *peens* she *teekes* to talk of the *teebles* and *cheers* . . . and with so much *teeste* to speak pure English."[32] Lady Clonbrony is struggling between two selves: one is her natural, "real," sensible Irish self; the other, her pretentious, novelesque, English self. In this sense she is another version of the female quixote. "A natural and unnatural manner seemed struggling in all her gestures . . . —a naturally free, familiar, good-natured, precipitate, Irish manner, had been schooled, and schooled late in life, into a sober, cold, still, stiff deportment, which she mistook for English" (5). Eventually she comes to her Irish senses, and the family returns to Ireland.

In Edgeworth, a political purpose of delegitimization is clearly at work—of both English and patriarchal dominance (one of the characters in *Castle Rackrent* is kept imprisoned in a room for several years by her husband, a signal instance of patriarchal oppression). Such delegitimization of dominant, oppressive ideologies and institutions is what the novel's demythification or *desengaños* process is all about.

To the extent that romance ideology worked as an opiate that prevented women from thinking critically and realistically about their situations, the women writers who took a stand against romance were furthering the feminist cause. But many women writers of the latter half of the eighteenth century may be faulted for encouraging a kind of conformist behavior. Particularly in the novels of manners of Fanny Burney and Jane Austen, the woman of sense has become the woman who best knows how to operate the marriage-market system to her advantage. Nevertheless, insofar as the women's resistance to female quixotism encouraged a strengthening of women's rational, critical faculties, it must be seen in positive terms.

In a recent analysis of Tenney's *Female Quixotism,* Sharon M. Harris suggests that it exhibits the carnivalesque satire lauded by Bakhtin in *Rabelais and His World.* Such satire, Harris notes, "exposes the two-world condition" of Western society where one has a culture of "officialdom and a world outside that officialdom, that is, a world of the people" (2). The carnivalesque undermines and delegitimizes the world of officialdom from the point of view of the marginalized—whether that marginalization be due to gender, class, or ethnicity. Women writers' early and long-standing critique of marriage-market rituals and continuing critique of the female quixote contributed to this project of destabilizing dominant and oppressive ideologies and institutions from the standpoint of the marginalized and oppressed.

Chapter Nine

Women and the
Latin Rhetorical Tradition

IN *THE DIALOGIC IMAGINATION*, MIKHAIL BAKHTIN notes that through much of Western history there has been a kind of linguistic dialectic between centripetal and centrifugal forces: the former tending toward a unitary "Cartesian," "official" language; the latter toward diffused regional dialects and vernaculars.[1] Underlying this linguistic struggle were imperialistic political movements—beginning with the Romans and continuing with the establishment of the modern nation-states—and regional resistances to them.

Throughout the Middle Ages and until the early modern period Latin was the language of the official culture. Vernaculars were unofficial, oral languages used in regional, rural, and domestic environments. Latin was employed in official institutions, such as the Church and the university. Walter J. Ong has noted that by the eighth century, C.E.,

> Learned Latin, which moved only in artificially controlled channels through the male world of the schools, was no longer anyone's mother tongue, in a quite literal sense. Although from the sixth or eighth century to the nineteenth Latin was spoken by millions of persons, it was never used by mothers cooing to their children. There was no Latin baby-talk or nursery language.[2]

Because they were barred from "the male world of the schools," women were in short denied access to the language of official culture for a very long time. Indeed, Ong points out that until the nineteenth century learning Latin meant entrance into the male-educated elite. Latin had become a "sex-linked language, a kind of badge of masculine identity" (250).

> Under these circumstances learning Latin took on the characteristics of a puberty rite, a *rite de passage* or initiation rite; it involved isolation from the family, the achievement of identity in a totally male group (the school), the learning of a body of relatively abstract tribal lore inaccessible to those outside the group. . . . The Latin world was a man's world. (251)

Women's exclusion from the language of official culture does much to explain why so few of them were writing during this period. Until serious written literature was being composed in the vernaculars (that is, until the fourteenth century) women were simply denied access to the modes of literary production. The gradual weakening of the Latin rhetorical influence was a major reason that women began to write.

The framed-novelle and the novel (along with the romance) were the first forms in Western prose fiction that did not require training in classical rhetoric. Ong theorizes that the characteristic conversational style of the novel is one of women's main contributions to the genre, deriving from their historical location in the unofficial world of oral, vernacular traditions. "Into the nineteenth century," Ong notes,

> most literary style throughout the west was formed by academic rhetoric . . . with one notable exception: the literary style of female authors. Of the females who became published authors, as many did from the 1600s on, almost none had any such training. . . . Women writers were no doubt influenced by works they had read emanating from the Latin-based, academic, rhetorical tradition, but they themselves normally expressed themselves in a different, far less oratorical voice, which had a great deal to do with the rise of the novel.[3]

Ong goes on to suggest that "a great gap in our understanding of the influence of women on literary genre and style could be bridged or closed through attention to the orality-literacy-print shift. . . . Certainly, non-rhetorical styles congenial to women writers helped make the novel what it is: more like a conversation than a platform performance" (159–60).

Women's struggle with and eventual repudiation of the Latin rhetorical tradition is an important but overlooked chapter in the history of the emergence of novelistic discourse. Paratactic syntax; the use of the plain style in prose (and its spin-off, the familiar "dashaway" epistolary mode); and the ironic use of indirect discourse or reported speech—the most important constituent elements of a prosaic stylistics—were all pioneered by and identified with early modern women writers.

In his survey of medieval women writers Peter Dronke notes the problematic relationship most of these women had with Latin rhetoric, because of their lack of training in it. Their Latin "may remain not only unclassical . . . but awkward or unclear."[4] Yet out of these "unconventional modes of Latin" (viii) emerged what is clearly an anti-theoretistic proclivity. In women's writing "there is," Dronke notes,

> more often than in men's writing, a lack of apriorism, of predetermined postures: again and again we encounter attempts to cope with human problems in their singularity—not imposing rules and categories from without, but seeking solutions that are apt and truthful existentially. (x)

In other words, these medieval women writers were inclined toward a novelistic prosaics, which suggests that the use of a nonclassical Latin may encourage a prosaic rhetoric.

One of the earliest of these women, the martyr Perpetua (d. 203 C.E.), known for her vivid account of her persecution and martyrdom, the "Acts of Perpetua" (*Passio SS. Perpetua et Felicitas*), wrote in a "colloqual and homely" style (Dronke 1). She "records her thoughts in an informal, graphic way . . . she is not striving to be literary" (6). In commenting on the same text Erich Auerbach notes, "there is no rhetorical art in Perpetua's narrative. . . . Her vocabulary is limited; her sentence structure is clumsy, the connectives (frequent use of *tunc* [then]) are not always clear. . . . [There are] many vulgarisms. . . . The language in general is brittle, quite unliterary, naïve, almost childlike."[5]

Subsequent medieval women writers similarly broke with classical Latin models. Hrotsvitha, an important tenth-century dramatist, had manifest difficulty with Latin construction and in a preface apologized for "the boorishness of my flawed style" (Dronke 69). Even the great Hildegarde of Bingen (1098–1179) wrote in a highly unorthodox Latin, "her command of Latin . . . [remaining] uncertain," according to Dronke (148). In a letter written in 1175 Hildegarde explained how she transcribed her visionary experience in immediate language without rhetorical embellishment:

> I am not educated, but I have simply been taught how to read. And what I write is what I see and hear in the vision. I compose no other words than those I hear, and I set them forth in unpolished Latin just as I hear them in the vision, for I am not taught in this vision to write as philosophers do.[6]

As Barbara Newman comments, "Hildegarde, despite her encyclopedic knowledge, never mastered Latin grammar well enough to write without a secretary to correct her cases and tenses" (23).

One senses, however, in Hildegarde's interesting comment not so much an expression of inferiority or inadequacy about her Latin constructions, but rather a rejection of the Latin tradition. "I am not taught . . . to write as philosophers do" certainly could be read as harboring a complaint about her lack of education but there is also a note of defiance; "I don't need Latin training," she seems to be saying, "because the authority of my vision is so compelling, it transcends such trivial concerns as grammar and syntax."

This ambivalence about the Latin rhetorical tradition continues in the women writers of the early modern period. On the one hand, they often apologize for their lack of Latinate sophistication; on the other hand, they often put down Latinate rhetoric as obfuscatory and mystifying. In a 1589 critique, for example, of John Lily's Latinate euphuistic style, "Jane Anger" (presumably a pseudonym) characterizes it as unnecessary and typically male bombast: "their minds are so carried away with the manner, as no care at all is had of the matter. They run so into rhetoric as often times they overrun the bounds of their own wits and go they know not whither."[7]

Beginning with Marguerite de Navarre, women writers seem to have consciously favored a non-Latinate, even an anti-Latinate rhetoric. Marguerite used a familiar, conversational plain style in the *Heptaméron*, and indeed specifically excluded the participation of men of letters from storytelling lest they engage in "rhetorical ornament [that] would . . . falsify the truth of the account" (69; see chapter three). Significantly, the first unauthorized editor of the *Heptaméron*, Pierre Boaistuau, took it upon himself to "correct" its style (as well as to eliminate the frame and devisants and to rearrange the order of the novellas). Correcting the style meant Latinizing it; imposing an "eloquent" style that was "ornamented with Latin turns of phrase."[8] In his preface to the work Boaistuau claimed he only "cleaned it up," correcting "an infinity of manifest errors" (xxxvii). But a modern critic has noted that Boaistuau employed a self-consciously Latinate syntax: "He affects certain turns and constructions inspired by Latin eloquence"; it is a "sinuous syntax" with "sentences studded with subordinate and relative propositions couched one upon another" (lxxii)—in other words, the hypotactic constructions of classical Latin.

Other early modern women writers explicitly reject Latin rhetoric. Margaret Cavendish is one of the most emphatic and insistent in her abjurement. In the Preface to her biography of her husband, *The Life of the Thrice Noble, High and Puissant Prince William Cavendish* (1667), Cavendish announces that she is "resolved to write, in a natural plain style, without Latin sentences."[9] Like Marguerite de Navarre and, to some extent, Hildegarde of Bingen, Cavendish sees rhetoric as obscuring the truth, not enhancing it. Her lack of education or training in what she calls "the rules" thus is seen as a virtue because it allows her to speak the truth directly without false ornamentation.

> When I first intended to write this History [biography of her husband], knowing my self to be no scholar, and as ignorant of the rules of writing histories, as I have in my other works acknowledged my self to be of the names and terms of art, I desired My Lord [her husband], that he would be pleased to let me have some elegant and learned historian to assist me. (9)

The duke, however, says he would have her write it in "my own plain style, without elegant flourishings, or exquisite method, relying intirely upon truth" (9). "[R]hetorick," he claims, "was fitter for falsehoods then [*sic*] truths" (9). Margaret follows his counsel and employs the non-Latinate, plain style in the work.

Elsewhere, she is even more emphatic in her repudiation of learned rhetoric. In her Preface to the *Sociable Letters,* for example, she offers this defiant apology for her style:

> [T]hey may say some Words are not Exactly Placed, which I confess to be very likely, and not only in that, but in all the rest of my Works there may be such Errors, for I was not bred in an University, or a Free-School, to learn the Art of Words; neither do I take it for a Disparagement of my Works, to have the Forms, Terms, Words, Numbers or Rymes found fault with . . . for I leave the Formal, or Worditive part to Fools, and the Material or Sensitive part to Wise Men. (C1ʳ)

While she similarly acknowledges in *Natures Pictures* that it is not "learned, studious, or methodical" (106), she nevertheless in that work has Jove throw into hell all works that are "Sophisterious, Tedious, Obscure, Pedanticall" (362).

Cavendish draws a clear distinction between what she calls the "Formal" or symbolic, on the one hand, and the "Material" or natural, on the other. The Formal aspects are the "rules" of rhetoric, logic, mathematics, which she has never learned; whereas the material or natural refers to the empirical aspects of reality available to the senses or to intuitional, Cartesian "reason." Like many women writers, Cavendish sees symbolic forms as impediments; she desires instead to connect to reality directly in as unmediated a way as possible. In my article "Ecofeminist Literary Criticism," I proposed that a number of later (nineteenth- and twentieth-century) women writers expressed a similar fear that figurative, symbolic representations obscure the literal, inscribing it in a dominative "chain of signifiers." Their own style, I contended, manifests an anti-theoretistic attempt to reconnect with the real, with the literal.[10] Cavendish's theory is strikingly similar to theirs.

In her "Epistle to the Reader" of her *Philosophical and Physical Opinions* (1663) she rearticulates her conception:

> It is Plain and Vulgarly Express'd, as having not so much Learning as to Puzle the Reader with Logistical, Metaphysical, Mathematical, or the like Terms; Wherefore you shall onely find therein Plain Sense and Reason, Plainly Declared, without Geometrical Demonstrations, Figures, Lines, and Letters; Nevertheless, since it concerns Sense and Reason in all Matter . . . it doth not Hinder or Obstruct.[11]

Cavendish elaborates that "Art proceeds from Nature, not Nature from Art, and Logick, Metaphysick, Mathematick, Chymistry, and the like" (b4^v)—a clear repudiation of deductive reasoning in favor of induction. Like Virginia Woolf she would "record the atoms as they fall upon the mind in the order in which they fall" (see chapter one). Unlike the formal branches of knowledge enumerated above, Cavendish claims, "my Philosophy doth not Obstruct Art" (c1^r).

In "Another Epistle to the Reader" in *Philosophical and Physical Opinions,* Cavendish amplifies, drawing a distinction between "Natural Philosphers" whose knowledge is derived from "the Clearest, Natural Observation, and the Least Artificial Learning" and "Scholars [who] are so in Love with Art, that they Despise or at least Neglect Nature" (d2^v). They thus fail to realize Cavendish's cardinal principle, which is that "Art proceeds from Nature, yet Nature doth not proceed from Art" (d2^r). Significantly, Cavendish's view of nature is animist (like the women artists I treat in "Ecofeminist Literary Criticism"); the literal is thus animated with a presence, and indeed much of Cavendish's writing is devoted to revealing the aliveness of the material world.

The gist of Cavendish's philosophy of style is given neatly in a 1653 poem:

> Give me a *Stile* that *Nature* frames, not *Art:*
> For *Art* doth seem to take the *Pedants* part.
> And that seemes *Noble,* which is *Easie, Free,*
> Not to be bound with ore-nice *Pedantry.*[12]

Cavendish was part of and contributed to the breakaway from classical rhetorical models and the transition to the "plain style" in prose that occurred during the seventeenth century. A number of factors encouraged the demise of classical rhetorical authority. The gradual replacement of literary patrons by capitalist booksellers as the primary source of remuneration for writers was one. Booksellers themselves generally had scanty classical training and were in any event primarily interested in marketing their products, not enforcing classical rules. They were quite willing to pander to a reading public that was by the turn of the seventeenth century increasingly dominated by women, who themselves, of course, knew little about and had little interest in Latin constructions.[13]

Another important factor in the transition to a non-Latinate rhetoric was the rise of the new scientific epistemology, the Baconian "new philosophy," which emphasized "the denotative function of language—'observation, fact-collecting, and classification.'"[14] Thomas Sprat called for the use of a plain simple prose in scientific treatises in his *History of the Royal Society* in 1667.

By then the battle had been joined between those who favored the use of classical rhetoric, the Ciceronian, "grand," or "Asiatic" style, exemplified by John Lily's *Euphues* and Sir Philip Sidney's *Arcadia,* and the anti-Ciceronians Montaigne and Bacon, who adopted a more conversational, less artificial rhetoric. Their style was "Senecan, terse, plain," as opposed to the "periodic, ornate" Ciceronianism (Adams 244).

One feature of the new style was the "loose period." Unlike the Ciceronian rounded period, which is hypotactic and subordinative, the loose period attempts

> to express . . . the order in which an idea presents itself when it is first experienced. It begins, therefore, without premeditation, stating its idea in the first form that occurs; the second member is determined by the situation in which the mind finds itself after the first has been spoken; and so on throughout the period, each member being an emergency of the situation.[15]

In the loose period, "everything was subordinated to the aim of expressing the ideas passing in the mind at the moment of writing" (Watt 194).

Such a stylistic method implies an inductive, empirical epistemology, in accordance with the seventeenth-century shift toward the experientially verifiable and away from received axioms as sources of truth. As Ian Watt notes, the novel was in part a response to these stylistic and philosophical shifts. "Previous literary forms had reflected the general tendency of their cultures to make conformity to traditional practice the major test of truth. . . . This literary traditionalism was first and most fully challenged by the novel, whose primary criterion was truth to individual experience" (13).

The loose period also allows for the relatively unmediated spontaneity that Cavendish (and Hildegarde of Bingen) saw as more truthful than labored artificial syntax. And it opened literary doors to uneducated outsiders because it required little or no rhetorical training to produce it. When used in an epistolary format, the loose period became known as the "dashaway" style. Its "breathless, disorganized, 'artless' informality" came to be identified as a feminine style.[16]

Samuel Richardson was perhaps the first male writer to capitalize on this "feminine" style in his novel *Pamela,* which became a model for subsequent writers, including Fanny Burney. Evelina's mentor enjoins her, for example, against writing letters that are "correct, nicely grammatical, and run in smooth periods." Rather, he urges her to "dash away, whatever comes uppermost" (Moers 97). Similarly, Anna Howe in Richardson's *Clarissa* "tells us that '*mere* scholars' too often 'spangle over their productions with *metaphors;* they rumble into *bombast . . .* ' while others 'sinking into the *classical* pits, there poke and scramble about, never seeking to show genius of their own.'"[17]

The demise of classical rhetorical authority also entailed the breakdown of the classical doctrine of separation of styles (*Stiltrennung*)—an issue that still greatly concerned theorists in the Renaissance and neoclassical periods. According to this Aristotelian doctrine, genres are ranked by the social class of the characters. The highest forms—tragedy and epic—dealt with royalty or the nobility; where comedy dealt with the middle and lower classes. The style of a work had similarly to correspond to the social level, with the grand style appropriate for tragedy and epic, and the low style for comedy. Under this doctrine the domestic world—women's everyday world—was not considered appropriate matter for serious literary attention, and thus a Bakhtinian prosaics—the kind of realism seen in the novel—is impossible in these genres, according to Aristotelian and neo-classical theory. Indeed, Erich Auerbach in *Mimesis* connects the breakdown of *Stiltrennung* with the rise of realism.[18] The novel thus represented a break with the classical doctrine of *Stiltrennung,* and it was so censured in the early years.

But women and others not trained in the classical tradition were advantaged by this development because it enabled them to use the plain style or low style to treat domestic matter seriously, and it freed them from the necessity of having to know classical "rules" in order to write. While the attempt to evaluate the novel in Aristotelian terms persisted—Samuel Johnson called it a "comedy of romance" and Henry Fielding "a comic epic in prose"—it was ultimately unsuccessful. Critical judgments on the novel could not be rooted in ancient authority. Women readers were known to be particularly receptive to nonclassical genres such as the heroic romance, the framed-novelle, and the novel, and as early as 1594, according to Torquato Tasso, defended them against the classicists.[19]

One of the characteristics of Ciceronian periodic rhetoric is its hypotactic syntax, as opposed to the parataxis seen in the low, familiar, or plain style with its loose period. Hypotaxis is a style or structure that involves subordination (it stems from the Greek *hypotassein* [to arrange under]), whereas parataxis entails a lateral, conjunctive, but nonsubordinative arrangement (from the Greek *paratassein* [to place side by side]). As Auerbach describes it, hypotaxis "looks at and organizes things from above" (*Mimesis* 62) unlike parataxis where no such subordination or ranking occurs. In his discussion of plot in the *Poetics,* Aristotle distinguishes between a complex *propter hoc* [because of which] plot and a simple *post hoc* [after which] pattern.[20] Hypotaxis corresponds to the former and parataxis the latter. Parataxis often proceeds by a string of *and*s or *then*s (Perpetua's style) where hypotaxis uses a lot of *that*s and *which*es.

The celebrated distinction Virginia Woolf made in *A Room of One's Own* between a "man's sentence" (79) and a woman's is largely a contrast between a hypotactic, Ciceronian period and paratactic syntax. Interestingly, in an earlier typescript version of *A Room* Woolf included as her example of a characteristically woman's sentence a Jane Austen passage that is strikingly paratactic. "She examined into their employments, looked at their work, & advised them to do it differently; found fault with the arrangement of the furniture, or detected the housemaid in negligence; & if she accepted any refreshment, seemed to do it only for the sake of finding out that Mrs. Collins's joints of meat were too large for her family."[21] This example was deleted for the published version of *A Room.*

Much oral literature is essentially paratactic in structure. As Walter J. Ong remarks in *Orality and Literacy* it tends to be "additive rather than subordinative" and "aggregative rather than analytic" (37–38). In an intriguing study of the thought-patterns of illiterate Russian peasants done in the 1930s, which Ong summarizes and Mary Belenky et al. refer to in *Women's Ways of Knowing* (1986), A. R. Luria notes that they exhibited an unfamiliarity with abstract analytical thought, such as the deductive syllogism, and use instead situational, pragmatic identifying patterns. Items are located in immediate operational contexts and not abstracted into generic categories (Ong 49–57). (Thus, when given four terms such as *hammer, saw, log, hatchet,* the illiterate subject would not group them under the generic term *tool,* excluding the log, but rather would envisage an operational narrative using the tools on the log [51]). While the latter provides for practical understanding, it does not allow for causal theorizing. Belenky et al. associate this kind of thinking with the extreme passivity of the disempowered.[22] For women such thinking does not allow them to name their pain or to theorize about its causes. Events are perceived to happen single file, as it were, one thing after another, in paratactic fashion.[23]

The women writers I treat in this study were not on the level of illiterate peasants because they were at least literate in the vernaculars (and some in Latin), but those who were not trained in the Latin tradition were inclined to use paratactic syntax. Indeed, in her study of seventeenth-century women poets Germaine Greer notes a pervasive use of paratactic syntactic patterns: "endless chains of clauses which may be related back and forwards with equal justification, rather than a hierarchy of main clauses with obvious subordinates."[24]

On the question of structure, however, the women writers treated here were torn between parataxis and hypotaxis. In fact, their structures appear to have been hypotactic to the extent that their feminist standpoint had crystalized. In the works of Christine de Pizan and María de Zayas, for example, a strong feminist thesis subordinates the inset material or novellas. At the same time one senses in Marguerite de Navarre, for example, a reluctance to subordinate everything to one governing thesis. A solution appears to have been reached by the later women writers in the framed-novelle tradition who reconceptualized the organizing principles of the genre. In particular, the British women (Cavendish, Manley, Barker, and Davys) came to focus on individual life-stories as their unifying plot. Episodes are arranged as "cases" or parts of a case that is designed to defend the woman; they are not ordered simply as one thing after another but are linked *propter hoc* to a feminist thesis or standpoint.

Those women trained in Latin rhetoric—for example Christine de Pizan and (perhaps) Jeanne Flore—do exhibit hypotactic syntax. The former, although one of the first to write a serious treatise in a vernacular language, used "Latin prose as her model, [employing] complicated periodic syntax," according to a recent translator.[25] Similarly, although Jeanne Flore apologized for her "rude and poorly managed language," a modern editor, Michel LeGuern considers the *Comptes amoureux* the work of a person trained in the classical tradition. The structure of the stories is not based on an "and-then" sequence but rather is organized hypotactically according to the principle of causality.[26]

LeGuern, correctly I believe, contrasts Flore to Marguerite de Navarre in this respect. Where Marguerite's stories unfold paratactically—one thing after another—with the thesis extracted metanarratively; in the *Comptes amoureux* the thesis is built into the story at the beginning, so that the story works to exemplify the thesis. In story number three, for example, which concerns an adolescent married to a decrepit elderly man after she has "scorned" Love by holding herself aloof from several youthful suitors, the deity's vengeance is introduced causally at the beginning of the story: "Cupid . . . not having forgotten the irreverence which she displayed toward him" ["non ayant mis en oubly l'irreverence que celle luy portoit" (159)], takes action. The rest of the story then flows from this cause, and acts as an exemplum of the thesis that you cannot scorn Love.

As a genre the framed-novelle is an interesting combination of paratactic and hyptactic structures, as Katherine S. Gittes points out in her study of the genre's history.[27] The stories are arranged paratactically but the frame can (but does not always) provide a unifying hypotaxis. Indeed, the genre seems to teeter between a centripetally ordered work and one that has yielded to centrifugal forces; providing a kind of synecdoche of the centripetal-centrifugal tension that underlies much of Western Europe's cultural history, as noted by Bakhtin. Where Bakhtin champions the novel as the form that retains a locus of resistance to the "centripetal forces in socio-linguistic and ideological life" (271) because of its "heteroglossia," which effects the work of "decentralization and disunification" (272); in fact, as Bakhtin himself acknowledges, the novel "combin[es] these subordinated, yet still relatively autonomous, unities . . . into the higher unity of the work as a whole" (262). It is really the framed-novelle that retains the resistance to dominative subordination that Bakhtin extols in the novel. Its paratactic character may well be another reason, as we suggested in chapter three, that women writers were attracted to the genre.

After Marguerite de Navarre, women writers in this tradition generally used a familiar paratactic, conversational style. Margaret Cavendish's style is determinedly paratactic and "dashaway." It is characterized by a heavy use of *asyndeton* (omission of conjunctions) as well as *polysyndeton* (repetition of conjunctions), characteristics of a paratactic style. As Mary Hyatt notes in her study of women's style, these devices "indicate a lack of subordination."

> A predilection for polysyndeton lessens the opportunity for grammatical subordination, for if a string of items is joined equally by the same connective, there can be no hierarchical value assigned to the items. And the emphasis is . . . of unpredictability, for the reader does not know when the list will end. But it is also the emphasis of *sameness*. The effect is often one of childishness and naiveté simply because no judgment is being made about the relative importance of the items.[28]

An example of Cavendish's use of asyndeton follows. Note, however, how she uses it to establish an ironic tone, which enables the expression of her (feminist) standpoint. This passage, which is very typical of Cavendish's style, occurs in "The Discreet Virgin," a feminist novella in *Natures Pictures*:

> [A]nd do not Men take more delight in idle pastimes, and foolish sports, than Women: and in all this time of their visiting, club, gossiping, news, travelling, news venting, news making, vain spending, mode fashioning, foolish quarrelling, and unprofitable journeying, what advantage do they bring to the Commonwealth [?][29]

The cumulative effect of this catalog of men's "idle pastimes" is satirical and has the effect of undercutting masculine authority, which is the point of the story. Thus, here we see parataxis, but being used to a coherent political effect.

By the 1690s women writers were beginning to realize some of the limitations of a strictly paratactic structure. Delarivier Manley in her preface to *The Secret History of Queen Zarah* criticizes romances for their failure to concentrate on "*one Principal Event*"; they "*overcharge* [the work] *with* Episodes."[30] At the same time Manley urges the use of natural conversation; "for if it be the *Heroe that speaks, then he ought to express himself Ingeniously, without affecting any Nicety of Points or Syllogisms, because he speaks without any Preparation*" (1:a4^{v}). And, although the body of the work may be written "in a more nice language," Manley stipulates, conversations of characters *"ought to be writ after an easie and free Manner; Fine Expressions and Elegant Turns agree little to the Stile of Conversation whose Principal Ornament consists in the Plainness, Simplicity, Free and Sincere Air*" (1:a5^{r}).

Mary Davys also indicates a concern about plot unity in various theoretical statements. In her important Preface to the *Works* (1725), she argues that one of the advantages of fictional "invention" is that it allows one to better order episodes than as they occur in reality, randomly and by happenstance: it "*gives us room to order Accidents better than Fortune.*"[31] "*This I have endeavour'd to do,*" she claims. "*I have in every Novel propos'd one entire Scheme or Plot, and the other adventures are only incident or collateral to it; which is the great Rule prescribed by the Criticks*" (1:v). The great rule is, of course, the Aristotelian one of plot unity.

Davys's theory thus heralds the novel, where there is generally "one entire scheme or plot" with all episodes subordinate in one way or another to it—a hypotactic arrangement. Davys's awareness of and concern about narrative structure is also expressed, as we have noted, in *The Lady's Tale* and *The Merry Wanderer* (see chapter six). And, although she puts down pedantic use of "*Greek* and *Latin* Motto's" in her Introduction to *The Reform'd Coquet,*[32] both *The Accomplished Rake* and *The Reform'd Coquet* are distinguished by their plot unity and coherence.

It may be that Davys was in this influenced by Mary Astell, who is said to have mastered "the art of eloquence" with a "bold invasion of the masculine stronghold of traditional rhetoric."[33] Her treatises were carefully organized according to classical rhetorical doctrine (99), but her principal rhetorical theory derived from Descartes and other Cartesian rhetoricians, who maintained that rational order is something that is innate in the mind, and therefore one has only to look within rather than to classical models to discover the elusive "rules" that so exercised Margaret Cavendish.

As Astell states in her *Serious Proposal:* "And since Truth is so near at hand . . . we are not oblig'd to tumble over many Authors . . . but may have it for enquiring after in our own Breasts" (as cited in Sutherland, 106). She continues, "All have not leisure to Learn Languages and pore on Books, nor Opportunity to Converse with the Learned; but all may *Think*, may use their own Faculties rightly, and consult the Master who is within them" (106). Like Cavendish, Astell concludes that "Nature . . . instruct[s] us in Rhetoric much better than Rules of Art, which if they are good ones are nothing else but those Judicious Observations which Men of Sense have drawn from Nature" (110). The only difference is that the Nature Astell is speaking of is "Nature methodized," to use Pope's term, a nature that is in the rationalist world-view of Newtonian and Cartesian mechanism itself classically ordered and unified.

Women writers thus struggled with the conflicting claims of hypotaxis and parataxis. They were, of course, influenced by the philosophical currents of their day, moving in the early eighteenth century away from the more paratactic structure of the framed-novelle toward the more hyptactic organization of the novel; Jane Barker being the last to manifest a strong attachment to the former. To the extent that hypotaxis is a subordinative dominative mode this abandonment of the framed-novelle structure may have been unfortunate. However, variations of the genre have resurfaced from time to time—for example, Sarah Orne Jewett's *The Country of the Pointed Firs* (1896). And it may be that we are now seeing a revival of the form with works like Julia Voznesenskaya's *The Women's Decameron* (1985), Whitney Otto's *How to Make an American Quilt* (1991), or Monique Wittig's *Les Guérillères* (1969), which Rachel Blau DuPlessis cites as an example of "radical parataxis," a form of "verbal quilt . . . everything joined with no subordination, no ranking."[34]

The final non-Latinate device seventeenth-century women writers helped to pioneer, undoubtedly contributing to its pervasive use in the novel, was the practice of indirect discourse, overheard or reported speech, the *style indirect libre.* We noted in chapter two an important instance of its use in Cavendish's *Sociable Letters* in which she ironically reports the conversation of the pundits about the origins of the universe. The inherent irony in indirect discourse, as seen in the Cavendish and other examples, did much to establish the novel's inherently ironic mood.

As Ann Banfield notes, indirect discourse or what she calls represented speech, was largely unknown in Latin texts; there are few, if any, examples of it in classical or medieval literature.[35] While the form has an oral context, a conversation, and in this way connects to oral culture, it is, according to Banfield, a strictly literary form, reflecting the advent of a literate culture; it is a "novelistic" device (241). While Jane Austen is often thought to have invented it, as I have indicated throughout this study, it was widely and effectively deployed by women writers over a century before her.

In his discussion in *The Rape of Clarissa* of the language used by Richardson's heroine Pamela, Terry Eagleton accentuates the political significance of the novel's rhetorical modes. By monitoring the transformation of her diction, one can trace Pamela's political subdual. In part two, "Pamela the pert colloquialist has become Pamela the genteel housewife—tirelessly producing anonymous platitudes." The transformation of her rhetoric indicates her "linguistic absorption into the ruling class," her domination as "collusive victim of patriarchy."[36]

The "epistemic choices"—to use Richard Ohmann's characterization of writers' prose styles[37]—made by the women writers of the early modern period were in part a result of practical pressures and in part similarly a manifestation of their own political position. The practical factors included the fact that, having been excluded from training in official Latin modes for centuries, women had no recourse but to use the vernacular, oral modes they knew.

It may also be that these and other women's inclination toward parataxis may have been rooted in their own domestic material practices, in use-value production, which does not entail a rigidly hierarchical division of labor. In their personal domestic practice these women performed a variety of tasks sequentially but none of these was necessarily given priority (unlike in exchange-value production where intellectual and manual labor are separated with the former held in higher esteem and with labor acutely specialized and repetitive). Cavendish's equation of spinning and writing, which we discussed earlier, suggests a refusal to rank one above the other. And Jane Barker's *Patch-Work Screen*, in which no ranking is given to the different patches, which are labor products, also suggests an aesthetic based on the nonhierarchical character of use-value production. While most of the women in this study were of the upper ranks in a highly stratified society, their own personal labor was production for use, as characterized above. To the extent that one's material practices impinge on one's epistemology and one's aesthetics (as held in Marxist theory), such nonhierarchical labor may have influenced their rhetorical modes, their epistemic choices.

Beyond this, it is clear that these women's political location in the unofficial margins and their resentment of and resistance to such subordination were determining factors in the epistemic choices they as a group made. Their style—characterized as we have seen by paratactic syntax, the plain style in prose, and the ironic use of indirect discourse (all non- or anti-Latinate forms)—reflects a political resistance both to their domination by official cultures and to hierarchical subordination. In this way, the rhetorical modes that characterized this body of women's writing provided a resistance to the official "word of the fathers," thereby enriching the subversive prosaics of the early modern era, which paved the way for the rise of the novel.

Conclusion

Had she been born in 1827, Dorothy Osborne would have written novels; had she been born in 1527, she would never have written at all, but she was born in 1627, and at that date though writing books was ridiculous for a woman there was nothing unseemly in writing a letter. And so by degrees the silence is broken.

—Virginia Woolf
"Dorothy Osborne's *Letters*"[1]

THIS BOOK HAS ATTEMPTED TO CHART THE DEGREES by which Western women's literary silence was broken. Woolf dates the emergence of the middle-class woman writer to the end of the eighteenth century, an event she considers "of greater importance than the Crusades or the War of the Roses. . . . For if *Pride and Prejudice* matters, and *Middlemarch* and *Villette* and *Wuthering Heights* matter, then it matters . . . that women generally . . . took to writing."[2]

In this study I have traced the origins of women's literary writing in the West back much farther than the end of the eighteenth century, and have claimed implicitly that not only do *Pride and Prejudice* and *Middlemarch* matter; so too do the *Heptaméron* by Marguerite de Navarre, the *Novelas amorosas* by María de Zayas, the *Sociable Letters* by Margaret Cavendish, *The Fugitive* by Mary Davys, and *A Patch-Work Screen for the Ladies* by Jane Barker—and many more.

In their pioneering works not only did these women break women's literary silence, they also articulated a feminist position or standpoint in one of the greatest dialogues in Western history, the *querelle des femmes*. In expressing a critical position against abusive and pejorative treatment of women—realized through modes of critical irony, satire, and burlesque— these women contributed to the subversive antiauthoritarianism of the early modern period that helped to define the novel's ethos. In their use of casuistry to particularize individual women's realities, these women encouraged attention to the detailed circumstances of individual lives, which helped to shape the novel's prosaics; its dense, anti-theoretistic and ultimately subversive realism.

The ethical hope behind such realistic presentations is that, as Iris Murdoch pointed out,

> the more the separateness and differentness of other people is realized, and the fact seen that another . . . has needs and wishes as demanding as one's own, the harder it is to treat a person as a thing.[3]

These women hoped to establish through their literary presentations the awareness that women were people, not things; that they were subjects of needs and desires, not objects to be used for others' purposes.

As noted in the beginning of this study, neocasuistry is an important branch of contemporary ethics. It is premised on the idea that focusing attention on an individual's reality helps to foster ethical awareness of that individual. In *The Waves*, perhaps Virginia Woolf's greatest novel, one character muses, "I am no mystic; something always plucks at me—curiosity, envy, admiration, interest in hairdressers and the like bring me to the surface."[4] It is this aesthetic and ethical attitude—interest in hairdressers and the like—that characterizes the novel's prosaics. The women writers of the early modern period contributed much to its emergence in Western culture.

Notes

Introduction

1. See Josephine Donovan, "From Avenger to Victim: Genealogy of a Renaissance Novella," *Tulsa Studies in Women's Literature* 15, no. 2 (1996): 248 n. 1. For a similar definition, see Ruth Perry, *The Celebrated Mary Astell* (Chicago: University of Chicago Press, 1986), pp. 17–18; also, Constance Jordan, *Renaissance Feminism* (Ithaca: Cornell University Press, 1990), pp. 2–9.

   The term *early modern*, which I use throughout, is also an imperfect designation, but I think the best currently available. See Heather Dubrow, "The Term *Early Modern*," *PMLA* 109, no. 5 (Oct. 1994):1025–26.
2. [Margaret Cavendish], the Lady Newcastle, *Poems, and Fancies* (London: J. Martin and J. Allestrye, 1653), p. A3ᵛ.
3. Predecessors here include especially Jane Spencer, *The Rise of the Woman Novelist* (Oxford: Blackwell, 1986); Dale Spender, *Mothers of the Novel* (London: Pandora, 1986); Joan DeJean, *Tender Geographies: Women and the Origins of the Novel in France* (New York: Columbia University Press, 1991); and John J. Richetti, *Popular Fiction before Richardson*, rev. ed. (Oxford: Oxford University Press, 1992).
4. See especially Spencer, *Rise of the Woman Novelist*, and Richetti, *Popular Fiction*.

Chapter One

1. Georg Lukács, *The Theory of the Novel* (1920; Cambridge: MIT Press, 1971), p. 88.
2. Ian Watt, *The Rise of the Novel* (Berkeley: University of California Press, 1957), p. 15. Further references follow in the text.
3. Clara Reeve, *The Progress of the Novel* (New York: Facsimile Text Society, 1930), p. 111.
4. Arthur Herrold Teije, *The Theory of Characterization in Prose Fiction Prior to 1740*, University of Minnesota Studies in Language and Literature, no. 5 (1916), pp. 16–18.
5. [Delarivier Manley], "To the Reader," *The Secret History of Queen Zarah, and the Zarazians* in *The Novels of Mary Delariviere Manley*, ed. Patricia Koster.

2 vols. (Gainesville, Fla.: Scholars' Facsimiles & Reprints, 1971), 1:A5ʳ. Further references follow in the text.

6. Gary Saul Morson and Caryl Emerson, *Mikhail Bakhtin: Creation of a Prosaics* (Stanford: Stanford University Press, 1990), p. 33. Further references follow in the text.

7. [Margaret Cavendish], the Marchioness of Newcastle, *CCXI Sociable Letters* (1664; facsimile reprint, Menston, England: Scholar Press, 1969), p. 257.

8. [Margaret Cavendish], the Lady Marchioness of Newcastle, *Natures Pictures Drawn by Fancies Pencil to the Life* (London: J. Martin and J. Allestrye, 1656), p. 349. Further references follow in the text.

9. M. M. Bakhtin, *The Dialogic Imagination,* ed. Michael Holquist (Austin: University of Texas Press, 1981), p. 20. Further references follow in the text.

10. An interesting theory proposed by Giovanni Dotoli, *Letteratura per il popolo in Francia (1600–1750)* (Fasano, Italy: Schena, 1991) is that the formation of the nation-state during the seventeenth century required the extirpation of regionalist, folk loyalties, many of which were ancient traditions connected to women. The forces of modernity too worked to marginalize these feminine, folk traditions. See also Benedetta Craveri, "Women in Retreat," *New York Review of Books,* 19 December 1991.

In various works, especially *Rabelais and His World* (Bloomington: Indiana University Press, 1984), Bakhtin locates the resistance to translocal officialdom in folk traditions of parody. Joan DeJean in *Tender Geographies* details French women's resistance to the absolutism of Louis XIV (though these were aristocratic women, not "folk" women), which is seen in some of their literature.

Certainly, several English women writers took aim at the political machinations of early modern statecraft, particularly Delarivier Manley in her romans à clef. See Catherine Gallagher, "Embracing the Absolute: The Politics of the Female Subject in Seventeenth-Century England," *Genders* 1 (Spring 1988):24–39, and Jerry C. Beasley, "Politics and Moral Idealism: The Achievement of Some Early Women Novelists," in *Fetter'd or Free: British Women Novelists, 1670–1815,* ed. Mary Anne Schofield and Cecelia Macheski (Athens: Ohio University Press, 1986), pp. 216–36.

11. See especially G. A. Starr, *Defoe and Casuistry* (Princeton, N.J.: Princeton University Press, 1971).

12. Mikhail Bakhtin, *Problems of Dostoievsky's Poetics* (n. p.: Ardis, 1973), p. 47. Further references follow in the text.

13. Iris Murdoch, *Metaphysics as a Guide to Morals* (New York: Penguin, 1992), p. 196. Further references follow in the text.

14. Iris Murdoch, *The Sovereignty of Good* (New York: Schocken, 1971), p. 66. Further references follow in the text.

15. Simone Weil, "Reflections on the Right Use of School Studies with a View to the Love of God," in *The Simone Weil Reader,* ed. George A. Panichas (New York: David McKay, 1977), p. 51.

16. Iris Murdoch, "The Sublime and the Beautiful Revisited," *Yale Review* 69 (Dec. 1959): 257.

17. Iris Murdoch, "The Sublime and the Good," *Chicago Review* 13 (Autumn 1959):51, 54.

18. Martha C. Nussbaum, *Poetic Justice* (Boston: Beacon Press, 1995), p. xvii. Further references follow in the text.

19. Margaret Anne Doody, *The True Story of the Novel* (New Brunswick, N.J.: Rutgers University Press, 1996), p. 441. Further references follow in the text.

20. Margaret Anne Doody, "Women's Novels and the Femaleness of the Novel," *The World and I,* November 1987, 366, 370.

21. Josephine Donovan, "Everyday Use and Moments of Being: Toward a Nondominative Aesthetic," in *Aesthetics in Feminist Perspective,* ed. Hilde Hein and Carolyn Korsmeyer (Bloomington: Indiana University Press, 1993), pp. 53–67.

22. Virginia Woolf, *A Room of One's Own* (New York: Harcourt, 1957), p. 25. Further references follow in the text.

23. Virginia Woolf, "Modern Fiction," *Collected Essays,* vol. 2 (London: Hogarth Press, 1966), p. 107.

24. Josephine Donovan, "Ecofeminist Literary Criticism: Reading the Orange," *Hypatia* 11, no. 2 (1996):161–84.

25. Sarah Orne Jewett, *Sarah Orne Jewett Letters,* ed. Richard Cary (Waterville, Maine: Colby College Press, 1967), p. 120.

26. On Gnosticism in Existentialist literature see Josephine Donovan, *Gnosticism in Modern Literature* (New York: Garland, 1990); for critiques of poststructuralism from the point of view suggested here, see Carol Bigwood, *Earth Muse* (Philadelphia: Temple University Press, 1993); Murdoch, *Metaphysics as a Guide to Morals,* and Doody, *The True Story of the Novel.*

27. Carol Gilligan, *In a Different Voice* (Cambridge: Harvard University Press, 1982), p. 19.

28. Catherine Gallagher, *Nobody's Story* (Berkeley: University of California Press, 1994), pp. 166–75.

29. Emile V. Telle, *L'Oeuvre de Marguerite d'Angoulême, Reine de Navarre et la querelle des femmes* (Toulouse: Lion et Fils, 1937), p. 75. My translation.

30. Marie de Gournay, *Egalité des hommes et des femmes; Grief des dames; suivi du Proumenoir de Monsieur de Montaigne,* ed. Constant Venesoen (Geneva: Droz, 1993), p. 85. My translation.

31. María de Zayas, *The Enchantments of Love,* trans. H. Patsy Boyer (Berkeley: University of California Press, 1990), p. xvii; Zayas, *Parte segunda del Sarao y entretenimiento honesto [Desengaños amorosos],* ed. Alicia Yllera (Madrid: Cátedra, 1983), p. 118.

32. [Margaret Cavendish], the Duchess of Newcastle, Preface, *Natures Picture* [*sic*] *Drawn by Fancies Pencil to the Life,* 2d ed. (London: A. Maxwell, 1671), p. C1^r.

33. See Josephine Donovan, *Uncle Tom's Cabin: Evil, Affliction, and Redemptive Love* (Boston: Twayne, 1991).

Chapter Two

1. Douglas Hay, as cited in Ellen Pollak, "*Moll Flanders*, Incest, and the Structure of Exchange," *Eighteenth Century* 30, no. 1 (1989): 9.
2. See ibid., and chapter five.
3. Ibid., p. 7
4. Georg Lukács, *History and Class Consciousness* (Cambridge: MIT Press, 1971), p. 166. Further references follow in the text.
5. Catharine A. MacKinnon, "Sexuality, Pornography, and Method: 'Pleasure under Patriarchy," in *Feminism and Philosophy*, ed. Nancy Tuana and Rosemarie Tong (Boulder: Westview, 1995), p. 135.
6. Karl Marx, Preface to *A Contribution to the Critique of Political Economy* (1859), in *Karl Marx: Selected Writings*, ed. David McLellan (Oxford: Oxford University Press, 1977), p. 389.
7. Nancy C. M. Hartsock, "The Feminist Standpoint: Developing the Ground for a Specifically Feminist Historical Materialism," in *Discovering Reality*, ed. Sandra Harding and Merrill B. Hintikka (Dordrecht: Reidel, 1983), p. 303.
8. Josephine Donovan, "Women and the Rise of the Novel: A Feminist-Marxist Theory," *Signs* 16, no. 3 (1991): 441–62. Portions of the remainder of this chapter were originally presented in a somewhat different form in this article. ©1991 by the University of Chicago.
9. Lucien Goldmann, *Pour une sociologie du roman* (Paris: Gallimard, 1964), pp. 21–57. Further references follow in the text. My translations throughout.
10. Alice Walker, "Everyday Use," in *Women and Fiction*, ed. Susan Cahill (New York: New American Library, 1975), pp. 364–72.
11. M. M. Bakhtin, *The Dialogic Imagination*, ed. Michael Holquist (Austin: University of Texas Press, 1981), pp. 30–31. Further references follow in the text.
12. Maurice Z. Shroder, "The Novel as a Genre" (1963), in *The Novel: Modern Essays in Criticism*, ed. Robert Murray Davis (Englewood Cliffs, N.J.: Prentice-Hall, 1969), pp. 43–58.
13. John J. Richetti, *Popular Fiction before Richardson*, rev. ed. (Oxford: Oxford University Press, 1992), p. 259. Further references follow in the text.
14. Jane Barker, *A Patch-Work Screen for the Ladies; Or, Love and Virtue Recommended* (1723; facsimile reprint, New York: Garland, l973), p. 7. Further references follow in the text.
15. [Margaret Cavendish], the Marchioness of Newcastle, *CCXI Sociable Letters* (1664; facsimile reprint, Menston, England: Scholar Press, 1969), pp. 311–12. Further references follow in the text.
16. [Margaret Cavendish], the Lady Newcastle, *Poems, and Fancies* (London: J. Martin and J. Allestrye, 1653), p. A5^r. Further references follow in the text.
17. Ruth Perry, *Women, Letters, and the Novel* (New York: AMS Press, l980), pp. 50, 52.
18. Judith Lowder Newton, *Women, Power, and Subversion: Social Strategies in British Fiction, 1778 - 1860* (Athens: University of Georgia Press, 1981), p. 10.

19. V. N. Vološinov, *Marxism and the Philosophy of Language*, 2d ed., trans. Ladislav Metejka and I. R. Titunik (New York and London: Seminar Press, 1973), pp. 141 n. 1, 144.

20. Gary Saul Morson, "Tolstoy's Absolute Language," in *Bakhtin: Essays and Dialogues on His Work*, ed. Gary Saul Morson (Chicago: University of Chicago Press, 1986), p. 130.

21. [Margaret Cavendish], the Lady Marchioness of Newcastle, "To the Two Universities," *Philosophical and Physical Opinions* (London: J. Martin and J. Allestrye, 1655), p. B2^v.

22. [Delarivier Manley], *The Adventures of Rivella* (1714; facsimile reprint, New York: Garland, 1972), pp. 53–57, 72–81. Further references follow in the text.

23. Nancy K. Miller, *The Heroine's Text: Readings in the French and English Novel, 1722–1782* (New York: Columbia University Press, 1980).

24. Erich Auerbach, *Zur Technik der Frührenaissancenovelle in Italien und Frankreich*, 2d ed. (Heidelberg: Carl Winter, 1971), p. 31. My translation.

Chapter Three

Note: An earlier version of this and the next chapter appeared as "Women and the Framed-Novelle: A Tradition of Their Own," *Signs* 22, no. 4 (Summer 1997). ©1997 by the University of Chicago.

1. Robert J. Clements and Joseph Gibaldi, *Anatomy of the Novella* (New York: New York University Press, 1977), p. 183. Further references follow in the text.

2. Victor Shklovsky, *Theory of Prose*, trans. Benjamin Sher (Elmond Park, Ill.: Dalkey Archive Press, 1990), pp. 65–71.

3. Gary Saul Morson and Caryl Emerson, *Mikhail Bakhtin: Creation of a Prosaics* (Stanford: Stanford University Press, 1990), p. 274.

4. See Katherine S. Gittes, *Framing the Canterbury Tales* (Westport, Conn.: Greenwood, 1991).

5. See Erich Auerbach, *Zur Technik der Frührenaissancenovelle in Italien und Frankreich*, 2d ed. (Heidelberg: Carl Winter, 1971), pp. vi, 19–20, 24–28; Patricia Francis Cholakian, *Rape and Writing in the "Heptaméron" of Marguerite de Navarre* (Carbondale: Southern Illinois University Press, 1991), pp. 7, 105; Janet M. Ferrier, *Forerunners of the French Novel* (Manchester, England: Manchester University Press, 1954), pp. 5, 26; Margaret Schlauch, *Antecedents of the English Novel 1400–1600 (From Chaucer to Deloney)* (Warsaw: PWN Polish Scientific Publishers; London: Oxford University Press, 1963), pp. 101, 123, 138.

6. For more on these transitions see Charles C. Mish, "English Short Fiction in the Seventeenth Century," *Studies in Short Fiction* 6 (1968–69): 247–59, 279–316; B. G. MacCarthy, *The Female Pen* (1946–47; reprint, New York: New York University Press, 1994), pp. 126–29; Corradina Caporello-Sykeman, *The Boccaccian Novella* (New York: Peter Lang, 1990), pp. 2–5.

7. It is appears likely that Bakhtin had not read even the best known of these works, the *Heptaméron*. In *Rabelais and His World* (Bloomington: Indiana University Press, 1984), he dismisses it as an expression of "official" court society (184, 138–39), contrasted to the folk "marketplace" or "billingsgate" roots of Rabelais's work. In fact, several of the *Heptaméron* stories exhibit the scatological humor that Bakhtin so admires in Rabelais as subversive; and many of the stories deal with peasants and the middle classes, which suggests that Bakhtin had not in fact read the *Heptaméron*.

The frame characters in the *Heptaméron* are aristocrats, but their discussion, which expresses a number of different points of view, is by no means a monolithic representation of upper-class interests. Indeed, the intellectual depth of their discussion is an aspect of dialogic discourse that Bakhtin neglects. In *Rabelais and His World*, in particular, Bakhtin's conception of the dialogic becomes a somewhat adolescent "in-your-face" anti-intellectualism. The concept itself would have been considerably enriched had he relied more upon Marguerite de Navarre than on Rabelais.

8. M. M. Bakhtin, *The Dialogic Imagination*, ed. Michael Holquist (Austin: University of Texas Press, 1981), p. 342. Further references follow in the text.

9. Walter J. Ong, *Orality and Literacy* (London: Routledge, 1988), p. 103; Margaret J. M. Ezell, *Writing Women's Literary History* (Baltimore: Johns Hopkins University Press, 1993), pp. 37–38, 55–57; Clements and Gilbaldi, *Anatomy*, pp. 5–6.

10. Lewis Hyde, *The Gift* (New York: Vintage, 1983), p. 51.

11. Juliet Mitchell, *Psychoanalysis and Feminism* (New York: Vintage, 1975), p. 408. Emphasis in original.

12. Elizabeth C. Goldsmith, *"Exclusive Conversations"* (Philadelphia: University of Pennsylvania Press,1988), p. 11.

13. [Margaret Cavendish], the Lady Marchioness of Newcastle, *Natures Pictures Drawn by Fancies Pencil to the Life* (London: J. Martin and J. Allestrye, 1656), p. 104.

14. Cholakian, *Rape and Writing*, p. 217. Further references follow in the text.

15. The editor of the most recent critical edition of her work, Constant Venesoen (see chap. 1, n. 30) says she was familiar with both of their works.

16. Domna C. Stanton, "Women as Object and Subject of Exchange: Marie de Gournay's *Le Proumenoir* (1594)," *L'Esprit créateur* 23, no. 2 (1983): 17. Further references follow in the text.

17. Giovanni Boccaccio, *Il Decameron* (Turin: Guilio Einaudi, 1966), p. 157; *The Decameron*, trans. Richard Aldington (New York: Dell, 1966), p. 167. Further references follow in the text.

18. Mihoko Suzuki, "Gender, Power, and the Female Reader: Boccaccio's *Decameron* and Marguerite de Navarre's *Heptameron*," *Comparative Literature Studies* 30, no. 3 (1993): 232.

19. Madeleine Jeay, ed., *Les Évangiles des quenouilles*, (Paris: J. Vrin; Montréal: Presses Universitaires de Montréal, 1985), p. 77. Further references follow in the text. My translations throughout.

20. See Denis Baril, "Des 'Quenouilles' aux 'Caquets': 150 ans de commérages," *Recherches et travaux* (University of Grenoble, France), no. 22 (1982): 53–64, for a discussion of *Les Évangiles* and a later similar work, *Les Caquets de l'accouchée* (1622). Like Jeay, Baril feels that despite the frame of "masculine derision" these works manifest a kind of "feminine affirmation" (63, my translation).

21. Denis Baril and Gabriel-André Perouse, "Histoire du Texte," *Contes amoureux par Madame Jeanne Flore*, ed. Gabriel-A. Perouse et al. (Lyon: Presses Universitaires de Lyon, 1980), pp. 9–15. Further references to this edition follow in the text. My translations throughout.

22. Florindo Cerrata, "Jeanne Flore and Early French Translations from Boiardo and F. Bello" in *La Nouvelle française à la Renaissance*, ed. Lionello Sozzi and V. L. Saulnier (Geneva: Slatkine, 1981), p. 256; for the former position see Cathleen M. Bauschatz, "Parodic Didacticism in the *Contes Amoureux* par Madame Jeanne Flore," *French Forum* 20, no. 1 (1995): 5–21.

23. Nazli Fathi-Rizk, "La Moralité finale dans les 'Comptes amoureux' de Jeanne Flore," in *La Nouvelle française*, ed. Sozzi end Saulnier, p. 268. My translation.

24. Ferrier, *Forerunners*, pp. 6, 86–91.

25. Pierre Jourda, *Marguerite d'Angoulême* (Paris: Champion, 1930), pp. 1288, 518, 534. Further references follow in the text. My translations throughout.

26. Marguerite de Navarre, *The Heptameron*, ed. and trans. P. A. Chilton (London: Penguin, 1984), p. 68; *L'Heptaméron*, ed. M. François (Paris: Garnier, 1991), p. 9. Further references follow in the text.

27. Ferrier, *Forerunners*, pp. 93–103, compares novella six with its source in the *Cent Nouvelles Nouvelles*; Cholakian, *Rape and Writing*, p. 46, 73–75, analyses novellas one, eight, and forty-eight. On the use of exempla in the *Heptaméron*, see John D. Lyons, *Exemplum* (Princeton, N.J.: Princeton University Press, 1989).

Chapter Four

1. Edwin B. Place, "María de Zayas, an Outstanding Woman Writer of Seventeenth-Century Spain," *University of Colorado Studies* 13(1923): 10.

2. H. Patsy Boyer, Introduction to *The Enchantments of Love* (Berkeley: University of California Press, 1990), p. xxxvi.

3. Zayas, "El prevenido engañado" and "El imposible vencido" in *Novelas amorosas y ejemplares* (Madrid: Aldus, 1948); "Forewarned but Not Forearmed" and "Triumph over the Impossible" in *Enchantments of Love*, trans. Boyer.

4. María de Zayas, "Too Late for Disillusionment," trans. Peter Cocozzella, in *Women Writers of the Seventeenth Century*, ed. Katharine M. Wilson and Frank J. Warnke (Athens: University of Georgia Press, 1989), p. 225; María de Zayas, *Parte segunda del Sarao y entretenimiento honesto [Desengaños*

amorosos], ed. Alicia Yllera (Madrid: Cátedra, 1983), pp. 254–55. Further references follow in the text.

5. Marguerite de Navarre, *The Heptameron*, ed. and trans. P. A. Chilton (London: Penguin, 1984), p. 371; *L'Heptaméron*, ed. M. François (Paris: Garnier, 1967), p. 278. Further references follow in the text.

6. María de Zayas y Sotomayor, *A Shameful Revenge and Other Stories*, trans. John Sturrock (London: Folio Society, 1963), p. 108; María de Zayas, *Parte segunda*, p. 374. Further references follow in the text.

7. *Enchantments of Love*, p. 1; *Novelas amorosas*, p. 21. Further references follow in the text.

8. With the possible exception of the heroic romance. See Mish, "English Short Fiction," pp. 308–9, for the use of the frame in the romance.

9. Alicia Yllera, Introduction to *Parte segunda*, pp. 83–88; J. E. Tucker, "The Earliest English Translations of Scarron's Nouvelles," *Revue de Littérature comparée* 24 (1950): 557–63; Frederick Alfred de Armas, *The Four Interpolated Stories in the "Roman Comique": Their Sources and Unifying Function* (Chapel Hill: University of North Carolina Press, 1971); *A Week's Entertainment at a Wedding, Containing Six Surprizing and Diverting Adventures Written in Spanish by the Author of Don Quixot* (London: J. Woodwart, 1710). Armas, pp. 103–05, and Place, "María de Zayas," p. 25, note that Scarron's translations are loose; he added and deleted episodes but retained the gist of her plots. Armas also comments, pp. 98–99, however, "Maria de Zayas, a believer in the superiority of woman . . . has no problem believing that a lady can surpass a man in battle. Scarron must find a plausible motive for the capacity" (in "Le Juge de sa propre cause"). See also Etienne Cabillon, "A Propos d'une traduction des *Novelas amorosas y ejemplares* de Maria de Zayas y Sotomayor," *Les Langues neo-latines*, no. 183–84 (1968): 48–65. In "Aphra Behn's Progressive Dialogization of the Spanish Voice" (Ph.D. diss., State University of New York at Stony Brook, 1992), Delors Altaba-Artal proposes that Zayas had a strong and direct influence on Behn.

10. [Mary Carleton], *The Case of Madam Mary Carleton* (London: Speed and March, 1663), p. A4ᵛ. Further references follow in the text.

11. [Margaret Cavendish], the Lady Marchioness of Newcastle, *Natures Pictures Drawn by Fancies Pencil to the Life* (London: J. Martin and J. Allestrye, 1656), pp. 47–48. Further references follow in the text.

12. [Delarivier Manley], *Secret Memoirs and Manners of Several Persons of Quality, of Both Sexes from the New Atalantis*, 2 vols. (London: John Morphew and J. Woodward, 1709), 1:1. Further references follow in the text.

13. [Delarivier Manley], *The Adventures of Rivella* (1714; facsimile reprint, New York: Garland, 1972), p. 7.

14. [Delarivier Manley], *The Power of Love: In Seven Novels* ([London]: John Barber and John Morphew, 1720), pp. 276–77. Further references follow in the text.

15. M. M. Bakhtin, *The Dialogic Imagination*, ed. Michael Holquist (Austin: University of Texas Press, 1981), p. 272.

16. Jane Barker, *A Patch-Work Screen for the Ladies; Or, Love and Virtue Recommended* (1723; facsimile reprint, New York: Garland, 1973), pp. v-vi. Further references follow in the text.

17. See Jacqueline Pearson, "History of *The History of the Nun,*" in *Rereading Aphra Behn,* ed. Heidi Hutner (Charlottesville: University Press of Virginia, 1993).

18. Jane Barker, *The Lining of the Patch Work Screen* (London: A. Bettisworth, 1726), p. 201.

Chapter Five

1. Lowell Gallagher, *Medusa's Gaze: Casuistry and Conscience in the Renaissance* (Stanford: Stanford University Press, 1991), p. 4. Further references follow in the text. Albert R. Jonsen and Stephen Toulmin in *The Abuse of Casuistry: A History of Moral Reasoning* (Berkeley: University of California Press, 1988) and Kathryn Montgomery Hunter, *Doctor's Stories: The Narrative Structure of Medical Knowledge* (Princeton, N.J.: Princeton University Press, 1991) revalidate casuistry as a form of moral reasoning.

2. Camille Wells Slights, *The Casuistical Tradition: In Shakespeare, Donne, Herbert, and Milton* (Princeton, N.J.: Princeton University Press, 1981), p. 8; Jonsen and Toulmin, *The Abuse of Casuistry,* p. 137.

   Other useful works on the history of casuistry consulted but not cited elsewhere include E. Dublanchy, "Casuistique," in *Dictionnaire de théologie catholique,* ed. A. Vacant, E. Mangenot, and E. Amann, 3d ed. (Paris: Librairie Letouzey, 1932), vol. 2, pt. 2; P. J. Holmes, ed. *Elizabethan Casuistry* (Thetford, England: Catholic Record Society, 1981); Henry Charles Lea, *A History of Auricular Confession and Indulgences in the Latin Church,* 3 vols. (Philadelphia: Lea Brothers, 1896), vol. 2; John T. McNeil, "Casuistry in the Puritan Age," *Religion in Life* 12 (1943): 76–89; Pierre Michaud-Quantin, *Sommes de casuistique et manuels de confession au moyen age (XII-XVI siècles)* (Louvain: Nauwelaerts, 1962); Elliot Rose, *Cases of Conscience* (Cambridge: Cambridge University Press, 1975); Thomas N. Tentler, *Sin and Confession on the Eve of the Reformation* (Princeton, N.J.: Princeton University Press, 1977).

3. Walter Pabst, *Novellentheorie und Novellendichtung: Zur Geschichte ihrer Antinomie in den romanischen Literaturen* (Heidelberg: Carl Winter, 1967), pp. 8–14; André Jolles, *Formes simples,* trans. Antoine Marie Buquet (1930; Paris: Editions du Seuil, 1972), pp. 145, 151; Alexander H. Schutz, "Provençal Poetry," *Princeton Encyclopedia of Poetry and Poetics,* enl. ed. Alex Preminger (Princeton, N.J.: Princeton University Press, 1974), p. 679. Further references to Pabst follow in the text.

4. Marguerite de Navarre, *L'Heptaméron,* ed. M. François (Paris: Garnier, 1991), p. 233.

5. Joseph Hall, *Resolutions and Decisions of Divers Practical Cases of Conscience* (1650), in *The Works,* ed. Philip Wynter, rev. ed., 10 vols. (Oxford: Oxford

University Press, 1863), 7:410. Further references follow in the text. For a detailed genealogy of this novella see John Colin Dunlop, *History of Prose Fiction* (1814), rev. ed., 2 vols. (New York: Burt Franklin, 1970), 2:219–24.

6. Patricia Francis Cholakian, *Rape and Writing in the "Heptaméron" of Marguerite de Navarre* (Carbondale: Southern Illinois University Press, 1991), p. 155.

7. J. Paul Hunter, *Before Novels: The Cultural Contexts of Eighteenth-Century English Fiction* (New York: Norton, 1990), p. 289.

8. G. A. Starr, *Defoe and Casuistry* (Princeton, N.J.: Princeton University Press, 1971), p. 134 n. 32. Further references follow in the text.

9. Jolles, *Formes simples,* 143, 150, my translation.

10. Nancy K. Miller, "Emphasis Added: Plots and Plausibilities in Women's Fiction," in *The New Feminist Criticism,* ed. Elaine Showalter (New York: Pantheon, 1981), pp. 339–60. Further references follow in the text. In her essay Miller is amplifying ideas presented by Gérard Genette in "Vraisemblance et motivation," *Figures II* (Paris: Editions de Seuil, 1969).

11. Madame de Lafayette, *The Princess of Clèves,* trans. Walter J. Cobb (New York: Penguin, 1989), p. 117; *La Princesse de Clèves,* ed. Jean-Claude Laborie (1678; reprint, Paris: Larousse, 1995), p. 175. Further references follow in the text.

12. See Moshé Lazar, *Amour courtois et "fin' amors" dans la littérature du XIIe siècle* (Paris: C. Klincksieck, 1964), pp. 52, 55, 57, 73–77; R. Howard Bloch, *Medieval French Literature and Law* (Berkeley: University of California Press, 1977), pp. 172–73.

13. René Nelli and René Lavaud, *Les Troubadours,* vol. 2, *Le Trésor poétique de l'Occitanie* (Bruges: Brouwer, 1966), pp. 134–37, my translation from the modern French.

   Another example may be seen in a *tenson* by Guillelma de Rosers (mid-thirteenth century) and Lanfranc Cigala. Here the debate is over whether a woman is better served by a knight who spends time with her or by one who honors her by serving others. Guillelma replies decisively in favor of the first; of the latter she asks, "if he was so moved as you say by chivalry,/ why didn't he first serve his lady?" ["pois bels servirs tan de cor li movia/ car non servi sidons premieiramen?"] (in Meg Bogin, *The Women Troubadours* [London: Paddington, 1976], pp. 136–37). Pabst, *Novellentheorie,* pp. 13–14, analyzes the *razos* that accompanies this *tenson* to support his claim that the *razos* as a form evolved into the casuistical frame discussions seen in the *Decameron* and the *Heptaméron.*

14. Bogin, *Women Troubadours,* p. 168.

15. William Allan Neilson, *The Origins and Sources of the "Court of Love"* (1899; reprint, New York: Russell and Russell, 1967), p. 242.

16. Christine de Pisan, *Oeuvres poétiques,* ed. Maurice Roy, 2 vols. (1891; New York: Johnson Reprint, 1965), 2:129.

17. It is significant to note that Western jurisprudence in its use of the case method, is rooted in casuistry (see Jonsen and Toulmin; K. Hunter; and

Harold J. Berman, *Law and Revolution: The Formation of the Western Legal Tradition* [Cambridge: Harvard University Press, 1983]). In fact, Justinian's *Corpus civile*, a major source of early modern law occasionally recounts its cases in anecdotes that resemble novellas. Indeed, the section of the code that deals primarily with domestic matters (and thus women) is labeled "The Novels" ([Justinian], *The Civil Law*, ed. S.P. Scott, 17 vols. [1932; reprint in 7 vols., New York: AMS Press, 1973], vol. 16 [in reprint vol. 7], sec. 4, 3–364). For example, in a section on guardianship of children, an anecdotal "case" is presented that clearly anticipates the novella; it begins "Martha, a woman of illustrious birth, has presented a petition to us which sets forth that Sergius, her father of magnificent memory, died while she was of extremely tender age. Auxentia, her mother . . . having had issue by her second marriage . . . manifested very little affection for Martha . . ." (Justinian, vol. 17 [in reprint vol. 7], p. 182).

The current reemphasis on narrative in legal theory may be seen as a return to the casuistical roots of Western jurisprudence. For an interesting feminist take on this development, see Catharine A. MacKinnon, "Law's Stories as Reality and Politics," in *Law's Stories: Narrative and Rhetoric in the Law*, ed. Peter Brooks and Paul Gewirtz (New Haven: Yale University Press, 1996), pp. 232–37.

18. Boccaccio, *The Decameron*, trans. Richard Aldington (New York: Dell, 1966), p. 383; *Il Decameron* (Turin: Guilio Einaudi, 1966), p. 388. Further references follow in the text.

19. The other two are IV.1 and IV.5. While these have a general feminist point, brutally illustrating male control in the family over women, neither uses casuistry extensively to make the point, although Ghismonda in IV.1 does argue other points casuistically.

The story of Bernabo's wife was a much-told tale, a source in fact for Shakespeare's *Cymbeline* (see A. C. Lee, *The Decameron: Its Sources and Analogues* [New York: Haskell House, 1971], pp. 42–57), but none of the other versions seems to highlight the woman's "case" in feminist terms as Boccaccio and Christine de Pizan do.

20. Christine de Pizan, *The Book of the City of Ladies*, trans. Earl Jeffrey Richards (New York: Persea, 1982), pp. 182–83; *The "Livre de la cité des dames" of Christine de Pisan*, ed. Maureen C. Curnow, 3 vols. (Ann Arbor, Mich.: UMI, 1975), 3:920–21.

21. Other than Boccaccio and Defoe no male authors that I'm aware of used casuistry in even a qualified feminist way. Rabelais broadly satirizes the *Summas* of scholastic theology in Book III of *Gargantua et Pantagruel*, but does not otherwise engage casuistry, and his work is in any event deeply informed with misogyny.

22. Pierre Jourda, *Marguerite d'Angoulême* (Paris: Champion, 1930), 22, 26–27. My translations throughout. Further references follow in the text.

23. She used the format of the casuistical love debate in her comedies and other short pieces. See Telle, *L'Oeuvre de Marguerite*, pp. 215–36.

24. Robert Codrington, Preface to *Heptameron or the History of the Fortunate Lovers* (London: Nath. Ekins, 1654), p. A3.

25. Marc Shell, *Elizabeth's Glass* (Lincoln: University of Nebraska Press, 1993), p. 46, suggests as an influence on Marguerite de Navarre's *Miroir* Marguerite Porete's antinomian *Miroir des simples âmes* (ca. 1285–95). Porete, a Beguine, was burned as a heretic in 1310 after the work was condemned. Navarre also had within her household for a time an antinomian heretic by the name of Quintin, who was burned for heresy in 1547.

26. Marguerite de Navarre, *The Heptameron,* ed. and trans. P. A. Chilton (London: Penguin, 1984), p. 196; *L'Heptaméron,* ed. M. François (Paris: Garnier, 1991), p. 123. Further references follow in the text.

27. The question of whether marriage can be dissolved by the partners was a hot issue in casuistry treatises (see Starr, *Defoe and Casuistry,* 146, 147 n. 52).

28. See Jonsen and Toulmin, *Abuse of Casuistry,* p. 179.

29. Boccaccio treats a variant of *Heptameron,* novella forty, in the *Decameron,* 4th day, 5th tale; Christine de Pizan retells it in the *Livre de la cité des dames,* and María de Zayas reworks it as novella eight, "El traidor contra su sangre" in the *Parte segunda* (see discussion in chapter four).

30. Bertha-Monica Stearnes, "The First English Periodical for Women," *Modern Philology* 28 (1930): 47. Further references follow in the text.

31. Ernest Bernbaum, *The Mary Carleton Narratives, 1663–1673: A Missing Chapter in the History of the Novel* (Cambridge: Cambridge University Press, 1914). Further references follow in the text.

32. There is some debate as to what extent Carleton was the sole author. Bernbaum seems to think much was written by a scribe (12, 22), and C. F. Main, "The German Princess; or Mary Carleton in Fact and Fiction," *Harvard Library Bulletin,* no. 10 (1956): 173, by a hack. But modern critics, especially Elaine Hobby, *Virtue of Necessity: English Women's Writing, 1649–88* (Ann Arbor: University of Michigan, 1988) and Mihoko Suzuki, "The Case of Madam Mary Carleton: Representing the Female Subject, 1663–73," *Tulsa Studies in Women's Literature* 12, no. 1 (1993), assume Carleton to be the principal author of *The Case.* Also there is considerable divergence among critics over whether her story was essentially true or whether largely a fabrication (Bernbaum, Main, and Michael McKeon, *The Origins of the English Novel, 1600–1740* [Baltimore: Johns Hopkins, 1987], p.242, doubt its veracity, where Janet Todd, *The Sign of Angellica: Women, Writing, and Fiction, 1660–1800* [New York: Columbia University Press, 1989], pp. 52–55, for example, assumes its validity.)

　　Recent historical scholarship verifies one aspect of Carleton's story, her accurate knowledge of German women's status, which tends to strengthen her credibility. Carleton claims to be of German origin and states that German women have greater power and legal status than English women. In her critique of the *feme covert* law Carleton contrasts it with her own country "where the wife shares an equal portion with her husband in all things . . .

and can *liber intentare,* begin and commence, and finish a suit in her own name" (126).

Merry E. Wiesner in *Working Women in Renaissance Germany* (New Brunswick, N.J.: Rutgers University Press, 1986) corroborates this assertion: "a married woman who owns property in her own name—and this was very common in the sixteenth century—was free to do with it as she wished . . . without the knowledge or approval of her husband" (26); "women of all marital statuses brought cases to court, evoking no comment that this was somehow unusual. . . . At no point in the sixteenth and seventeenth centuries did a woman completely lose her legal identity when she married" (31).

My view is that Mary Carleton was either an amazing fiction-writer (and thus an important transitional figure in the history of fiction) or telling the truth about a life which used novella paradigms as models—in which case she was the first of the female quixotes.

33. [Mary Carleton], *The Case of Madam Mary Carleton* (London: Speed and March, 1663), p. A3ʳ. Further references follow in the text.

34. Daniel Defoe, *Roxana: The Fortunate Mistress,* ed. Jane Jack (New York: Oxford University Press, 1964), p. 271. Further references follow in the text.

35. There has been considerable debate over Defoe's attitude toward his heroines. As Starr, *Defoe and Casuistry,* comments, "Those who find *Moll Flanders* and *Roxana* works of consistent irony will so interpret the casuistical manoeuvering" in them (186). While I agree with Starr that Defoe has some sympathy for his protagonists and may have identified with them, he nevertheless casts their story in a pejorative, moralizing, and ironizing frame.

36. Karl Stanglmaier, *Mrs. Jane Barker: Ein Beitrag zur englishen Literaturgeschichte* (Berlin: E. Eberling, 1906), pp. 48–50.

37. Thomas Philip Haviland, *The "Roman de Longue Haleine" on English Soil* (Philadelphia: University of Pennsylvania Press, 1931), p. 55.

38. Ibid., p. 137.

39. Jane Barker, *Exilius; or, the Banish'd Roman,* 2 vols. in 1 (1715; facsimile reprint, New York: Garland, 1973), 1:7–9. Further references follow in the text.

Chapter Six

1. See Ruth Perry, *The Celebrated Mary Astell,* (Chicago: University of Chicago Press, 1986), pp. 14–15; also *The Polemics and Poems of Rachel Speght,* ed. Barbara Kiefer Lewalski (New York: Oxford University Press, 1996).

2. See Ruth Perry, "Radical Doubt and the Liberation of Women," *Eighteenth-Century Studies* 18, no. 4 (1985): 471–93; Margaret Atherton, ed., *Women Philosophers of the Early Modern Period* (Indianapolis: Hackett, 1994); Hilda Smith, *Reason's Disciples* (Urbana: University of Illinois Press, 1982).

3. Mary Astell, "A Serious Proposal to the Ladies" and "Some Reflections upon Marriage" (excerpts), in *The Meridian Anthology of Early Women Writers,*

ed. Katherine M. Rogers and William McCarthy (New York: Penguin, 1987), p. 120. Further references follow in the text.

4. See Melissa A. Butler, "Early Liberal Roots of Feminism: John Locke and the Attack on Patriarchy," in *Feminist Interpretation and Political Theory,* ed. Mary Lyndon Shanley and Carole Pateman (University Park: Penn State University Press, 1991), pp. 74–94.

5. See Melvin D. Palmer, "Madame d'Aulnoy in England," *Comparative Literature* 27 (1975): 237–53. Another, though probably less important continental influence on the English women writers was Paul Scarron's *Roman comique.* I trace the complexities of this influence in chapter eight. It is of particular interest because Scarron incorporated several Zayas novellas without attribution. Of course, the structural prototype of the picaresque framed-novelle is *Don Quixote.*

6. B. G. MacCarthy, *The Female Pen* (1946–47; reprint, New York: New York University Press, 1994), p. 263.

7. Madame [Marie-Catherine le Jumel de Barneville, Baroness] d'Aulnoy, *Travels into Spain,* ed. R. Foulché-Delbosc (London: Routledge, 1930), p. 3; Madame d'Aulnoy, *Relation du voyage d'Espagne,* ed. R. Foulché-Delbosc (Paris: C. Klincksieck, 1926), p. 155. Further references follow in the text.

8. Percy G. Adams, *Travel Literature and the Evolution of the Novel* (Lexington: University Press of Kentucky, 1983), pp. 74, 76. See his chapter, "Truth-Lie Dichotomy" for a further discussion of this issue. D'Aulnoy's modern French editor, R. Foulché-Delbosc (see n. 7) holds a similar position.

9. [Delarivier Manley], *Letters Writen* [sic] *by Mrs. Manley* (London: R. B., 1696), p. 29. Further references follow in the text. Robert Adams Day, *Told in Letters* (Ann Arbor: University of Michigan Press, 1966), p. 43, states that Manley "indubitably imitated" d'Aulnoy.

10. Ibid., p. 158.

11. Another of Manley's friends, Mary Pix, also published a work of prose fiction in the 1690s. Manley, Trotter, and Pix were lampooned in a 1697 comedy *The Female Wits: or, The Triumvirate of Poets at Rehearsal.* Pix's *The Inhumane Cardinal,* ed. Constance Clark (1696; Delmar, N.Y.: Scholars Facsimiles & Reprints, 1984) is not particularly innovative, being a lengthy rehearsal of the traditional novella seduction plot. Pix does see it as a cautionary tale, however, that should "raise Compassion in the tender Bosoms of the Young and Fair" (p. 236).

12. Introduction to *Olinda's Adventures* by Catherine Trotter (Los Angeles: Clark Memorial Library, 1969), pp. vi, vii.

13. Included in *Women Philosophers of the Early Modern Period,* ed. Margaret Atherton (Indianapolis: Hackett, 1994), pp. 126–46.

14. Trotter, *Olinda's Adventures,* p. 137. Further references follow in the text.

15. See Emma Donohue, *Passions between Women* (New York: Harper, 1993), pp. 131–32, 238.

16. Fidelia Morgan, *A Woman of No Character* (London: Faber and Faber, 1986), p. 103.

17. Mary Davys, *The Fugitive* (London: G. Sawbridge, 1705), p. A6^v. Further references follow in the text. I have silently corrected the original incorrect pagination.

18. Mary Davys, *The Merry Wanderer,* in *The Works of Mrs. Davys,* 2 vols. (London: H. Woodfall, 1725), 1:161. Further references follow in the text.

19. Mary Davys, *The Lady's Tale,* in *The Works of Mrs. Davys,* 2:125. The 1704 version is apparently no longer extant.

20. Virginia Woolf, *A Room of One's Own* (New York: Harcourt, 1957), p. 69.

21. See Naomi Jacobs, "The Seduction of Aphra Behn," *Women's Studies* 18 (1991):395–403; also Judith Kegan Gardiner, "The First English Novel: Aphra Behn's *Love Letters,* the Canon, and Women's Tastes," *Tulsa Studies in Women's Literature* 8, no. 2 (Fall 1989): 201–22.

22. *The Works of Aphra Behn,* ed. Montague Summers, vol. 5 (London: Heinemann, 1915), p. 96. Though not entirely reliable, says it may have appeared as "The Amorous Convent" in 1678. Summers.

23. Aphra Behn, *Oroonoko and Other Stories,* ed. Maureen Duffy (London: Methuen, 1986), p. 125.

24. Lennard Davis, *Factual Fictions* (New York: Columbia University Press, 1983), p. 107.

25. Aphra Behn, "The Black Lady," in *The Works of Aphra Behn,* ed. Summers, p. 3.

26. Aphra Behn, "The Wandering Beauty," in *The Works of Aphra Behn,* ed. Summers, p. 448.

27. Altaba-Artal, "Behn's Progressive Dialogization," pp. 297–305, considers that this novella derived from the Violenta novella that we consider in detail in chapter seven. Altaba-Artal argues for a strong Zayas influence on Behn.

28. Mary Davys, *Familiar Letters, Betwixt a Gentleman and a Lady,* in *The Works of Mrs. Davys,* 2:272, 227. Further references follow in the text.

29. William McBurney, "Mrs. Mary Davys: Forerunner of Fielding," *PMLA* 74 (Sept. 1979): 354.

30. Jane Spencer, *The Rise of the Woman Novelist* (Oxford: Blackwell, 1986), p. 146.

31. Mary Davys, *The Reform'd Coquet* (1724; facsimile reprint, New York: Garland, 1973), pp. 80–81. Further references follow in the text.

Chapter Seven

Note: An earlier version of this chapter appeared as "From Avenger to Victim: The Genealogy of a Renaissance Novella," *Tulsa Studies in Women's Literature* 15, no. 2 (1996): 269–88. ©1996 The University of Tulsa. Reprinted by permission of the publisher.

1. An example of the "backlash" is the 1697 lampoon *The Female Wits* (see chap. six, n. 11). See also Jane Spencer, *The Rise of the Woman Novelist* (Oxford: Blackwell, 1986), pp. 5–6.

2. See especially Alice Clark's classic study *Working Life of Women in the Seventeenth Century* (1919; reprint, London: Frank Cass, 1968), pp. 11–13, 295–308; Ruth Perry, *Women, Letters, and the Novel* (New York: AMS Press, 1980), pp. 27–62; Bridget Hill, *Women, Work, and Sexual Politics in Eighteenth-Century England* (Oxford: Blackwell, 1989), pp. 10–11, 48, 262; Spencer, *Rise of the Woman Novelist*, pp. 11–15, 91–92, 118–22; and Josephine Donovan, "Women and the Rise of the Novel: A Feminist-Marxist Theory," *Signs* 16, no. 3 (Spring 1991): 447–49, esp. 448, n. 14.

3. Another English Renaissance version is Beaumont and Fletcher's "Triumph of Death," a short play, the third in "Four Plays in One" (in *The Works of Beaumont and Fletcher*, ed. Henry Weber, 14 vols. [Edinburgh: James Ballantyne, 1812], 11:80–109). In this variant a long-lost fiancé of Violante (here Gabriella) returns from the wars in time to help with the vendetta. He persuades her against torturing Didaco (here Lavall), but Lavall, who has been drugged, wakes up and kills the fiancé (Perlot). Gabriella then stabs and kills Lavall, and then kills herself in order to join Perlot in death. A somewhat similar plot also obtains in Beaumont and Fletcher's "The Spanish Curate" (1622).

There also was apparently another Spanish version of the novella. Both William Painter and Delarivier Manley mention as a source for their versions a "Paludanus" who wrote in Latin, but Laura Tortonese says, in her analysis of the novella, "Bandello, Boaistuau e la novella di Didaco e Violante," in *La Nouvelle française*, ed. Sozzi and Saulnier, p. 465, n. 14, that she was unable to locate this version, having combed the *Sermones* of Pierre de la Palud, the likely source. Richard A. Carr, the editor of the modern critical edition of Pierre Boaistuau's adaptation of Bandello, *Histoires tragiques* (1559; Paris: Champion, 1977) also doubts the existence of a Spanish Paludanus, as does René Sturel, another scholar (p. 167, n. 2). There is one piece of evidence, however, which suggests a common source for Zayas and Boaistuau (other than Bandello) and that is the emerald ring that appears in both, which is not in Bandello.

The novella also appears to have become used as an exemplum in the misogynist writings of the Counterreformation in the late sixteenth and early seventeenth centuries. Jean de Marconville cites the Bandello version in his *De la bonté et mauvaistie des femmes* (Paris: Jean Dallier Librairie, 1571), pp. 60–61. The work is largely a catalog of "bad women" meant to warn of their inherent depravity. Since, however, none of the fictional writers I am concerned with appear to have been familiar with Marconville's summary (and only Boaistuau expresses a similarly virulent misogyny toward Violenta), I have not included him in my genealogy of the story. See, however, Giovanni Dotoli, *Letteratura per il populo in Francia (1600–1750)* (Fasano, Italy: Schena, 1991), pp. 143–48, 167, for more on this.

4. Since the extant *Heptaméron* is not complete, it is possible that the last missing section may have included the Violenta tale—that is, if such a section ever existed. A seventeenth-century English translator, Robert Codrington,

speculates in his preface that the last section was destroyed in the Counter-reformation: "I am informed that the Queen had fully finished the Tenth days work; but the Friers [sic] and Religious Men, who have deprived us of the two last Journals, and of the greatest part of the eighth, would have deprived us also of all the Rest, if possibly they could have prevented it" (Robert Codrington, Preface to *Heptameron or the History of the Fortunate Lovers* [London: Nath. Ekins, 1654], pp. A3ʳ-A3ᵛ). The *Heptaméron* was to have included one hundred tales, but only seventy-two (with a few variants) were completed, or at least remain.

5. *Tutte le Opere di Matteo Bandello,* ed. Francesco Flora, 2 vols. (1934; reprint, Verona: Arnoldo Montadori, 1966), 1:495. Further references to this edition follow in the text. My translations throughout.

6. According to Edwin B. Place, "María de Zayas: An Outstanding Woman Writer of Seventeenth-Century Spain," *University of Colorado Studies* 13 (1923): 11.

7. María de Zayas y Sotomayor, *A Shameful Revenge and Other Stories,* trans. John Sturrock (London: Folio Society, 1963), p. 64; María de Zayas, *Parte segunda del Sarao y entretenimiento honesto [Desengaños amorosos],* ed. Alicia Yllera (Madrid: Cátedra, 1983), p. 189; Further references follow in the text.

8. Zayas has one other novella in which the woman successfully avenges herself against her violator by killing him: "Just Desserts" ("Al fin se paga todo," *Novelas amorosas,* novella seven).

9. As noted in chapter eight, the main English vehicles for Zayas were translations of Paul Scarron's works; however, the Violenta novella was not among them. "La burlada Aminta" did appear in a French adaptation in 1656–57 as "La Vengeance d'Aminte affrontée" in *Les Nouvelles amoureuses et exemplaires, composées en espagnol par cette merveille de son sexe, Doña Maria de Zayas y Sotto Maior,* trans. Antoine de Méthel Escuier Sieur Douville (Paris: Guyillaume de Luynes). Source of the above information: Alicia Yllera, bibliography in *Parte segunda,* pp. 83–88.

10. Tortonese, "Bandello, Boaistuau," in *La Nouvelle française,* pp. 461–70. Pierre Boaistuau, *Histoires tragiques extraictes des oeuvres Italiennes de Bandel* (Paris: Vincent Sertenas, 1559); for modern critical edition see n. 3. Boaistuau also put together the first, truncated edition of Marguerite de Navarre's *Heptaméron* in 1558. Interestingly, with both Bandello and Marguerite, Boaistuau was concerned to "correct" (i.e., Latinize) their style. See further discussion in chapter nine.

11. William Painter, *The Palace of Pleasure* (1575; reprint, ed. Joseph Haslewood, London: Robert Triphook, 1813), pp. 209, 217. Further references follow in the text. This edition uses the old "I" for a "J" in Janique, which I am retaining here.

12 [Delarivier Manley], *The Power of Love: In Seven Novels* ([London]: John Berber and John Morphew, 1720), p. 180. Further references follow in the text.

13. Robert Adams Day, *Told in Letters* (Ann Arbor, University of Michigan Press, 1966), p. 253.

14. Eliza Haywood, *Love in Its Variety: Being a Collection of Select Novels; Written in Spanish by Signior Michael Bandello* (London: W. Feales, 1727), p. 106. Further references follow in the text.

In *Love Intrigues: Or, the History of the Amours of Bosvil and Galesia* (1713) (in *The Galesia Trilogy and Selected Manuscript Poems of Jane Barker*, ed. Carol Shiner Wilson [New York: Oxford University Press, 1997], pp. 1–47), Jane Barker's jilted protagonist Galesia fantasizes doing a job on faithless Bosvil (p. 31) that is reminiscent of Violenta's treatment of Roderigo; Barker's novella may therefore be another link in the Violenta genealogy.

15. See Nancy K. Miller, *The Heroine's Text: Readings in the French and English Novel, 1722 - 1782* (New York: Columbia University Press, 1980), pp. ix, xi.

Chapter Eight

1. Charles C. Mish, Preface to *Restoration Prose Fiction 1666 - 1700* (Lincoln: University of Nebraska Press, 1970), p. x. These stories may well have been intended for a masculine audience since they were published in *The Gentleman's Journal*, but it is Mish's assumption that the anti-romance would not appeal to women that I wish to highlight.

2. Ian Watt, "Serious Reflections on *The Rise of the Novel*," in *Towards a Poetics of Fiction*, ed. Mark Spilka (Bloomington: Indiana University Press, 1977), p. 103. Further references follow in the text.

3. Gilbert Highet, *The Anatomy of Satire* (Princeton, N.J.: Princeton University Press, 1962), p. 235.

4. Northrup Frye, *Anatomy of Criticism* (Princeton, N.J.: Princeton University Press, 1957), p. 172.

5. Maria de Zayas, *The Enchantments of Love*, trans H. Patsy Boyer (Berkeley: University of California Press, 1990), p. xvii; María de Zayas, *Parte segunda del Sarao y entretenimiento honesto [Desengaños amorosos]*, ed. Alicia Yllera (Madrid: Cátedra, 1983), p. 118.

6. Maurice Z. Shroder, "The Novel as a Genre" (1963), in *The Novel: Modern Essays in Criticism*, ed. Robert Murray Davis (Englewood Cliffs, N.J.: Prentice-Hall, 1969), p. 46.

7. Vladimir Jankélévitch, as cited in ibid., p. 50.

8. M. M. Bakhtin, *The Dialogic Imagination*, ed. Michael Holquist (Austin: University of Texas Press, 1981), p. 24. Further references follow in the text.

9. Mikhail Bakhtin, *Rabelais and His World*, trans. Helene Iswolsky (Bloomington: Indiana University Press, 1984), p. 239. Further references follow in the text.

10. Wayne C. Booth, "Freedom of Interpretation: Bakhtin and the Challenge of Feminist Criticism," in *Bakhtin*, ed. Gary Saul Morson (Chicago: University of Chicago Press, 1986), p. 154. Further references follow in the text.

11. Erich Auerbach, *Zur Technik der Frührenaissancenovelle in Italien und Frankreich*, 2d ed (Heidelberg: Carl Winter, 1971), p. 26. My translation.

12. Christine de Pisan, *Oeuvres poétiques,* ed. Maurice Roy, 2 vols. (1891; New York: Johnson Reprint, 1965), 2:14. My translation.

13. Paul Salzman, *English Prose Fiction, 1558 - 1700* (Oxford: Clarendon Press, 1985), pp. 274–76.

14. [Subligny, Adrien Thomas Perdou de], *The Mock Clelia, or, Madam Quixote* (London: Simon Neale and Charles Blount, 1678), p. 268.

15. Jane Barker, *The Lining of the Patch Work Screen* (London: A. Bettisworth, 1726), p. A5^r.

16. Joan DeJean, *Tender Geographies: Women and the Origins of the Novel in France* (New York: Columbia University Press, 1990), pp. 37–40.

17. Jean Regnault de Segrais, *Les Nouvelles françaises,* ed. Roger Guichemarre, vol. 1 (Paris: STFM, 1991), pp. 93–103, for example. Further references follow in the text. My translations throughout.

18. [Margaret Cavendish], the Duchess of Newcastle, Preface to *Natures Picture [sic] Drawn by Fancies Pencil to the Life,* 2d ed. (London: A. Maxwell, 1671), p. B2^v.

19. [Margaret Cavendish], the Marchioness of Newcastle, *CCXI Sociable Letters* (1664; facsimile reprint, Menston, England: Scholar Press, 1969), pp. 39–40. Further references follow in the text.

20. Mary Davys, *The Fugitive* (London: G. Sawbridge, 1705), pp. A4^v-A5^r.

21. Nancy K. Miller, *The Heroine's Text: Readings in the French and English Novel, 1722 - 1782* (New York: Columbia University Press, 1980), p. 4. Further references follow in the text.

22. Margaret Anne Doody, "George Eliot and the Eighteenth-Century Novel," *Nineteenth-Century Fiction* 35, no. 3 (1980): 268.

23. This the local-color realism of writers like Harriet Beecher Stowe, Rose Terry Cooke, and Sarah Orne Jewett. See Josephine Donovan, *New England Local Color Literature: A Women's Tradition* (New York: Ungar, 1983).

24. Sarah Fielding, *The Adventures of David Simple* (1744; reprint, London: Oxford University Press, 1973), p. 101. Further references follow in the text.

25. Charlotte Lennox, *Henrietta,* 2 vols. in 1 (1758; facsimile reprint, New York: Garland, 1974), 1:11–12. Further references follow in the text.

26. Charlotte Lennox, *The Female Quixote* (1752; reprint, London: Oxford University Press, 1970), p. 23. Further references follow in the text.

27. See Sharon M. Harris, "Lost Boundaries: The Use of the Carnivalesque in Tabitha Tenney's *Female Quixotism,*" unpublished article, p. 2. Further references follow in the text.

28. Tabitha Tenney, *Female Quixotism,* 2 vols. (Boston: I. Thomas and E. T. Andrews, 1801), 1:6. Further references follow in the text.

29. Maria Edgeworth, *Castle Rackrent,* in *Tales and Novels,* 10 vols. (New York: Harper, 1835), 1:11. Further references follow in the text.

30. Sandra M. Gilbert and Susan Gubar, *The Madwoman in the Attic* (New Haven: Yale University Press, 1979), p. 149.

31. As cited in O. Elizabeth McWhorter Harden, *Maria Edgeworth's Art of Prose Fiction* (The Hague: Mouton, 1971), p. 114.

32. Maria Edgeworth, *The Absentee* (1818; reprint, Oxford: Oxford University Press, 1988), p. 2. Further references follow in the text.

Chapter Nine

1. M. M. Bakhtin, *The Dialogic Imagination,* ed. Michael Holquist (Austin: University of Texas Press, 1981), p. 271. Further references follow in the text.
2. Walter J. Ong, *The Presence of the Word* (New Haven: Yale University Press, 1967), pp. 250–51. Further references follow in the text.
3. Walter J. Ong, *Orality and Literacy* (London: Routledge, 1988) p. 11. Further references follow in the text.
4. Peter Dronke, *Women Writers of the Middle Ages* (Cambridge: Cambridge University Press, 1984), p. viii. Further references follow in the text.
5. Erich Auerbach, *Literary Language and Its Public in Late Latin Antiquity and in the Middle Ages* (New York: Bollingen, 1965), p. 60.
6. As cited in Barbara Newman, *Sister of Wisdom* (Berkeley: University of California Press, 1987), p. 7. Further references follow in the text.
7. Jane Anger, "Her Protection for Women," in *by a woman writt,* ed. Joan Goulianos (Indianapolis: Bobbs-Merrill, 1973), p. 24.
8. Richard A. Carr, Introduction to *Histoires tragiques* by Pierre Boaistuau (Paris: Champion, 1977), p. xxxviii. My translation. Further references follow in the text.
9. [Margaret Cavendish], Lady Marchioness of Newcastle, *The Life of the (1st) Duke of Newcastle and Other Writings by Margaret Duchess,* ed. Ernest Rhys (London: J. M. Dent, n. d.), p. 12. Further references follow in the text.
10. Josephine Donovan, "Ecofeminist Literary Criticism: Reading the Orange," *Hypatia* 11, no. 2 (1996): 161–84; also see discussion in chapter one.
11. [Margaret Cavendish], the Lady Marchioness of Newcastle, *Philosophical and Physical Opinions* (London: William Wilson, 1663), pp. b4^r-b4^v. Further references follow in the text.
12. [Margaret Cavendish], the Lady Newcastle, *Poems, and Fancies* (London; J. Martin and J. Allestrye, 1653), p. 110.
13. John J. Richetti, *Popular Fiction before Richardson,* rev. ed. (Oxford: Oxford University Press, 1992), pp. 126–27, states that this largely feminine reading public "required the plain style . . . because ornate style, intricate plot, and psychological complication were beyond its comprehension and appreciation."
14. Percy G. Adams, *Travel Literature and the Evolution of the Novel* (Lexington: University Press of Kentucky, 1983), p. 247. Further references follow in the text.
15. Morris Croll, *Style, Rhetoric, and Rhythm,* ed. J. Max Patrick and Robert O. Evans (Princeton, N.J.: Princeton University Press, 1966), p. 224.
16. Ellen Moers, *Literary Women* (Garden City, N.Y.: Doubleday, 1977), p. 97. Further references follow in the text.

17. Ian Watt, *The Rise of the Novel* (Berkeley: University of California Press, 1957), p. 194.

18. Erich Auerbach, *Mimesis* (Garden City, N.Y.: Doubleday, 1953), pp. 95, 161, 189–92, 272, 274, 410–11.

19. Torquato Tasso, "Discourse on the Heroic Poem," in *Literary Criticism from Plato to Dryden*, ed. Allan H. Gilbert (Detroit: Wayne State University Press, 1962), p. 465.

20. Aristotle, *Poetics* 10.20, in *The Basic Works of Aristotle*, ed. Richard McKeon (New York: Random, 1941), p. 1465.

21. Virginia Woolf, *Women & Fiction: The Manuscript Versions of "A Room of One's Own,"* ed. S. P. Rosenbaum (Oxford: Blackwell, 1992), p. 182. Other than using an ampersand for "and," Woolf transcribes the passage accurately. It is found in *Pride and Prejudice*, in *The Novels of Jane Austen*, ed. R. W. Chapman, 3d ed., 5 vols. (Oxford: Oxford University Press, 1923), 2:169.

22. Mary Field Belenky et al., *Women's Ways of Knowing* (New York: Basic, 1986), pp. 24–28.

23. In his analysis of the sentimentalist tradition, *Hard Facts* (New York: Oxford University Press, 1985), pp. 116–17, Philip Fisher suggests that for an oppressed group, which lacks an analysis of the causes of its oppression, events do seem to happen as just one thing after another: "Sentimental narrative avoids the roots of actions in the past, [because to do so provides] . . . understanding why the act occurred . . . [allowing the reader to] identify with the actor rather than the victim, for [whom] such acts are unexplained."

24. Germaine Greer, Introduction to *Kissing the Rod: An Anthology of Seventeenth-Century Women's Verse*, ed. Greer et al. (New York: Farrar, Straus, Giroux, 1988), p. 9.

25. Earl Jeffrey Richards, Introduction to *The Book of the City of Ladies* by Christine de Pizan (New York: Persea, 1982), pp. xxi, xli.

26. Michel LeGuern, Preface to *Contes amoureux par Madame Jeanne Flore*, ed. Gabriel-A. Perouse et al. (Lyon: Presses Universitaires de Lyon, 1980), pp. 84–86. Further references to this edition follow in the text. My translation.

27. Katherine S. Gittes, *Framing the Canterbury Tales* (Westport, Conn.: Greenwood, 1991), p. 29.

28. Mary Hyatt, *The Way Women Write* (New York: Teachers College Press, 1977), p. 67.

29. [Margaret Cavendish], the Lady Marchioness of Newcastle, *Natures Pictures Drawn by Fancies Pencil to the Life* (London: J. Martin and J. Allestrye, 1656), 112.

30. [Delarivier Manley], "To the Reader," *The Secret History of Queen Zarah, and the Zarazians*, in *The Novels of Mary Delariviere Manley*, ed. Patricia Koster, 2 vols. (Gainesville, Fla.: Scholars' Facsimiles & Reprints, 1971), 1:A3[r]. Further references follow in the text.

31. Mary Davys, Preface to *The Works of Mrs. Davys*, 2 vols. (London: H. Woodfall, 1725), 1:iv. Further references follow in the text.

32. Mary Davys, *The Reform'd Coquet* (1724; facsimile reprint, New York: Garland, 1973), p. 2.

33. Christine Mason Sutherland, "Mary Astell: Reclaiming Rhetorica in the Seventeenth Century," in *Reclaiming Rhetorica,* ed. Andrea A. Lunsford (Pittsburgh: University of Pittsburgh Press, 1995), p. 93. Further references follow in the text.

34. Rachel Blau DuPlessis, "For the Etruscans," in *The New Feminist Criticism,* ed. Elaine Showalter (New York: Pantheon, 1981), p. 278.

35. Ann Banfield, *Unspeakable Sentences* (Boston: Routledge & Kegan Paul, 1982), pp. 228–29. Further references follow in the text.

36. Terry Eagleton, *The Rape of Clarissa* (Minneapolis: University of Minnesota Press, 1982), p. 36.

37. Richard Ohmann, "Prolegomena to an Analysis of Prose Style," in *Style in Prose Fiction* (New York: Columbia University Press, 1959), p. 14.

Conclusion

1. Virginia Woolf, "Dorothy Osborne's *Letters,*" in *Collected Essays,* vol. 3 (London: Hogarth, 1967), p. 60.

2. Virginia Woolf, *A Room of One's Own* (New York: Harcourt, 1957), p. 68.

3. Iris Murdoch, *The Sovereignty of Good* (New York: Schocken, 1971), p. 66.

4. Virginia Woolf, *"Jacob's Room" and "The Waves"* (New York: Harcourt, 1959), p. 371.

Index